Greek

A ROUGH GUIDE
PHRASEBOOK

Compiled
by Lexus

Credits

Compiled by Lexus with Costas Panayotakis

Lexus Series Editor:	Sally Davies
Rough Guides Phrase Book Editor:	Jonathan Buckley
Rough Guides Series Editor:	Mark Ellingham

This first edition published in 1995 by Rough Guides Ltd, 1 Mercer Street, London WC2H 9QJ.

Distributed by the Penguin Group.

Penguin Books Ltd, 27 Wrights Lane, London W8 5TZ
Penguin Books USA Inc., 375 Hudson Street, New York 10014, USA
Penguin Books Australia Ltd, 487 Maroondah Highway, PO Box 257, Ringwood, Victoria 3134, Australia
Penguin Books Canada Ltd, Alcorn Avenue, Toronto, Ontario, Canada M4V 1E4
Penguin Books (NZ) Ltd, 182–190 Wairau Road, Auckland 10, New Zealand

Typeset in Rough Serif and Rough Sans to an original design by Henry Iles.
Printed by Cox & Wyman Ltd, Reading.

British Library Cataloguing in Publication Data
A catalogue for this book is available from the British Library.

ISBN 1-85828-145-8

CONTENTS

INTRODUCTION

The Rough Guide Greek phrasebook is a highly practical introduction to the contemporary language. Laid out in clear A-Z style, it uses key-word referencing to lead you straight to the words and phrases you want – so if you need to book a room, just look up 'room'. The Rough Guide gets straight to the point in every situation, in bars and shops, on trains and buses, and in hotels and banks.

The main part of the Rough Guide is a double dictionary: English-Greek then Greek-English. Before that, there's a page explaining the pronunciation system we've used, then a section called **The Basics**, which sets out the fundamental rules of the language, with plenty of practical examples. You'll also find here other essentials like numbers, dates and telling the time.

Forming the heart of the guide, the **English-Greek** section gives easy-to-use transliterations of the Greek words wherever pronunciation might be a problem, and to get you involved quickly in two-way communication, the Rough Guide includes dialogues featuring typical responses on key topics – such as renting a car and asking directions. Feature boxes fill you in on cultural pitfalls as well as the simple mechanics of how to make a phone call, what to do in an emergency, where to change money, and more. Throughout this section, cross-references enable you to pinpoint key facts and phrases, while asterisked words indicate where further information can be found in the Basics.

In the **Greek-English** dictionary, we've given not just the phrases you're likely to hear, but also all the signs, labels, instructions and other basic words you might come across in print or in public places.

Finally the Rough Guide rounds off with an extensive **Menu Reader**, giving a run-down of food and drink terms that you'll find indispensable whether you're eating out, stopping for a quick drink, or browsing through a local food market.

καλό ταξίδι!
kal**o** tax**i**thi!
have a good trip!

vi

THE GREEK ALPHABET

Set out below is the Greek alphabet, the names of the Greek letters, and the system of transliteration used in this book:

Α, α	alfa	a as in cat
Β, β	vita	v as in vet
Γ, γ	Gama	y as in yes, except before consonants and a, o or long i, when it's g as in goat or a breathy, throaty version of the g in gap (represented by G)
Δ, δ	thelta	th as in then
Ε, ε	epsilon	e as in get
Ζ, ζ	zita	z
Η, η	ita	i as in ski
Θ, θ	THita	as the th in theme (represented by TH)
Ι, ι	yota	i as in bit
Κ, κ	kapa	k
Λ, λ	lamtha	l
Μ, μ	mi	m
Ν, ν	ni	n
Ξ, ξ	ksi	x
Ο, ο	omikron	o as in hot
Π, π	pi	p
Ρ, ρ	ro	r
Σ, σ, ς*	siGma	s
Τ, τ	taf	t
Υ, υ	ipsilon	long i, indistinguishable from ita
Φ, φ	fi	f
Χ, χ	khi	h as in hat or harsh ch in the Scottish word loch (represented by kh)
Ψ, ψ	psi	ps as in lips
Ω, ω	omeGa	o as in hot, indistinguishable from omikron

* this letter is used only at the end of a word in lower case

Combinations and diphthongs:

AI, αι	e as in g**e**t
AY, αυ	av or af depending on following consonant
EI, ει	long i, exactly like **i**ta
OI, οι	long i, exactly like **i**ta
EY, ευ	ev or ef depending on following consonant
OY, ου	oo as in m**oo**n
ΓΓ, γγ	ng as in a**ng**le
ΓΚ, γκ	g as in **g**oat at the beginning of a word; ng in the middle
ΜΠ, μπ	b as in bar and sometimes mb as in e**mb**assy in the middle of a word
ΝΤ, ντ	d at the beginning of a word and sometimes nd as in e**nd** in the middle
ΤΣ, τσ	ts as in hi**ts**

PRONUNCIATION

Throughout this book Greek words have been transliterated into romanized form (see The Greek Alphabet page vi) so that they can be read as though they were English bearing in mind the notes on pronunciation given below:

a	as in cat
e	as in get
eh	represents e at end of a word; should always be pronounced as in get
g	always hard as in goat
G	a breathy, throaty version of the g in gap
i	as in ski
kh	like the ch in the Scottish way of saying loch
o	as in hot
th	as in then
TH	as in theme

Letters given in bold type indicate the part of the word to be stressed. When two vowels (such as 'ea') are next to each other in the pronunciation, both should be pronounced, as for example in the word: amfiTHeatro (amphitheatre).

ABBREVIATIONS

acc	accusative case
adj	adjective
fam	familiar
fem	feminine
gen	genitive case
masc	masculine
neut	neuter
nom	nominative case
pl	plural
pol	polite
sing	singular

NOTE

An asterisk (*) next to a word in the dictionaries means that you should refer to the Basics section for further information.

The Basics

BASIC PHRASES

yes
ναί
neh

no
όχι
okhi

OK
εντάξει
endaxi

hello
χαίρετε
khereteh

good morning
καλημέρα
kalimera

good evening
καλησπέρα
kalispera

good night
καληνύχτα
kalinikhta

goodbye
αντίο
andio

hi
γειά
ya

see you
γειά, θα τα πούμε
ya, тна ta poomeh

please
παρακαλώ
parakalo

thank you
ευχαριστώ
efkharisto

yes, please
ναί, παρακαλώ
neh, parakalo

no thank you
όχι, ευχαριστώ
okhi, efkharisto

excuse me, please (to attract
    attention, to get past someone)
συγγνώμη, παρακαλώ
signomi, parakalo

sorry!
συγγνώμη!
signomi!

pardon? (sorry? what did you say?)
ορίστε;
oristeh?

what did you say?
πώς είπατε;
pos ipateh?

I don't understand
δεν καταλαβαίνω
then katalaveno

do you speak English?
μιλάτε Αγγλικά;
milateh Anglika?

I don't speak Greek
δεν μιλάω Ελληνικά
then milao Elinika

please speak more slowly
παρακαλώ, μιλάτε πιό αργά;
parakalo, milateh pio arga?

could you repeat that?
το ξαναλέτε αυτό, σας
 παρακαλώ;
to xanaleteh afto, sas
 parakalo?

please write it down
μου το γράφετε, παρακαλώ;
moo to grafeteh, parakalo?

I would like ...
θα ήθελα ...
тнa itнela ...

can I have ...?
μπορώ να έχω ...;
boro na ekho ...?

how much is it?
πόσο κάνει;
poso kani?

cheers!
εις υγείαν!
is iyian!

where is/are the ...?
πού είναι ...;
poo ineh ...?

NOUNS AND ARTICLES

Articles

Greek nouns have one of three genders – masculine, feminine or neuter. The indefinite article (a, an) for each gender is:

masc	fem	neut
ένας	μία	ένα
enas	mia	ena

ένας άνδρας	μία γυναίκα
enas anthras	mia yineka
a man	a woman

ένα παιδί
ena pethi
a child

The definite article (the) is:

	masc	fem	neut
sing	o	η	το
	o	i	to
plural	οι	οι	τα
	i	i	ta

ο πατέρας	οι πατεράδες
o pateras	i paterathes
the father	the fathers

η μητέρα	οι μητέρες
i mitera	i miteres
the mother	the mothers

το μωρό	τα μωρά
to moro	ta mora
the baby	the babies

ο δρόμος	οι δρόμοι
o thromos	i thromi
the street	the streets

η χώρα	οι χώρες
i khora	i khores
the country	the countries

το βουνό	τα βουνά
o voono	ta voona
the mountain	the mountains

Cases

There are three main cases in Greek – nominative, genitive and accusative. The forms of articles, nouns, adjectives and most pronouns change according to their gender, number and case. The indefinite article (a, an) declines as follows:

sing	masc	fem	neut
nom	ένας	μία	ένα
	enas	mia	ena
gen	ενός	μιάς	ενός
	enos	mias	enos
acc	ένα(ν)*	μία	ένα
	ena(n)	mia	ena

The definite article (the) declines as follows:

sing	masc	fem	neut
nom	o	η	το
	o	i	to
gen	του	της	του
	too	tis	too
acc	το(ν)*	τη(ν)*	το
	to(n)	ti(n)	to

*The forms έναν and τον/την should be used before nouns beginning with a vowel.

plural	masc	fem	neut
nom	οι	οι	τα
	i	i	ta
gen	των	των	των
	ton	ton	ton
acc	τους	τις	τα
	toos	tis	ta

Nominative Case

The nominative case is used for the subject of sentences:

το δωμάτιό μου είναι μικρό
to thom**a**tio moo **i**neh mik**r**o
my room is small

ο Γιάννης διαβάζει ένα βιβλίο
o Y**a**nis thiav**a**zi **e**na vivl**i**o
John is reading a book

Genitive Case

The genitive case is used to indicate possession and to translate 'of':

αυτό είναι το αυτοκίνητο του Γιώργου
aft**o i**neh to aftok**i**nito too Y**o**rgoo
this is George's car

ο σκύλος του γείτονα
o sk**i**los too y**i**tona
the neighbour's dog

Accusative Case

The accusative case is used for direct objects:

μπορείτε να μας φέρετε το λογαριασμό, παρακαλώ;
bor**i**teh na mas f**e**reteh to logariasm**o**, parakal**o**?
could you bring us the bill, please?

έχασα το λεωφορείο
ekhasa to leofor**i**o
I missed the bus

The accusative case is also used with some prepositions (to, from, with etc):

αυτή πήγε στην παραλία
aft**i** p**i**yeh stin paral**i**a
she has gone to the beach

αυτός είναι από τη Σκωτία
aft**o**s **i**neh ap**o** ti Skot**i**a
he comes from Scotland

αυτοί πηγαίνουν με τα πόδια
aft**i** piy**e**noon meh ta p**o**thia
they are going on foot

προτιμάμε να ταξιδεύουμε με το τρένο
protim**a**meh na taxith**e**voomeh meh to tr**e**no
we prefer to travel by train

Vocative Case

Another case in Greek is the vocative case which is used to address someone directly. The vocative has the same endings as the nominative case, apart from masculine nouns and names where the final ς is dropped:

Μαρία, πού είναι ο
  Γιάννης;
Maria, poo **i**neh o **Y**anis?
Mary, where is John?

Γιάννη, πού είναι η
  Μαρία;
Yani, poo **i**neh i Maria?
John, where is Mary?

Noun Endings

The endings of nouns change according to whether they are singular or plural and depending on whether they are in the nominative, genitive or accusative cases.

Masculine Nouns

Masculine nouns usually have one of three endings:

	-ας	-ης	-ος
	ο χειμώνας	ο εργάτης	ο δάσκαλος
	the winter	the workman	the teacher
sing			
nom	ο χειμώνας	ο εργάτης	ο δάσκαλος
	o khim**o**nas	o erg**a**tis	o th**a**skalos
gen	του χειμώνα	του εργάτη	του δασκάλου
	too khim**o**na	too erg**a**ti	too thask**a**loo
acc	το χειμώνα	τον εργάτη	τον δάσκαλο
	to khim**o**na	ton erg**a**ti	ton th**a**skalo
plural			
nom	οι χειμώνες	οι εργάτες	οι δάσκαλοι
	i khim**o**nes	i erg**a**tes	i th**a**skali
gen	των χειμώνων	των εργατών	των δασκάλων
	ton khim**o**non	ton ergat**o**n	ton thask**a**lon
acc	τους χειμώνες	τους εργάτες	τους δασκάλους
	toos khim**o**nes	toos erg**a**tes	toos thask**a**loos

A few masculine nouns end in:

-άς, -ές or -ούς

but for these only the plural differs from the above endings:

ο ψαράς	οι ψαράδες
o psaras	i psarathes
fisherman	fishermen
ο παπάς	οι παπάδες
o papas	i papathes
the priest	the priests
ο καφές	οι καφέδες
o kafes	i kafethes
the coffee	the coffees
ο καναπές	οι καναπέδες
o kanapes	i kanapethes
the couch	the couches
ο παππούς	οι παππούδες
o papoos	i papoothes
the grandfather	the grandfathers

Feminine Nouns

Feminine nouns either end in:

-α or -η

η γλώσσα	η νίκη
the tongue, the language	the victory

sing		
nom	η γλώσσα	η νίκη
	i glosa	i niki
gen	της γλώσσας	της νίκης
	tis glosas	tis nikis
acc	τη γλώσσα	τη νίκη
	ti glosa	ti niki

plural		
nom	οι γλώσσες	οι νίκες
	i gloses	i nikes
gen	των γλωσσών	των νικών
	ton gloson	ton nikon
acc	τις γλώσσες	τις νίκες
	tis gloses	tis nikes

Some irregular feminine nouns ending in -η, take the plural ending -εις, for example:

η λέξη	οι λέξεις
i lexi	i lexis
the word	the words
η απόφαση	οι αποφάσεις
i apofasi	i apofasis
the decision	the decisions

Feminine nouns ending in -ος decline like masculine nouns. For example:

η έξοδος	η είσοδος
i exothos	i isothos
the exit	the entrance

Neuter Nouns

Neuter nouns have one of the following endings:

-ο, -ι or -μα

		το δέντρο the tree	το ψωμί the bread, the loaf	το όνομα the name
sing	nom	το δέντρο to th**e**ndro	το ψωμί to psom**i**	το όνομα to **o**noma
	gen	του δέντρου too th**e**ndroo	του ψωμιού too psomi-**oo**	του ονόματος too on**o**matos
	acc	το δέντρο to th**e**ndro	το ψωμί to psom**i**	το όνομα to **o**noma
plural	nom	τα δέντρα ta th**e**ndra	τα ψωμιά ta psomi**a**	τα ονόματα ta on**o**mata
	gen	των δέντρων ton th**e**ndron	των ψωμιών ton psomi**on**	των ονομάτων ton onom**a**ton
	acc	τα δέντρα ta th**e**ndra	τα ψωμιά ta psomi**a**	τα ονόματα ta on**o**mata

Several neuter nouns end in -ος:

το είδος to **i**thos the kind	τα είδη ta **i**thi the kinds	το μέγεθος to me**y**eTHos the size	τα μεγέθη ta mey**e**THi the sizes

ADJECTIVES AND ADVERBS

Most adjectives also change as follows according to gender and number:

masc	fem	neut	masc	fem	neut
ακριβός expensive			γλυκός sweet		
ακριβός akriv**os**	ακριβή akriv**i**	ακριβό akriv**o**	γλυκός glik**os**	γλυκιά glik**ia**	γλυκό glik**o**
όμορφος beautiful			ελαφρύς light		
όμορφος **o**morfos	όμορφη **o**morfi	όμορφο **o**morfo	ελαφρύς elafr**is**	ελαφριά elafr**ia**	ελαφρύ elafr**i**

Adjective endings follow the pattern of the corresponding noun endings. Adjectives should agree with their nouns in gender, number, and case:

ο καλός φίλος
o kalos filos
the good friend

έχω μερικούς καλούς φίλους
ekho merikoos kaloos filoos
I have some good friends

η όμορφη πόλη
i omorfi poli
the beautiful town

είδαμε ένα ωραίο έργο
ithame enah oreo ergo
we saw a good film

The most common irregular adjective is:

ο πολύς a lot of, much, many

	sing	plural
masc	ο πολύς o polis	οι πολλοί i poli
fem	η πολλή i poli	οι πολλές i poles
neut	το πολύ to poli	τα πολλά ta pola

Comparatives

The comparative is formed by putting the word πιό [pio] 'more' in front of the adjective:

αυτό το ξενοδοχείο είναι πιό/λιγότερο ακριβό από εκείνο
afto to xenothokhio ineh pio/ligotero akrivo apo ekino
this hotel is more/less expensive than that one

είναι πιό ήσυχα εδώ
ineh pio isikha etho
it's quieter here

Superlatives

Superlatives are formed by putting the definite article in front of the comparative:

η Ομόνοια είναι η πιό διάσημη πλατεία στην Αθήνα
i Omoni-a ineh i pio thiasimi plati-a stin ATHina
Omonia Square is the most famous square in Athens

αυτός ο δρόμος είναι ο λιγότερο επικίνδυνος
aftos o thromos ineh o ligotero epikinthinos
this route is the least dangerous

η ταβέρνα Ο Γιάννης είναι η πιο δημοφιλής ταβέρνα στη Μυτιλήνη
i taverna O Yanis ineh i pio thimofilis taverna sti Mitilini
the O Yanis taverna is the most popular in Mitilini

'As ... as' is translated as τόσο ... όσο:

αυτό το εστιατόριο είναι
τόσο ακριβό όσο και το
άλλο
afto to estiatorio ineh toso
akrivo oso keh to alo
this restaurant is as
expensive as that one

αυτή η πόλη δεν είναι
τόσο ενδιαφέρουσα όσο
νόμιζα
afti i poli then ineh toso
enthiaferoosa oso nomiza
this town is not as
interesting as I thought

The following common
adjectives have irregular
comparatives and
superlatives:

κακός	χειρότερος	χείριστος
kakos	khiroteros	khiristos
bad	worse	worst

καλός	καλύτερος	κάλλιστος
kalos	kaliteros	kalistos
good	better	best

μικρός	μικρότερος	ελάχιστος
mikros	mikroteros	elakhistos
small	smaller	smallest

μεγάλος	μεγαλύτερος
megalos	megaliteros
big	bigger

μέγιστος
meyistos
biggest

λίγος	λιγότερος	ελάχιστος
ligos	ligoteros	elakhistos
few	fewer	fewest

πολύς	περισσότερος
polis	perisoteros
a lot of	a lot more of

Adverbs

If the adjective ends in -ος,
remove this ending and add
-α to create the adverb:

adjective	adverb
καλός	καλά
kalos	kala
good	well
κακός	κακά
kakos	kaka
bad	badly
ωραίος	ωραία
oreos	oreh-a
nice	nicely
τυχερός	τυχερά
tikheros	tikhera
lucky	luckily

If the adjective ends in -ης,
remove this ending and add
-ως to create the adverb:

adjective	adverb
συνεχής	συνεχώς
sinekhis	sinekhos
continuous	continuously
ακριβής	ακριβώς
akrivis	akrivos
precise	precisely

<table>
<tr><td>διεθνής</td><td>διεθνώς</td></tr>
<tr><td>thi-ethnis</td><td>thi-ethnos</td></tr>
<tr><td>international</td><td>internationally</td></tr>
</table>

Possessive Adjectives

my	μου	moo
your (sing, fam)	σου	soo
his	του	too
her	της	tis
its	του	too
our	μας	mas
your (pl, pol)	σας	sas
their	τους	toos

Possessive adjectives do not change according to case, gender or number. They follow the noun they refer to, but note that the definite article is placed in front of the noun:

το διαβατήριό μου
to thiavat**i**rio moo
my passport

τα λεφτά τους
ta left**a** toos
their money

το βιβλίο της
to vivl**i**o tis
her book

PRONOUNS

Possessive Pronouns

Possessive pronouns (mine, hers etc) are formed by placing the word δικός in front of the possessive. δικός declines like an adjective, agreeing with the object possessed in case, gender and number:

	masc	fem	neut
mine	δικός μου	δική μου	δικό μου
	thik**o**s moo	thik**i** moo	thik**o** moo
yours (sing, fam)	δικός σου	δική σου	δικό σου
	thik**o**s soo	thik**i** soo	thik**o** soo
his	δικός του	δική του	δικό του
	thik**o**s too	thik**i** too	thik**o** too
hers	δικός της	δική της	δικό της
	thik**o**s tis	thik**i** tis	thik**o** tis
its	δικός του	δική του	δικό του
	thik**o**s too	thik**i** too	thik**o** too
ours	δικός μας	δική μας	δικό μας
	thik**o**s mas	thik**i** mas	thik**o** mas
yours (pl, pol)	δικός σας	δική σας	δικό σας
	thik**o**s sas	thik**i** sas	thik**o** sas
theirs	δικός τους	δική τους	δικό τους
	thik**o**s toos	thik**i** toos	thik**o** toos

Plurals take the usual adjective endings:

αυτές είναι οι δικές μας
aftes ineh i thikes mas
these are ours

Personal Pronouns

nom	gen	acc
εγώ [ego] I	μου [moo] me	με/εμένα [meh/emena] me
εσύ [esi] you*	σου [soo] you	σε/εσένα [seh/esena] you
αυτός [aftos] he	του [too] him	τον [ton] him
αυτή [afti] she	της [tis] her	την [tin] her
αυτό [afto] it	του [too] it	το [to] it
εμείς [emis] we	μας [mas] us	μας/εμάς [mas/emas] us
εσείς [esis] you**	σας/εσάς [sas/esas] you	σας/εσάς [sas/esas] you
αυτοί [afti] they (m)	τους [toos] them	τους/αυτούς [toos/aftoos] them
αυτές [aftes] they (f)	τους [toos] them	τις/αυτές [tis/aftes] them
αυτά [afta] they (n)	τους [toos] them	τα/αυτά [ta/afta] them

GRAMMAR

* εσύ used when speaking to one person and is the familiar form generally used when speaking to family, friends and children.
** εσείς is the polite form which can be used to address one person or several people.

αυτή του έδωσε τα
χρήματα
afti too **e**thoseh ta khr**i**mata
she gave him the money

εγώ τους είδα να το
κλέβουν
eg**o** toos **i**tha na to kl**e**voon
I saw them stealing it

Where two forms are given
for the accusative, the second
is used after prepositions:

θα πάω μαζί με αυτές
THa p**a**o mazi meh aft**e**s
I will go with them

αυτό είναι ένα δώρο γιά
εσένα
aft**o** ineh **e**na th**o**ro ya es**e**na
this is a present for you

In Greek the subject pronoun
(nominative) is usually
omitted:

έφυγε χθές
efiyeh khTH**e**s
he left yesterday

θα ήθελα να παραγγείλω
THa **i**THela na parang**i**lo
I'd like to order

Although it may be retained
for emphasis:

αυτή ήταν πρώτη
aft**i** itan pr**o**ti
SHE was first

αυτός έκλεψε το
πορτοφόλι μου
aft**o**s **e**klepseh to portof**o**li moo
HE stole my wallet

εσύ φταίς
esi ftes
YOU are to blame

Examples using pronouns in
genitive and accusative:

το πήρε από την τσάντα
μου
to p**i**reh ap**o** tin ts**a**nda moo
he took it from my bag

εσύ τους το έδωσες;
es**i** toos to **e**thoses?
did YOU give it to them?

την πήρα μαζί μου
tin p**i**ra mazi moo
I took her with me

τα αγόρασε χθες
ta ag**o**raseh khTH**e**s
she bought them yesterday

θα σου τον συστήσω
THa soo ton sist**i**so
I shall introduce you to him

την είδα
tin **i**tha
I saw her

δε σε ακούω καλά
theh seh ak**oo**-o kal**a**
I cannot hear you very well

VERBS

The form of the verb given in dictionaries is usually the first person singular of the present tense. This is the basic form (equivalent to the infinitive) and the endings are either -ω (active verbs) or -μαι (passive verbs).

Although there are two categories of Greek verbs (active and passive), many verbs that are not passive in English are considered passive in Greek.

Present Tense

Present tense endings for verbs ending in -ω depend on whether or not the stress falls on the last syllable:

	stress not on last syllable	stress on last syllable	
	αγοράζω buy	πουλώ sell	μπορώ be able
I	αγοράζ-ω	πουλ-ώ	μπορ-ώ
	agorazo	poolo	boro
you	αγοράζ-εις	πουλ-άς	μπορ-είς
	agorazis	poolas	boris
he/she	αγοράζ-ει	πουλ-ά	μπορ-εί
	agorazi	poola	bori
we	αγοράζ-ουμε	πουλ-άμε	μπορ-ούμε
	agorazoomeh	poolameh	boroomeh
you	αγοράζ-ετε	πουλ-άτε	μπορ-είτε
	agorazeteh	poolateh	boriteh
they	αγοράζ-ουν	πουλ-ούν	μπορ-ούν
	agorazoon	pooloon	boroon

πόσο το πουλάς;
poso to poolas?
how much are you selling it for?

το αγοράζω για χίλιες δραχμές
to agorazo ya khili-es thrakhmes
I am buying it for 1,000 drachmas

δεν μπορεί να περπατήσει
then bori na perpatisi
he can't walk

Passive verbs ending in -μαι take the following endings:

ντύνομαι be dressed, dress (oneself)

I	ντύν-ομαι
	dinomeh
you	ντύν-εσαι
	dineseh
he/she	ντύν-εται
	dineteh
we	ντυν-όμαστε
	dinomasteh
you	ντύν-εστε
	dinesteh
they	ντύν-ονται
	dinondeh

The verbs 'to be' and 'to have' are irregular:

είμαι I am	είμαστε we are
imeh	imasteh
είσαι you are	είσαστε/είστε you are
iseh	isasteh/isteh
είναι he/she/it is	είναι they are
ineh	ineh
έχω I have	έχουμε we have
ekho	ekhoomeh
έχεις you have	έχετε you have
ekhis	ekheteh
έχει he/she/it has	έχουν they have
ekhi	ekhoon

Past Simple Tense

To describe an action that has taken place in the past, use the past simple tense in Greek. To form this, take the basic form of the verb and add the following endings. Note that in the simple past, the stress moves back one syllable and sometimes changes have to be made to the form of the verb which comes before these endings. For example, where necessary, the letter ε is added to the beginning of the verb so that the stress can move back a syllable:

ακού-ω (I hear)	κάν-ω (I do)
άκου-σ-α I heard **a**koosa	έκαν-α I did **e**kana
άκου-σ-ες you heard **a**kooses	έκανες you did **e**kanes
άκου-σ-ε he/she heard **a**kooseh	έκανε he/she/it did **e**kaneh
ακού-σ-αμε we heard ak**oo**sameh	εκάναμε we did ek**a**nameh
ακού-σ-ατε you heard ak**oo**sateh	εκάνατε you did ek**a**nateh
άκου-σ-αν they heard **a**koosan	έκαναν they did **e**kanan

The past tense of 'to be' and 'to have' is:

ήμουν I was **i**moon	ήμασταν we were **i**mastan
ήσουν you were **i**soon	ήσασταν you were **i**sastan
ήταν he/she/it was **i**tan	ήταν they were **i**tan

είχα I had **i**kha	είχαμε we had **i**khameh
είχες you had **i**khes	είχατε you had **i**khateh
είχε he/she/it had **i**kheh	είχαν they had **i**khan

πόσα χρήματα είχατε στην τσάντα σας;
p**o**sa khr**i**mata **i**khateh stin ts**a**nda sas?
how much money did you have in your handbag?

επισκεφτήκατε το Αρχαιολογικό Μουσείο;
episkeft**i**kateh to Arkheoloyik**o** Moos**i**o?
did you visit the Archaeological Museum?

οι τιμές ήταν πιό φτηνές πέρυσι
i tim**e**s **i**tan pi**o** ftin**e**s p**e**risi
prices were cheaper last year

υπογράψατε στο βιβλίο;
ipograpsateh sto vivlio?
did you sign the book?

The Indefinite

The Greek indefinite form of
the verb has no direct
equivalent in English
although its use often
corresponds to the infinitive
used after verbs such as 'to
want', 'to be able to', 'can',
etc, and has the following
pattern:

να + basic form of verb +
ending of the verb preceding
it.

It must agree in person and
number with the main verb
preceding it:

θα μπορούσα να πληρώσω
με επιταγή;
THα boroosa na pliroso meh
epitayi?
could I pay by cheque?

The exception to this is the
impersonal verb 'to have to',
'must' which always takes the
same form πρέπει:

πρέπει να πηγαίνουμε
τώρα
prepi na piyenoomeh tora
we must go now

Here is a list of some useful verbs with their indefinite and
past simple in the first person:

present	indefinite	past simple	perfect
βλέπω see	να δω	είδα	έχω δει
vlepo	na tho	itha	ekho thi
βρίσκω find	να βρω	βρήκα	έχω βρει
vrisko	na vro	vrika	ekho vri
δίνω give	να δώσω	έδωσα	έχω δώσει
thino	na thoso	ethosa	ekho thosi
έρχομαι come	να έλθω	ήλθα	έχω έλθει
erkhomeh	na elTHo	ilTHa	ekho elTHi
κάνω do	να κάνω	έκανα	έχω κάνει
kano	na kano	ekana	ekho kani
λέω say	να πω	είπα	έχω πει
le-o	na po	ipa	ekho pi
μένω stay	να μείνω	έμεινα	έχω μείνει
meno	na mino	emina	ekho mini
παίρνω take	να πάρω	πήρα	έχω πάρει
perno	na paro	pira	ekho pari

πηγαίνω go	να πάω	πήγα	έχω πάει
piyeno	na pao	piga	ekho pa-i
πίνω drink	να πιώ	ήπια	έχω πιεί
pino	na pio	ipia	ekho pi-i
στέλνω send	να στείλω	έστειλα	έχω στείλει
stelno	na stilo	estila	ekho stili
τρώω eat	να φάω	έφαγα	έχω φάει
tro-o	na fa-o	efaga	ekho fa-i
ρωτώ ask	να ρωτήσω	ρώτησα	έχω ρωτήσει
roto	na rotiso	rotisa	ekho rotisi
αγοράζω buy	να αγοράσω	αγόρασα	έχω αγοράσει
agorazo	na agoraso	agorasa	ekho agorasi
κλείνω close	να κλείσω	έκλεισα	έχω κλείσει
klino	na kliso	eklisa	ekho klisi
κοιτάζω look	να κοιτάξω	κοίταξα	έχω κοιτάξει
kitazo	na kitaxo	kitaxa	ekho kitaxi
σταματώ stop	να σταματήσω	σταμάτησα	έχω σταματήσει
stamato	na stamatiso	stamatisa	ekho stamatisi
νομίζω think	να νομίσω	νόμισα	έχω νομίσει
nomizo	na nomiso	nomisa	ekho nomisi
γράφω write	να γράψω	έγραψα	έχω γράψει
grafo	na grapso	egrapsa	ekho grapsi

Future Tense

The simplest way to form the continuous future tense in Greek is to take the present tense forms and add the word θα in front of them:

I will be waiting	θα περιμένω
	THa perimeno
you will ...	θα περιμένεις
	THa perimenis
he/she will ...	θα περιμένει
	THa perimeni
we will ...	θα περιμένουμε
	THa perimenoomeh
you will ...	θα περιμένετε
	THa perimeneteh
they will ...	θα περιμένουν
	THa perimenoon

GRAMMAR

To form the simple future tense you use θα and the appropriate forms of the indefinite (without the να):

I will buy	θα αγοράσω
	THa agoraso
you will ...	θα αγοράσεις
	THa agorasis
he/she/it will ...	θα αγοράσει
	THa agorasi
we will ...	θα αγοράσουμε
	THa agorasoomeh
you will ...	θα αγοράσετε
	THa agoraseteh
they will ...	θα αγοράσουν
	THa agorasoon

θα σε δω το βράδυ
THa seh tho to vrathi
I'll see you tonight

Imperatives

The imperative form of the verb is used to give commands. To create the singular, familiar imperative, take the indefinite form of the verb (without the να) and change the final -ω to -ε:

κοίταξε εκεί!
kitaxeh eki!
look over there!

πρόσεξε!
prosexeh!
watch out!

Polite and plural forms of the imperative are created by changing the final -ω of the indefinite form (without the να) to -ετε or -τε :

ρωτήστε τον αστυνόμο
εκεί πέρα
rotisteh ton astinomo eki pera
ask the policeman over there

υπογράψτε εδώ, παρακαλώ
ipograpsteh etho, parakalo
sign here, please

Negative imperatives are formed by placing μη or μην in front of the second person of the indefinite form (without the να) of the verb:

μην πάτε από αυτόν το
δρόμο
min pateh apo afton ton thromo
don't go along this street

μην πιείς αυτό το νερό
min pi-is afto to nero
do not drink this water

Some common irregular imperatives are:

familiar	polite/plural
βρες find	βρείτε
vres	vriteh
δες see	δείτε or δέστε
thes	thiteh or thesteh
πιές drink	πιείτε or πιέστε
pies	pi-iteh or pi-esteh

πες say   πείτε or πέστε
pes   pesteh
ελα come   ελάτε
e**l**a   el**a**teh

Negatives

To form the negative, place the word δε or δεν in front of the verb:

δε μου αρέσει αυτό
theh moo a**r**esi aft**o**
I don't like this

δε μιλάω καλά Ελληνικά
theh mil**a**-o kal**a** Elinik**a**
my Greek is not very good

δεν μπορώ να βρώ το ξενοδοχείο
then bo**r**o na vro to xenothokh**i**o
I cannot find the hotel

QUESTIONS

The word order and intonation for questions in Greek are the same as in English:

πού είναι το γραφείο του ΕΟΤ, παρακαλώ;
poo **i**neh to graf**i**o too **E**-OT, parakal**o**?
where is the tourist information office, please?

Note that in questions in Greek, a semi-colon is used instead of a question mark.

DATES

To say the date take the ordinal number then the genitive of the month. The exception is 'the first' when you should use the ordinal number:

σήμερα είναι εικοσιεφτά Φεβρουαρίου
simera **i**neh **i**kosi-eft**a** Fevroo-ar**i**oo
today is the 27th of February

αύριο είναι πρώτη Ιουλίου
avrio **i**neh pr**o**ti Iool**i**-oo
tomorrow is the first of July

χθες ήταν τρεις Δεκεμβρίου
khТΗes **i**tan tris thekemvr**i**oo
yesterday was the 3rd of December

Πρωταπριλιά
protaprili**a**
1st of April

Πρωτομαγιά
protomay**a**
1st of May

Instead of saying 'nineteen ninety-five' you literally say 'nine thousand, nine hundred, ninety five':

χίλια εννιακόσια ενενήντα πέντε
kh**i**lia enniak**o**sia enen**i**nda p**e**ndeh

TIME

what time is it?	τί ώρα είναι;	ti ora ineh?
one o'clock	μία η ώρα	mia i ora
two o'clock	δύο η ώρα	thio i ora
it's one o'clock	είναι μία η ώρα	ineh mia i ora
it's two o'clock	είναι δύο η ώρα	ineh thio i ora
it's ten o'clock	είναι δέκα η ώρα	ineh theka i ora
five past one	μία και πέντε	mia keh pendeh
ten past two	δύο και δέκα	thio keh theka
quarter past one	μία και τέταρτο	mia keh tetarto
quarter past two	δύο και τέταρτο	thio keh tetarto
twenty past ten	δέκα και είκοσι	theka keh ikosi
half past ten	δέκα και μισή	theka keh misi
twenty to ten	δέκα παρά είκοσι	theka para ikosi
quarter to two	δύο παρά τέταρτο	thio para tetarto
at half past four	στις τέσσερις και μισή	stis teseris keh misi
at eight o'clock	στις οκτώ	stis okto
14.00	δεκατέσσερις	theka-teseris
17.30	δεκαεφτά και τριάντα	theka-efta keh trianda
2 a.m.	δύο η ώρα το βράδυ	thio i ora to vrathi
2 p.m.	δύο η ώρα το μεσημέρι	thio i ora to mesimeri
6 a.m.	έξι η ώρα το πρωί	exi i ora to pro-i
6 p.m.	έξι η ώρα το απόγευμα	exi i ora to apoyevma
noon	το μεσημέρι	to mesimeri
midnight	τα μεσάνυχτα	ta mesanikhta
an hour	η ώρα	i ora
a minute	το λεπτό	to lepto
one minute	ένα λεπτό	ena lepto
two minutes	δύο λεπτά	thio lepta
a second	το δευτερόλεπτο	to thefterolepto
a quarter of an hour	ένα τέταρτο	ena tetarto
half an hour	μισή ώρα	misi ora
three quarters of an hour	τρία τέταρτα της ώρας	tria tetarta tis oras

NUMBERS

0	μηδέν mithen
1	ένα ena
2	δύο thio
3	τρία tria
4	τέσσερα tesera
5	πέντε pendeh
6	έξι exi
7	επτά epta
8	οχτώ okhto
9	εννιά enia
10	δέκα theka
11	έντεκα endeka
12	δώδεκα thotheka
13	δεκατρία theka-tria
14	δεκατέσσερα theka-tesera
15	δεκαπέντε theka-pendeh
16	δεκαέξι theka-exi
17	δεκαεπτά theka-epta
18	δεκαοχτώ theka-okhto
19	δεκαεννιά theka-enia
20	είκοσι ikosi
21	εικοσιένα ikosi-ena
22	εικοσιδύο ikosi-thio
30	τριάντα trianda
31	τριανταένα trianda-ena
40	σαράντα saranda
50	πενήντα peninda
60	εξήντα exinda
70	εβδομήντα evthominda
80	ογδόντα ogthonda
90	ενενήντα eneninda
100	εκατό ekato
110	εκατό δέκα ekato theka
200	διακόσια thiakosia

300	τριακόσια triakosia
1,000	χίλια khilia
2,000	δύο χιλιάδες thio khiliathes
5,000	πέντε χιλιάδες pendeh khiliathes
10,000	δέκα χιλιάδες theka khiliathes
20,000	είκοσι χιλιάδες ikosi khiliathes
50,000	πενήντα χιλιάδες peninda khiliathes
100,000	εκατό χιλιάδες ekato khiliathes
1,000,000	ένα εκατομμύριο ena ekatomirio

Ordinals

Ordinal numbers decline like regular adjectives:

1st	πρώτος protos
2nd	δεύτερος thefteros
3rd	τρίτος tritos
4th	τέταρτος tetartos
5th	πέμπτος pemptos
6th	έκτος ektos
7th	έβδομος evthomos
8th	όγδοος ogtho-os
9th	ένατος enatos
10th	δέκατος thekatos

CONVERSION TABLES

1 centimetre = 0.39 inches	1 inch = 2.54 cm

1 metre = 39.37 inches = 1.09 yards

1 foot = 30.48 cm

1 yard = 0.91 m

1 kilometre = 0.62 miles = 5/8 mile

1 mile = 1.61 km

km	1	2	3	4	5	10	20	30	40	50	100
miles	0.6	1.2	1.9	2.5	3.1	6.2	12.4	18.6	24.8	31.0	62.1

miles	1	2	3	4	5	10	20	30	40	50	100
km	1.6	3.2	4.8	6.4	8.0	16.1	32.2	48.3	64.4	80.5	161

1 gram = 0.035 ounces

1 kilo = 1000 g = 2.2 pounds

g	100	250	500
oz	3.5	8.75	17.5

1 oz = 28.35 g

1 lb = 0.45 kg

kg	0.5	1	2	3	4	5	6	7	8	9	10
lb	1.1	2.2	4.4	6.6	8.8	11.0	13.2	15.4	17.6	19.8	22.0

kg	20	30	40	50	60	70	80	90	100
lb	44	66	88	110	132	154	176	198	220

lb	0.5	1	2	3	4	5	6	7	8	9	10	20
kg	0.2	0.5	0.9	1.4	1.8	2.3	2.7	3.2	3.6	4.1	4.5	9.0

1 litre = 1.75 UK pints / 2.13 US pints

1 UK pint = 0.57 l	1 UK gallon = 4.55 l
1 US pint = 0.47 l	1 US gallon = 3.79 l

centigrade / Celsius

$C = (F - 32) \times 5/9$

C	-5	0	5	10	15	18	20	25	30	36.8	38
F	23	32	41	50	59	64	68	77	86	98.4	100.4

Fahrenheit

$F = (C \times 9/5) + 32$

F	23	32	40	50	60	65	70	80	85	98.4	101
C	-5	0	4	10	16	18	21	27	29	36.8	38.3

English-Greek

A

a, an* enas, mia, ena

about: about 20 peripoo ikosi
  it's about 5 o'clock ineh yiro
  stis pendeh
  a film about Greece ena ergo
  ya tin Elatha

above pano apo

abroad sto exoteriko

absolutely! (I agree) apolitos!

accelerator to gazi

accept thekhomeh

accident to thistikhima
  there's been an accident
  eyineh ena thistikhima

accommodation i thiamoni
  see room

accurate akrivis

ache o ponos
  my back aches pona-i i plati
  moo

across: across the road
  apenandi sto thromo

adapter (plug) i priza taf
  (electrical) to polaplo

address i thi-efTHinsi
  what's your address? pia ineh
  i thi-efTHinsi soo?

Addresses are written with the
street number after the name of
the street, e.g.

Γιάννης Παπαδόπουλος
Ελευθερίου Βενιζέλου 28
Χανιά 73100
Κρήτη   →

Yiannis Papadopoulos
Eleutheriou Venizelou 28
Khania 73100
Kriti

When sending mail, always use
postcodes; they can be found in
special lists in post offices. You
can write Greek addresses in the
Greek or Roman alphabet.

---

address book i adzenda ton
  thi-efTHinseon

admission charge timi isothoo

adult (man/woman) o enilikos/i
  eniliki

advance: in advance
  prokatavolika

aeroplane to a-eroplano

after meta
  after you meta apo sas
  after lunch meta apo to
  yevma

afternoon apo-yevma
  in the afternoon kata to apo-
  yevma
  this afternoon afto to apo-
  yevma

aftershave i kolonia meta to
  xirisma

aftersun cream to galaktoma ya
  ton ilio

afterwards meta

again xana

against enandion

age i ilikia

ago: a week ago prin apo mia
  evthomatha
  an hour ago prin apo

mia ora
agree: I agree simfono
AIDS to AIDS
air o a-eras
  by air a-eroporikos
air-conditioning o klimatismos
airmail: by airmail
  a-eroporikos
airmail envelope o
  a-eroporikos fakelos
airport to a-erothromio
  to the airport, please sto
  a-erothromio, parakalo
airport bus to leoforio
  a-erothromi-oo
aisle seat THesi thipla sto
  thiathromo
alarm clock to xipnitiri
Albania i Alvania
Albanian (adj) Alvanikos
alcohol to alko-ol
alcoholic inopnevmatothis
all: all the boys ola ta agoria
  all the girls ola ta koritsia
  all the men oli i andres
  all the women oles i yinekes
  all of it olokliro
  all of them ola afta
  that's all, thanks afta ineh
  ola, efkharisto
allergic: I'm allergic to ... imeh
  aleryikos meh ...
allowed: is it allowed?
  epitrepeteh?
all right entaxi
  I'm all right imeh entaxi
  are you all right? iseh entaxi?
almond to amigthalo
almost skhethon

alone monos
alphabet to alfavito
  see page vi
already ithi
also episis
although an keh
altogether sinolika
always panda
am*: I am imeh
a.m.: at seven a.m. stis efta pro
  mesimvrias
amazing (surprising) ekpliktikos
  (very good) thavmasios
ambulance to asTHenoforo
  call an ambulance! kalesteh
  ena asTHenoforo!

Dial 166 for an ambulance.

America i Ameriki
American (adj) Amerikanikos
  I'm American (man/woman)
  imeh Amerikanos/
  Amerikana
among anamesa
amount to poso
  (money) ta khrimata
amp: a 13-amp fuse mia asfalia
  thekatria amper
amphitheatre to amfiTHeatro
Ancient Greece i arkhea Elatha
Ancient Greek ta arkhea Elinika
and keh
angry THimomenos
animal to zo-o
ankle o astraGalos
anniversary (wedding) i epetios
  too Gamoo
annoy: this man's annoying me

aftos o andras meh enokhli
annoying enokhlitikos
another alos, ali, alo
   can we have another room?
   boroomeh na ekhoomeh
   ena alo thomatio?
   another beer, please ali mia
   bira, parakalo
antibiotics to andiviotiko
antihistamine to andi-
   istaminiko farmako
antique: is it an antique? ineh
   antika?
antique shop to paleopolio
antiseptic to andisiptiko
any: have you got any bread/
   tomatoes? ekheteh psomi/
   domates?

•••••• DIALOGUE ••••••

   do you have any change? ekhis
   kaTHoloo psila?
   sorry, I don't have any lipameh,
   then ekho kaTHoloo

anybody kanis
   does anybody speak English?
   mila-i kanis Anglika?
   there wasn't anybody there
   then itan kanis eki
anything otithipoteh

•••••• DIALOGUES ••••••

   anything else? tipoteh alo?
   nothing else, thanks tipoteh,
   efkharisto

   would you like anything to drink?
   THa THelateh na pi-iteh kati?
   I don't want anything, thanks then
   THelo tipoteh, efkharisto

apart from ektos apo
apartment to thiamerisma
appendicitis i skoliko-ithitis
appetizer to proto piato
   appetizers ta orektika
aperitif to aperitif
apology i signomi
apple to milo
appointment to randevoo

•••••• DIALOGUE ••••••

   good afternoon, sir, how can I help
   you? kalispera sas, kiri-eh, pos
   boro na sas vo-iTHiso?
   I'd like to make an appointment
   THa iTHela na kliso ena
   randevoo
   what time would you like? ti ora
   THeleteh?
   three o'clock tris i ora
   I'm afraid that's not possible; is four
   o'clock all right? fovameh oti afto
   then yineteh; boriteh stis
   teseris?
   yes, that will be fine neh, poli kala
   the name was ...? to onoma sas?

apricot to verikoko
April o Aprilios
archaeology i arkheoloyia
are*: we are imasteh
   you are isteh
   they are ineh
area i periokhi
area code o kothikos ariTHmos
arm to kheri
arrange: will you arrange it for
   us? THa to kanonisis ya mas?
arrival i afixi
arrive ftano

when do we arrive? poteh
ftanoomeh?
has my fax arrived yet?
eftaseh to fax moo?
we arrived today ftasameh
simera
art i tekhni
art gallery i pinakoTHiki
artist (man/woman) o kalitekhnis/
i kalitekhnitha
as: as big as ... megalo san ...
as soon as possible oso pio
grigora yineteh
ashtray to tasaki, to stokhto-
thokhio
ask roto
I didn't ask for this then zitisa
afto
could you ask him to ...? boris
na too pis na ...?
asleep: she's asleep kimateh
aspirin i aspirini
asthma to asTHma
astonishing ekpliktikos
at: at the hotel sto
xenothokhio
at the station sto staTHmo
at six o'clock stis exi i ora
at Yanni's stoo Yanni
Athens i ATHina
athletics o aTHlitismos
attractive elkistikos
aubergine i melidzana
August o AvGoostos
aunt i THia
Australia i Afstralia
Australian (adj) Afstralezikos
I'm Australian (man/woman)
imeh Afstralos/Afstraleza

automatic (adj) aftomatos
(car) to aftomato aftokinito
automatic teller i mikhani ya
metrita
autumn to fTHinoporo
in the autumn sto fTHinoporo
avenue i leoforos
average (not good) metrio
on average kata meson oro
awake: is he awake? ineh
xipnios?
away: go away! fiyeh
is it far away? ineh poli
makria?
awful apesios
axle o axonas

B

baby to moro
baby food i pethiki trofi
baby's bottle to bibero
baby-sitter i baby-sitter
back (of body) i plati
(back part) piso
at the back sto piso meros
can I have my money back?
boro na ekho ta lefta moo
piso?
to come/go back epistrefo,
yirizo piso
backache ponos stin plati
bacon to bacon
bad kakos
a bad headache enas
askhimos ponokefalos
badly askhima
bag i tsanda
(suitcase) i valitsa

baggage i aposkeves
baggage check o khoros filaxis
   aposkevon
baggage claim anazitisi
   aposkevon
bakery o foornaris
balcony to balkoni
   a room with a balcony ena
   thomatio meh balkoni
bald falakros
ball (large) i bala
   (small) to balaki
ballet to baleto
banana i banana
band (musical) to singrotima
bandage o epithesmos
Bandaid® to lefkoplast
bank i trapeza

Banks are usually open Monday
to Thursday from 8 a.m. to 2
p.m., and Fridays from 8 a.m. to
1.30 p.m. Certain branches in
the major cities and tourist
centres open extra hours in the
evenings and on Saturday
mornings for exchanging money.
Usually you have to queue twice,
once to get the transaction
approved and a second time to
pick up the cash. The best rates
for exchanging money or
travellers' cheques are to be
found in banks and post offices
(where there's usually less of a
queue) rather than hotels,
tourist shops etc.

bank account o trapezikos

logariasmos
bar to bar

Bars, 'barakia' in the plural, are
a recent transplant confined to
big cities and holiday resorts.
They range from unappealing
clones of Parisian bars to
imitation British pubs and are
invariably more expensive than
cafés. They are, however, most
likely to stock a range of foreign
label beers. Some bars and cafés
close in the afternoon but many
remain open from early in the
morning until late at night. In
summer, the chief socializing
time is rarely before 8 p.m. and
can often start around 10 p.m.
It is not offensive to be drunk
as long as you don't annoy other
people. Driving after drinking
any alcohol is strictly forbidden.
see also café

a bar of chocolate mia
   sokolata
barber's to koorio
basket to kalaTHi
basketball to basketball, i
   kalaTHosferisi
bath to banio
   can I have a bath? boro na
   kano ena banio?
bathroom to lootro, to banio
   with a private bathroom meh
   ithiotiko lootro
bath towel i petseta too
   banioo

battery i bataria
bay o kolpos
be* imeh
beach i paralia
beach mat i psaTHa
beach umbrella i ombrela
beans ta fasolia
  green beans ta fasolakia
  runner beans ta kokina
  fasolia
  broad beans ta kookia
beard ta yenia
beautiful oreos
because epithi
  because of ... exetias ...
bed to krevati
  I'm going to bed now pao ya
  ipno tora
bed and breakfast thomatio
  meh pro-ino
bedroom to ipnothomatio
beef to moskhari
beer i bira
  two beers, please thio bires,
  parakalo

Most bars serve foreign label
beers in bottles or cans (Amstel,
Heineken, Becks, etc.) You will
not often find places which serve
draught beer.

---

before prin
begin arkhizo
  when does it begin? poteh
  arkhizi?
beginner (man/woman) o
  arkharios/i arkharia
beginning: at the beginning kat

arkhas
behind piso
  behind me apo piso moo
beige bez
believe pistevo
belly-dancing to tsifteteli
below apo kato
belt i zoni
bend (in road) i strofi
berth (on ship) i klini
beside: beside the ... thipla
  sto ...
best aristos
better kaliteros
  better than ... kaliteros apo ...
  are you feeling better?
  esTHaneseh kalitera?
between metaxi
beyond pera apo
bicycle to pothilato
big meGalos
  too big poli meGalo
  it's not big enough then ineh
  arketa meGalo
bike to pothilato
  (motorbike) to mikhanaki
bikini to bikini
bill o loGariasmos
  (US) to khartonomisma
  could I have the bill, please?
  boro na ekho ton
  loGariasmo, parakalo?
bin o skoopithotenekes
bin liners i sakoola
  skoopithion
bird to pooli
biro® to stilo
birthday ta yeneTHlia
  happy birthday! khronia pola!

biscuit to biskoto
bit: a little bit liGo
  a big bit ena megalo komati
  a bit of ... ligo apo ...
  a bit expensive ligo akrivo,
    akrivootsiko
bite (by insect) to tsibima
  (by dog) i thagonia
bitter (taste etc) pikros
black mavros
blanket i kooverta
bleach (for toilet) to Harpik®
bless you! ya soo!
blind tiflos
blinds ta pantzooria
blister i fooskala
blocked (road, pipe)
  frakarismenos
  (sink) voolomenos
block of flats i polikatikia
blond xanTHos
blood to ema
  high blood pressure ipsili
  pi-esi ematos
blouse i blooza
blow-dry to khtenisma
  I'd like a cut and blow-dry THa
  iTHela kopsimo keh
  khtenisma
blue bleh
  blue eyes galana matia
blusher i poothra
boarding house i pansion
boarding pass i karta
  epivivaseos
boat (small) to ka-iki
  (for passengers) to plio
body to soma
boil (verb) vrazo

boiled egg to vrasto avgo
boiler o vrastiras
bone to kokalo
bonnet (of car) to kapo
book to vivlio
  (verb) klino
  can I book a seat? boro na
  kliso mia THesi?

•••••• DIALOGUE ••••••

I'd like to book a table for two THa
iTHela na kliso ena trapezi ya
thio atoma
what time would you like it booked
for? ti ora to THeleteh?
half past seven stis efta keh misi
that's fine entaxi
and your name? to onoma sas,
parakalo?

bookshop to vivliopolio
bookstore to vivliopolio
boot (footwear) i bota
  (of car) to port-bagaz
border (of country) ta sinora
bored: I'm bored vari-emeh
boring varetos
born: I was born in Manchester
yeniTHika sto Manchester
I was born in 1960 yeniTHika
to 1960 (khilia eniakosia
exinda)
borrow thanizomeh
  may I borrow ...? boro na
  thanisto ...?
both keh i thio
bother: sorry to bother you
signomi poo sas enokhlo
bottle to bookali
  a bottle of house red ena

bookali kokino spitiko krasi
bottle-opener to anikhtiri
bottom (of person) o kolos
  at the bottom of the hill sto
  vaTHos too lofoo
  at the bottom of the road sto
  telos too thromoo
box to kooti
box office to tamio
boy to aGori
boyfriend o filos
bra to sooti-en
bracelet to vrakhioli
brake to freno
  (verb) frenaro
brandy to koniak
bread to psomi
  white bread to aspro psomi
  brown bread to mavro psomi
  wholemeal bread to starenio
  psomi
break (verb) spao
  I've broken the ... espasa to ...
  I think I've broken my wrist
  nomizo oti espasa ton
  karpo moo
break down (car) paTHeno
  vlavi
  I've broken down khalaseh to
  aftokinito moo
breakdown (car) i vlavi

The place where you hire a car
should give you the telephone
number for the local Express
Service in case of breakdowns.
Tourists driving their own car
with proof of AA/RAC or similar
→

membership are given free
road assistance from the ELPA,
the Greek equivalent, which
runs breakdown services based
in Athens, Patra, Larissa,
Volos, Ioannina, Corfu, Tripoli,
Crete and Thessaloniki. The
information number is 174. In
an emergency ring their road
assistance service on 104,
anywhere in the country.

breakdown service i vlaves
  aftokiniton
breakfast to pro-ino
break-in: I've had a break-in
  meh listepsan
breast to stiTHos
breathe anapneo
breeze to aeraki
bridge (over river) i yefira
brief sindomos
briefcase o khartofilakas
bright (light etc) fotinos
  bright red khtipitos kokinos
brilliant (idea, person)
  katapliktikos
bring ferno
  I'll bring it back later THa to
  fero piso argotera
Britain i Vretania
British Vretanikos
brochure to prospektoos
broken spasmenos
  it's broken ineh spasmeno
bronchitis i vronkhititha
brooch i karfitsa
broom i skoopa

brother o athelfos
brother-in-law o Gambros
brown kafeh
　brown hair kastana malia
　brown eyes kastana matia
bruise i melania
brush i voortsa
　(for hair) i voortsa ya ta malia
　(artist's) to pinelo
bucket o koovas
buffet car to boofeh
buggy (for child) to pethiko
　amaxaki
building to ktirio
bulb (light bulb) i lamba
Bulgaria i Voolgaria
Bulgarian (adj) Voolgarikos
bumper o profilaktiras
bunk i kooketa
bureau de change Sinalagma
　see bank
burglary i thiarixi
burn (noun) to kapsimo
　(verb) keo
burnt: this is burnt afto ineh
　kameno
burst: a burst pipe mia
　spasmeni solina
bus to leoforio
　what number bus is it to ...? ti
　ariTHmo ekhi to leoforio
　ya ...?
　when is the next bus to ...?
　poteh ineh to epomeno
　leoforio ya ...?
　what time is the last bus? ti
　ora ineh to telefteo
　leoforio?
　could you let me know when

we get there? boriteh na moo
to piteh, otan ftasoomeh
eki?

For city buses, tickets should be
bought in advance from
newspaper or cigarette kiosks.
You can use the same type of
ticket for buses and trolleybuses
in Athens. When you get on,
always validate your ticket by
inserting it into the machine on
the bus/trolleybus. Buses have
their destination written on the
front; check this carefully, rather
than the number, to make sure
you are not on the wrong bus.
For the major inter-city lines,
ticketing is now computerized,
with assigned seating and sold-
out vehicles common. On
smaller rural/island routes, it's
generally first-come, first-served
with some standing allowed and
tickets dispensed on the spot by
a conductor.

•••••• DIALOGUE ••••••
does this bus go to ...? piyeni afto
to leoforio sto ...?
no, you need a number ... okhi,
prepi na pareteh to leoforio
ariTHmos ...

business i thooli-es
bus station to praktorio
　leoforion, o staTHmos
　leoforion
bus stop i stasi leoforioo

bust (sculpture) i protomi
  (measurement) to stiTHos
busy (restaurant etc)
  polisikhnastos
  I'm busy tomorrow imeh
  apaskholimenos avrio
but ala
butcher's o khasapis
butter to vootiro
button to koobi
buy aGorazo
  where can I buy ...? poo boro
  na agoraso ...?
by: by bus/car meh to leoforio/
  aftokinito
  written by ... grameno apo ...
  by the window thipla sto
  paraTHiro
  by the sea konda sti THalasa
  by Thursday prin apo tin
  Pempti
bye yasoo

C

cabbage to lakhano
cabin (on ship) i kabina
cable car to teleferik
café i kafeteria, to kafenio

The 'kafenio' is the traditional
Greek coffee shop or café.
Although its main business is
Greek coffee it also serves
spirits, beer, tea and soft drinks.
A 'zakharoplastio' is a cross
between café and patisserie and
it serves coffee, alcohol, yoghurt
→

and honey, sticky cakes etc, both
to eat in and take away. A
'galaktopolio' is a type of take-
away café, specializing more in
dairy products (yoghurt, ice
cream, custard desserts etc).
These last two types of café are
usually more family-oriented
than a 'kafenio' and many also
serve a basic continental
breakfast. Usually the only
edibles sold in cafés are very
sweet cakes and preserves,
although some city cafés serve
savoury snacks and sandwiches.
See also bar

cagoule to athiavrokho
cake to cake
cake shop to zakharoplastio
call fonazo
  (to phone) tilefono
  what's it called? pos to
  leneh?
  he/she is called ... ton/tin
  leneh ...
  please call a doctor seh
  parakalo, tilefoniseh seh
  ena yatro
  please give me a call at 7.30
  a.m. tomorrow seh parakalo,
  tilefoniseh moo avrio to
  pro-i stis efta keh misi
  please ask him to call me seh
  parakalo, pes too na moo
  tilefonisi
call back: I'll call back later THa
  xanarTHo argotera

(phone back) THa seh paro
piso
call round: I'll call round
tomorrow THa peraso avrio
camcorder i mikhani lipseos
camera i fotoGrafiki mikhani
camera shop to katastima
fotografikon ithon
camp (verb) kataskinono
can we camp here?
boroomeh na
kataskinosoomeh etho?
camping gas to iGra-erio

Camping gas canisters can be
bought either from a hardware
store, supermarkets or from
campsite shops; you can't carry
canisters on planes.

campsite to kambing

Official campsites range from
ramshackle compounds on the
islands to highly organized sites
run by EOT (Greek Tourist
Organization). Freelance
camping is officially illegal and
police crack down on people
camping rough in popular
tourist resorts. However, in
quiet rural inland areas you may
find that nobody is very
bothered about it. It is always
best to ask permission first in
the village taverna or café before
pitching a tent.

can to kooti, i konserva

a can of beer mia bira seh
kooti
can: can you ...? boriteh na ...?
can I have ...? boro na
ekho ...?
I can't ... then boro ...
Canada o Kanathas
Canadian Kanathezikos
I'm Canadian (man/woman)
imeh Kanathos/Kanatheza
canal to kanali
cancel akirono
candies i karameles
candle to keri
canoe to kano
canoeing kano kano
can-opener to anikhtiri
cap (hat) to kapelo
(of bottle) to kapaki
car to aftokinito
by car meh to aftokinito
carafe i karafa
a carafe of house white, please
mia karafa aspro spitiko
krasi, parakalo
caravan to trokhospito
caravan site topoTHesia ya
trokhospita
carburettor to karbirater
card (birthday etc) i karta
here's my (business) card
oristeh, i karta moo
cardigan i zaketa
cardphone i tilekarta
see phone
careful prosektikos
be careful! prosekheh!
caretaker o/i epistatis
car ferry to feri-bot

car hire enikiasis aftokiniton
see **rent**
car park to **parking**
carpet to khali
  (fitted) i mok**e**ta
carriage (of train) to va**G**oni
carrier bag i sak**oo**la
carrot to kar**o**to
carry metaf**e**ro
carry-cot to port-beh-b**e**h
carton i k**oo**ta
carwash to plindirio
  aftokiniton
case (suitcase) i val**i**tsa
cash ta metrit**a**
  will you cash this for me? TH**a**
  moo to exaryir**o**seteh?
cash desk to tam**i**o
cash dispenser i mikhani ya
  metrit**a**
cashier o/i tam**i**as
cassette i kas**e**ta
cassette recorder to kaset**o**fono
castle to k**a**stro
casualty department Protes Vo-
  ITH**i**-es
cat i **G**ata
catch p**i**ano
  where do we catch the bus
  to ...? ap**o** poo TH**a** par**oo**meh
  to leoforio?
cathedral o kaTH**e**drikos naos
Catholic (adj) kaTH**o**likos
cauliflower to koonoop**i**thi
cave i spil**i**a
ceiling to tav**a**ni
celery to sel**i**no
cellar (for wine) to kel**a**ri
cemetery to nekrot**a**fio

Centigrade* Kelsioo
centimetre* **e**na ekat**o**sto
central kendrik**o**s
central heating i kendrik**i**
  TH**e**rmansi
centre to k**e**ndro
  how do we get to the city
  centre? pos TH**a** p**a**meh sto
  k**e**ndro?
cereal ta cornflakes
certainly sig**oo**ra
  certainly not fisik**a** **o**khi
chair i kar**e**kla
champagne i samp**a**nia
change (money) ta r**e**sta
  (verb: money, trains) al**a**zo
  can I change this for ...? bor**o**
  na al**a**xo aft**o** ya ...?
  I don't have any change then
  ekho ps**i**la
  can you give me change for a
  5,000 drachma note? bor**i**teh
  na moo khal**a**seteh p**e**ndeh
  khili**a**thes thrakhm**e**s?

> Kiosks may sometimes refuse to
> change a 1,000 or 5,000
> drachma note for you, unless
> you buy something from them.

•••••• DIALOGUE ••••••

do we have to change (trains)?
pr**e**pi na alax**oo**meh tr**e**no?
yes, change at Corinth/no, it's a
direct train neh, al**a**xteh stin
Kor**i**nTHo/**o**khi, p**i**yeni
katefTH**i**an

changed: to get changed al**a**zo
r**oo**kha

chapel to eklisaki
charge i timi, i thapani
　(verb) khreono
charge card i pistotiki karta
　see credit card
cheap ftinos
　do you have anything cheaper?
　ekheteh tipoteh ftinotero?
check (verb) epaliTHevo
　(US: cheque) i epitayi
　see cheque
　(US: bill) o loGariasmos
　see bill
　could you check the ..., please?
　boriteh na elenxeteh to ...,
　parakalo?
checkbook to karneh epitaGon
check-in to check-in
check in kano check-in
　where do we have to check in?
　poo prepi na kanoomeh
　check-in?
cheek (on face) to magoolo
cheerio! yasoo!
cheers! (toast) stin iya sas!, is
　iyian!
cheese to tiri
chemist's to farmakio

> Greek chemists are well-
> qualified to give you advice on
> minor ailments; there's
> generally an all-night chemist's
> in bigger towns and cities; they
> work on a rota system and you
> generally find the address of the
> one currently open on the door
> of any chemist's.

cheque i epitayi
　do you take cheques?
　perneteh epitayes?
　see credit card
cheque book to karneh
　epitaGon
cheque card i karta epitaGon
cherry to kerasi
chess to skaki
chest to stiTHos
chewing gum i tsikhla
chicken to kotopoolo
chickenpox i anemovloyia
child to pethi
　children ta pethia
child minder i dada
children's pool i pisina ton
　pethion
children's portion i pethiki
　meritha
chin to piGooni
china i porselani
Chinese (adj) Kinezikos
chips i tiGanites patates
chocolate i sokolata
　milk chocolate i sokolata
　Galaktos
　plain chocolate sokolata sketi
　a hot chocolate i zesti
　sokolata, mia sokolata
　rofima
choose thialeGo
Christian name to mikro
　onoma
Christmas ta khristooyena
　Christmas Eve i paramoni ton
　khristooyenon
　merry Christmas! kala
　khristooyena!

church i eklisia
cicada o tzitzikas
cider cider
cigar to pooro
cigarette to tsiGaro
cigarette lighter o anaptiras
cinema o kinimatografos, to
  sinema
circle o kiklos
  (in theatre) o exostis
city i poli
city centre to kendro tis polis
clean (adj) kaTHaros
  can you clean these for me?
  moo pleneteh afta?
cleaning solution (for contact
  lenses) to kaTHaristiko
  thialima
cleansing lotion to Galaktoma
  kaTHarismoo
clear kaTHaros
  (obvious) profanis
clever exipnos
cliff o apotomos vrakhos
climbing i orivasia
cling film to na-ilon
clinic i kliniki
cloakroom i Gardaroba
clock to rolo-i
close klino

•••••• DIALOGUE ••••••
what time do you close? ti ora
klineteh?
we close at 8 pm on weekdays
and 6 pm on Saturdays klinoomeh
stis okto to vrathi tis
kaTHimerines keh stis exi to
apoyevma ta Savata

do you close for lunch? klineteh ya
mesimeriano fayito?
yes, between 1 and 3.30 pm neh,
apo ti mia mekhri tis tris keh
misi

closed klistos
cloth (fabric) to ifasma
  (for cleaning etc) to pani
clothes ta rookha
clothes line i aplostra
clothes peg to mandalaki
cloud to sinefo
cloudy sinefiasmenos
clutch to debrayaz, o siblektis
coach (bus) to poolman
  (on train) to vagoni
coach station o staTHmos
  iperastikon leoforion
coach trip to taxithi meh
  poolman
coast i akti
  on the coast stin akti
coat (long coat) to palto
  (jacket) to sakaki
coathanger i kremastra
cockroach i katsaritha
cocoa to kakao
coconut i karitha
code (for phoning) o kothikos
  what's the (dialling) code for
  Athens? pios ineh o kothikos
  ya tin ATHina?
  see dialling code
coffee o kafes
  two Greek coffees, please thio
  Elinikoos kafethes,
  parakalo

When you ask for a coffee, say what kind you want:

Eliniko Greek/Turkish coffee
Galliko filter coffee
Nescafeh zesto/pagomeno
hot/iced instant coffee

Other useful terms are:

sketo unsweetened
metrio medium-sweet
Gliko very sweet

coin to kerma
Coke® i koka-kola
cold krios
  I'm cold kriono
  I have a cold imeh kriomenos
collapse: he's collapsed katarefseh
collar o yakas
collect paralamvano
  I've come to collect ... ilTHa ya na paro ...
collect call tilefono collect
college to koleyio
colour to khroma
  do you have this in other colours? to ekheteh seh ala khromata?
colour film to enkhromo film
comb i khtena
come erkhomeh

•••••• DIALOGUE ••••••

where do you come from? apo poo iseh?
I come from Edinburgh imeh apo to Ethimvoorgo

come back epistrefo
  I'll come back tomorrow THa epistrepso avrio
come in beno mesa
comfortable (chair) anapaftikos
  (clothes) anetos
  (room, hotel) volikos
compact disc to compact disc
company (business) i eteria
compartment (on train) to koopeh
compass i pixitha
complain paraponoomeh
complaint to parapono
  I have a complaint ekho ena parapono
completely telios
computer o ipolo-yistis
concert i sinavlia
concussion i thiasisi engefaloo
conditioner (for hair) to kondisioner
condom to profilaktiko
conference to sinethrio
confirm epiveveono
congratulations! sinkharitiria!
connecting flight sinthesi ptisis
connection (travel) i sinthesi
conscious sinesTHanomenos
constipation i thiskiliotis
consulate to proxenio
contact erkhomeh seh epafi
contact lenses i faki epafis
contraceptive (pill) to andisiliptiko
  (condom) to profilaktiko
convenient volikos
  that's not convenient then meh volevi

convent to monastiri
cook (verb) ma-yirevo
  not cooked misopsimeno
cooker i koozina
cookie to biskoto
cooking utensils ta ma-yirika
  skevi
cool throseros
Corfu i Kerkira
cork o felos
corkscrew to anikhtiri
corner: on the corner sti gonia
  in the corner sti gonia
cornflakes ta cornflakes
correct (right) sostos
corridor o thiathromos
cosmetics ta kalindika
cost (verb) stikhizo
  how much does it cost? poso
  kani?
cot i koonia
cotton to vamvaki
cotton wool to vamvaki
couch o kanapes
couchette i kooketa
cough o vikhas
cough medicine to farmako ya
  ton vikha
could: could you ...? boriteh
  na ...?
  could I have ...? boro na
  ekho ...?
  I couldn't ... then boroosa
  na ...
country (nation) i khora
  (countryside) i exokhi
countryside i exokhi
couple (man and woman) to
  zevgari

a couple of ... thio apo ...
courgette to kolokiTHaki
courier o/i sinothos
course (main course etc) to piato
  of course veveh-a
  of course not fisika okhi
cousin (male/female) o xathelfos/
  i xathelfi
cow i a-yelatha
crab to kavoori
cracker to krakeraki
craft shop to ergastiri
crash i sigroosi
  I've had a crash trakara
crazy trelos
cream (on milk, in cake) i
  krema
  (lotion) i krema thermatos
  (colour) krem
creche o pethikos staTHmos
credit card i pistotiki karta

Credit/charge cards are useful –
indeed almost essential – for
renting cars. However, most
hotels, restaurants and shops
prefer cash, rather than cheques
or cards, so check in advance if
they are accepted.

• • • • • • DIALOGUE • • • • • •

can I pay by credit card? boro
na pliroso meh pistotiki
karta?
which card do you want to use? ti
karta THeleteh na khrisimopi-
iseteh?
yes, sir entaxi, kiri-eh
what's the number? ti ariTHmo

ekhi?
and the expiry date? keh poteh
ineh i imerominia lixeos?

Crete i Kriti
crisps ta tsips
crockery ta piatika
crossing (by sea) to THalasio
  taxithi
crossroads to stavrothromi
crowd o kosmos
crowded yematos kosmo
crown (on tooth) i korona
cruise i krooazi-era
crutches i pateritses
cry (weep) kleo
  (shout) fonazo
cucumber to agoori
cup to flidzani
  a cup of ..., please ena
  flidzani ..., parakalo
cupboard to doolapi
cure i THerapia
curly sgooros, katsaros
current to revma
curtains i koortines
cushion to maxilaraki
custom to eTHimo
Customs to Telonio
cut to kopsimo
  (verb) kovo
  I've cut myself kopika
cutlery ta makheropiroona
cycling i pothilasia
cyclist o/i pothilatis
Cyprus i Kipros

D

dad o babas
daily kaTHimerina
damage (verb) katastrefo
  damaged katastrafikeh
  I'm sorry, I've damaged this
  lipameh, to khalasa
damn! na pari i oryi!
damp (adj) iGros
dance o khoros
  (verb) khorevo
  would you like to dance?
  THelis na khorepsoomeh?
dangerous epikinthinos
Danish thanos
dark (adj: colour) skotinos
  (hair) mavros
  it's getting dark skotiniazi
date*: what's the date today?
  poso ekhi o minas simera?
  let's make a date for next
  Monday as sinandiTHoomeh
  tin epomeni theftera
dates (fruit) i khoormathes
daughter i kori
daughter-in-law i nifi
dawn i avgi
  at dawn tin avgi
day i mera
  the day after tin epomeni
  mera
  the day after tomorrow
  meTHavrio
  the day before tin pro-
  igoomeni mera
  the day before yesterday
  prokhtes
  every day kaTHeh mera

all day oli tin imera
in two days' time meta apo
thio meres
day trip to taxithi afTHimeron
dead peTHamenos, nekros
deaf koofos
deal (business) i simfonia
it's a deal simfonisameh,
entaxi
death o THanatos
decaffeinated coffee o kafes
khoris kafe-ini
December o thekemvrios
decide apofasizo
we haven't decided yet then
ekhoomeh apofasisi akoma
decision i apofasi
deck (on ship) to katastroma
deckchair i poliTHrona, i sez
long
deduct afero
deep vaTHis
definitely oposthipoteh
definitely not seh kamia
periptosi
degree (qualification) to ptikhio
delay i kaTHisterisi
deliberately epitithes
delicatessen ta delicatessen
delicious nostimotatos
deliver thianemo
delivery (of mail) i thianomi, i
parathosi
demotic i dimotiki
Denmark i thania
dental floss to othondiko
nima
dentist o/i othondiatros

•••••• DIALOGUE ••••••

it's this one here afto etho ineh
this one? afto?
no, that one okhi, ekino
here? etho?
yes neh

dentures i masela
deodorant to aposmitiko
department to tmima
department store to meGalo
katastima
departure i anakhorisi
departure lounge i eTHoosa
anakhoriseos
depend: it depends exartateh
it depends on ... exartateh
apo ...
deposit (as security) i kataTHesi
(as part payment) i prokatavoli
description i perigrafi
dessert to Glikisma
destination o pro-orismos
develop anaptiso
(a film) emfanizo

•••••• DIALOGUE ••••••

could you develop these films?
boriteh na emfaniseteh afta ta
film?
when will they be ready? poteh
THa ineh etima?
tomorrow afternoon avrio to
apoyevma
how much is the four-hour service?
poso kani i emfanisi seh teseris
ores?

diabetic (man/woman) o
thiavitikos/i thiavitiki

diabetic foods i thiavitiki trofi
dial (verb) kalo, perno ariTHmo
dialling code o kothikos
ariTHmos

For direct international calls
from Greece, dial the country
code (given below), the area
code (minus the first 0), and
finally the subscriber number:
UK: 0044   Australia: 0061
Ireland: 00353
New Zealand: 0064
US & Canada: 001

diamond to thiamandi
diaper i pana
diarrhoea i thiaria
diary to imerolo-yio
dictionary to lexiko
didn't
  see not
die peTHeno
diesel i dizel
diet i thi-eta
  I'm on a diet kano thi-eta
  I have to follow a special diet
  prepi na kano ithiki thi-eta
difference i thiafora
  what's the difference? pia ineh
  i thiafora?
different thiaforetikos
  this one is different afto etho
  ineh thiaforetiko
  a different table ena alo
  trapezi
difficult thiskolos
difficulty i thiskolia
dinghy to zodiak®

dining room i trapezaria
dinner (evening meal) to thipno
  to have dinner tro-o vrathino
direct (adj) kat-efTHian
  is there a direct train? iparkhi
  kat-efTHian treno ya ...?
direction i katefTHinsi
  which direction is it? pros ta
  poo ineh?
  is it in this direction? ineh
  pros afti tin katefTHinsi?
directory enquiries i plirofori-es

The number for directory
enquiries is 131 for Athens
numbers, 132 for other numbers
in Greece and 161 for
international numbers.

dirt i vroma
dirty vromikos
disabled anapiros
  is there access for the
  disabled? iparkhi prosvasi ya
  toos anapiroos?
disappear exafanizomeh
  it's disappeared exafanistikh
disappointed apoGo-itevmenos
disappointing apoGo-iteftiko
disaster i katastrofi
disco i diskotek
discount i ekptosi
  is there a discount? kaneteh
  ekptosi?
disease i arostia
disgusting a-ithiastikos
dish (meal) to piato
  (bowl) to bol
dishcloth i patsavoora

disinfectant to apolimandiko

disk (for computer) i thisketa

disposable diapers i khartines panes

disposable nappies i khartines panes

distance i apostasi
in the distance eki kato

distilled water apestagmeno nero

district i sinikia

disturb enokhlo

diversion (detour) i parakampsi

diving board i sanitha vootias

divorced: I'm divorced (man/ woman) khorismenos/ khorismeni

dizzy: I feel dizzy zalizomeh

do kano
what shall we do? ti THa kanoomeh?
how do you do it? pos to kaneteh?
will you do it for me? boriteh na moo to kaneteh?

•••••• DIALOGUES ••••••

how do you do? ti kaneteh?
nice to meet you kharika ya ti gnorimia
what do you do? ti thoolia kaneteh?
I'm a teacher, and you? imeh thaskalos, ki esis?
I'm a student imeh fititis
what are you doing this evening? ti THa kaneteh apopseh?
we're going out for a drink; do you

want to join us? THa pameh ya ena poto – THeleteh na elTHeteh mazi mas?

do you want cream? THeleteh krema?
I do, but she doesn't ego neh, ekini, omos, okhi

doctor o/i yatros
we need a doctor khriazomasteh enan yatro
please call a doctor seh parakalo, kaleseh enan yatro

Any chemist's will have a list of the nearest doctor's surgeries; if you're a citizen of an EU country, take the form E111 (obtainable from post offices in the UK) with you – this should enable you to get free treatment and pay for prescriptions at the local rate. In practice, hospital staff often meet the E111 with uncomprehending looks and you may have to request reimbursal from the NHS on your return. Some form of travel insurance is therefore advisable and is essential for non-EU citizens. In tourist areas, it should be easy to find an English-speaking doctor and the tourist police (phone 171) may be able to help with some names if you have any difficulty.

•••••• DIALOGUE ••••••

where does it hurt? poo ponateh?
right here akrivos etho
does that hurt more? sas pona-i
afto pio poli?
yes neh
take this to a chemist thosteh afto
seh ena farmaki-o

document to enGrafo
dog o skilos
doll i kookla
domestic flight ptisi esoterikoo
donkey o Ga-itharos
don't! mi!
don't do that! min to kanis
afto!
(stop) stamata!
see not
door i porta
doorman o THiroros
double thiplo
double bed to thiplo krevati
double room to thiplo
thomatio
doughnut to donat
down kato
down here etho kato
put it down over there valeh
to eki kato
it's down there on the right
vrisketeh eki kato sta thexia
it's further down the road ineh
ligo parakato
downmarket (restaurant etc)
ftinos
downstairs kato
dozen mia doozina
half a dozen misi doozina
drain o okhetos

draught beer varelisia bira
draughty: it's draughty kani
revma
drawer to sirtari
drawing to skhethio
dreadful friktos
dream to oniro
dress to forema
dressed: to get dressed
dinomeh
dressing (for cut) i gaza
(for salad) to lathoxitho
dressing gown i roba
drink (alcoholic) to poto
(non-alcoholic) mi alko-
olookho poto, to
anapsiktiko
(verb) pino
a cold drink to anapsiktiko
can I get you a drink? boro na
seh keraso kanena poto?
what would you like (to drink)?
ti THa THelateh na pi-iteh?
no thanks, I don't drink okhi,
efkharisto, then pino
I'll just have a drink of water
THa paro monon ena potiri
nero
drinking water to posimo nero
is this drinking water? ineh
posimo afto to nero?

Although water in villages is
pure (and tastes wonderful)
because it comes from the
mountains, mineral water is
preferable to tap water in big
towns or on some of the drier
and more remote islands.

drive othiGa-o
 we drove here othiyisameh
 etho
 I'll drive you home THa seh
 pao spiti

Cars have obvious advantages
for getting to the more
inaccessible parts of mainland
Greece, but this is one of the
more expensive countries in
Europe to rent a car. If you drive
your own vehicle to and through
Greece, you'll need international third party insurance,
the so-called Green Card, as well
as an International Driving
Licence and the registration
documents. Upon arrival your
passport will get a carnet stamp;
this normally allows you to keep
a vehicle in Greece for up to
six months, exempt from road
tax.

Greece has the highest accident
rate in Europe after Portugal,
and many of the roads can be
quite perilous – asphalt can
turn into a dirt track without
warning on the smaller routes,
and railway crossings are rarely
guarded. Uphill drivers insist on
their right of way, as do those
first to approach a one-lane
bridge – headlights flashed at
you mean the opposite of what
they mean in the UK or North
America and signify that the
→

driver is coming through.
Wearing a seatbelt is
compulsory and children under
10 are not allowed to sit in the
front seats. If you are involved
in any kind of accident it's
illegal to drive away, and you
can be held at a police station
for up to 24 hours. If this
happens, ring your consulate
immediately, in order to get a
lawyer (you have this right).
Don't make a statement to
anyone who doesn't speak, and
write, very good English.

There are a limited number of
express highways between
Pátra, Athens, Vólos and
Thessaloníki, on which tolls are
levied – currently between
400dr and 700dr at each
sporadically placed gate.
They're nearly twice as quick as
the old roads, and well worth
using.

---

driver o/i othiGos
driving licence i athia
 othiyiseos, to thiploma
 othiyiseos
drop: just a drop, please
 (of drink) poli ligo,
 parakalo
drug to farmako
 drugs (narcotics) ta narkotika
drunk (adj) meTHismenos
drunken driving methismeno
 othiyima

The legal limit is 0.5% but don't
drink and drive.

dry (adj) steGnos
  (wine) xiros
dry-cleaner to steGno-
  kaTHaristirio
duck i papia
due: he was due to arrive
  yesterday eprokito na ftasi
  khtes
  when is the train due? poteh
  ftani to treno?
dull (pain) exasTHenimenos
  (weather) moondos
  (boring) varetos
dummy (baby's) i pipila
during kata ti thiarkia
dust i skoni
dusty skonismeno
dustbin o skoopithodenekes
duty-free (goods) ta aforolo-yita
duty-free shop to katastima
  aforolo-yiton
duvet to paploma

E

each kaTHeh
  how much are they each?
  poso ekhi to kaTHena?
ear to afti
earache: I have earache ekho
  pono sto afti
early noris
  early in the morning noris to
  pro-i
  I called by earlier perasa pro-

  igoomenos
earrings ta skoolarikia
east i anatoli
  in the east stin anatoli
Easter to Paskha
Easter Sunday i Kiriaki too
  Paskha

Easter is by far the most
important festival of the Greek
year and taken much more
seriously than it is anywhere
in western Europe. From
Wednesday of Holy Week the
state radio and TV networks are
given over solely to religious
programmes until the following
Monday. The festival is an
excellent time to be in Greece,
both for the beautiful and
moving religious ceremonies
and for the days of feasting that
follow. In the week leading up
to Easter Sunday you should
wish people a Happy Easter
'kalo paskha'.

easy efkolos
eat tro-o
  we've already eaten, thanks
  fagameh ithi, efkharisto

eating habits
Greeks don't generally eat
breakfast; however, you can get
a continental-style breakfast of
bread, jam, yoghurt and coffee
at most cafés. Greeks usually →

ENGLISH ◆ GREEK | Ea

have a late lunch – between 2-3 p.m. The evening meal is also eaten late – between 9 and 11 p.m., although it is possible to eat earlier in some more touristic establishments. Greek cuisine and restaurants are simple and straightforward. There's no snobbery about eating out.

eau de toilette i kolonia
EC i eok
economy class tooristiki THesi
Edinburgh to Ethimvoorgo
egg to avGo
  hard-boiled egg avGo sfikhto
  fried egg tiganito avGo
eggplant i melidzana
Eire i Notios Irlanthia
either: either ... or ... i ... i ...
  either of them opio naneh
elastic to lastikho
elastic band to lastikhaki
elbow o angonas
electric ilektrikos
electrical appliances ilektrikes siskeves
electric fire i ilektriki somba
electrician o ilektrologos
electricity to ilektriko revma

The supply is 220V, though anything requiring 240V will work. Most plugs are two round pins: a travel plug is useful.

elevator to asanser

else: something else kati alo
  somewhere else kapoo aloo

•••••• DIALOGUE ••••••

would you like anything else? THa THelateh tipoteh alo?
no, nothing else, thanks okhi, tipoteh alo, efkharisto

embassy i presvia
emergency i ektakti anangi
  this is an emergency! ineh epigon!
emergency exit i exothos kinthinoo
empty (adj) athios
end to telos
  (verb) teliono
  at the end of the street sto telos too thromoo
  when does it end? poteh telioni?
engaged (toilet, telephone) katilimenos
  (to be married: man/woman) aravoniasmenos/ aravoniasmeni
engine (car) i mikhani too aftokinitoo
England i Anglia
English ta Anglika
  I'm English (man/woman) imeh Anglos/Anglitha
  do you speak English? milateh anglika?
enjoy: to enjoy oneself thiaskethazo

how did you like the film? pos soo
fanikeh to ergo?
I enjoyed it very much; did you
enjoy it? moo areseh para poli;
esena soo areseh?

enjoyable efkharistos
enlargement (of photo) i
  me-yenTHisi
enormous terastios
enough arketa
  there's not enough then
  iparkhi arketo
  it's not big enough then ineh
  arketa meGalo
  that's enough ftani, arki
entrance i isothos
envelope o fakelos
epileptic (man/woman) o
  epiliptikos/i epiliptiki
equipment o exoplismos
error to laTHos
especially ithika
essential vasikos, aparetitos
  it is essential that ... ineh
  aparetito na ...
EU Evropa-iki Enosi
Eurocheque to Eurocheque
Eurocheque card i karta
  Eurocheque
Europe i Evropi
European (adj) Evropa-ikos
European Union Evropa-iki
  Enosi
even: even the Greeks akoma
  keh i Elines
  even if ... akoma ki an ...
evening to vrathi

this evening simera to vrathi
in the evening to vrathi
evening meal to thipno
eventually telika
ever poteh

have you ever been to Crete?
ekheteh pa-i poteh stin Kriti?
yes, I was there two years ago
neh, imoon eki prin apo thio
khronia

every kaTHeh
  every day kaTHeh mera
everyone oli
everything kaTHeh ti
everywhere pandoo
exactly! akrivos!
exam to thiagonisma
example to parathiGma
  for example parathiGmatos
  kharin
excellent exokhos
  excellent! exokha!
except ektos
excess baggage to ipervaro
exchange rate sinalaGmatiki
  isotimia
exciting sinarpastikos
excuse me (to get past) siGnomi
  (to get attention) parakalo
  (to say sorry) meh sinkhoriteh
exhaust (pipe) i exatmisi
exhausted (tired) exandlimenos
exhibition i ekTHesi
exit i exothos
  where's the nearest exit? poo
  ineh i plisi-esteri exothos?
expect perimeno

expensive akrivos
experienced embiros
explain exiGo
  can you explain that? boris na
  moo to exiyisis?
express mail to katepigon
express train to treno express
extension (telephone) i sinthesi
  tilefonoo
  could you get me extension
  221, please? meh sintheh-
  eteh meh to 221 (thiakosia
  ikosi ena), parakalo?
extension lead i pro-ektasi
extra: can we have an extra
  chair? boroomeh na
  ekhoomeh mia karekla
  akoma?
  do you charge extra for that?
  khreoneteh epipleon ya
  afto?
extraordinary asiniTHistos
extremely ipervolika
eye to mati
  will you keep an eye on my
  suitcase for me? THa moo to
  prosekheteh?
eyebrow pencil to molivi ya ta
  frithia
eye drops i stagones ya ta
  matia
eyeglasses (US) ta yialia
eyeliner to eyeliner
eye make-up remover to
  galaktoma kaTHarismoo
eye shadow i skia mation

F

face to prosopo
factory to erGostasio
Fahrenheit* vaTHmi Farena-it
faint (verb) lipoTHimao
  she's fainted lipoTHimiseh
  I feel faint esTHanomeh
  lipoTHimia
fair (funfair) to paniyiri
  (trade) i ekTHesi
  (adj) thikeos
fairly arketa
fake i apomimisi
Fall to fTHinoporo
  see autumn
fall (verb) pefto
  she's had a fall epeseh
false pseftikos
family i iko-yenia
famous thiasimos
fan (electrical) o anemistiras
  (hand held) i ventalia
  (sports) o/i opathos
fan belt to vendilater
fantastic fandastikos
far makria

•••••• DIALOGUE ••••••

is it far from here? ineh makria
apo etho?
no, not very far okhi, okhi keh
poli makria
well how far? poso makria,
thilathi?
it's about 20 kilometres ineh
peripoo ikosi khiliometra

fare i timi too isitirioo
farm to aGroktima

fashionable tis **mo**thas
fast Gri**Go**ros
fat (person) pak**his**
  (on meat) to **li**pos
father o pa**te**ras
father-in-law o pe**THe**ros
faucet i **vri**si
fault to e**la**toma
  sorry, it was my fault sig**no**mi,
  itan s**fal**ma moo
  it's not my fault then f**te**o e**go**
faulty elatomati**kos**
favourite a**Ga**pimenos
fax to fax
  (verb: person) **ste**lno fax seh ...
  (document) **ste**lno seh fax
February o Fevroo**a**rios
feel es**THa**nomeh
  I feel hot zes**te**nomeh
  I feel unwell then
  es**THa**nomeh ka**la**
  I feel like going for a walk
  ekho o**re**xi na **pa**o mia **vol**ta
  how are you feeling? pos
  es**THa**neseh?
  I'm feeling better es**THa**nomeh
  kali**te**ra
felt-tip pen o markat**ho**ros
fence o fra**ktis**
fender o profila**kti**ras
ferry to **fe**ri bot

There are three different
varieties of vessel: medium-
sized to large ordinary ferries
(which operate the main
services), hydrofoils (run by the
Ceres "Flying Dolphins" and →

Dodecanese Hydrofoils, among
other companies), and local
'kaikia' (small boats which in
season cover short island hops
and excursions). Costs are very
reasonable on longer journeys,
though proportion-ately more
expensive for shorter, inter-
island connections. The most
reliable, up-to-date information
is available from the local port
police ('limenark**hi**o'), which
main-tains offices at Piraeus
and on virtually all fair-sized
islands.

festival to festi**val**
fetch **pa**-o na **fe**ro
  I'll fetch him THa **pa**-o na ton
  fero
  will you come and fetch me
  later? THa **el**THis na meh
  pa**ris** argo**te**ra?
feverish empi**re**tos
few: a few **li**yi, **li**yes, **li**ga
  a few days **li**yes **me**res
fiancé o aravonias**ti**kos
fiancée i aravonias**ti**kia
field to kho**ra**fi
fight o a**Go**nas
figs ta **si**ka
fill ye**mi**zo
fill in ye**mi**zo
  do I have to fill this in? **pre**pi
  na to ye**mi**so?
fill up ye**mi**zo **te**lios
  fill it up, please ye**mis**teh tin,
  paraka**lo**

filling (in cake, sandwich) i yemisi
   (in tooth) to sfra-yisma
film to film

•••••• DIALOGUE ••••••

do you have this kind of film?
ekheteh tetio film?
yes; how many exposures? neh;
meh poses stasis?
36 trianda-exi

film processing i emfanisi too
film
filter coffee o kafes filtroo
filter papers ta filtra ya kafeh
filthy vromeros
find vrisko
   I can't find it then to vrisko
   I've found it to vrika
find out anakalipto
   could you find out for me?
   boris na maTHis?
fine (weather) oreos
   (punishment) to prostimo

•••••• DIALOGUES ••••••

how are you? ti kanis?
I'm fine thanks mia khara,
efkharisto

is that OK? afto ineh entaxi?
that's fine thanks ineh mia khara,
efkharisto

finger to thakhtilo
finish teliono
   I haven't finished yet then
   ekho teliosi akomi
   when does it finish? poteh
   telioni?
fire: fire! pirkaya!

can we light a fire here?
boroomeh na anapsoomeh
fotia etho?
   it's on fire pireh fotia
fire alarm o sinayermos
pirkayas
fire brigade i pirosvestiki
ipiresia

In the event of a fire, phone 199.

fire escape i exothos pirkayas
fire extinguisher o pirosvestiras
first protos
   I was first imoon protos
   at first stin arkhi
   the first time i proti fora
   first on the left protos sta
   aristera
first aid i protes vo-ITHi-es
first aid kit to kooti proton vo-
   ITHi-on
first class (travel etc) proti THesi
first floor to proto patoma
   (US) to iso-yio
first name to onoma
fish to psari
fisherman o psaras
fishing village to psarokhori
fishmonger's to psarathiko
fit (attack) i prosvoli
   it doesn't fit me then moo
   khora-i
fitting room to thokimastirio
fix ftiakhno
   (arrange) kanonizo
   can you fix this? boris na to
   ftiaxis?
fizzy meh anTHrakiko

flag i simea
flannel to sfoogari
flash (for camera) to flas
flat (apartment) to thiamerisma
(adj) epipethos
I've got a flat tyre me epiaseh
lastikho
flavour i Gefsi
flea o psilos
flight i ptisi
flight number ariTHmos ptisis
flippers ta vatrakhopethila
flood i plimira
floor (of room) to patoma
(of building) o orofos
on the floor sto patoma
florist o anTHopolis
flour to alevri
flower to looloothi
flu i Gripi
fluent: he speaks fluent Greek
mila-i aptesta elinika
fly i miGa
(verb) peto
can we fly there? boroomeh
na pameh eki a-eroporikos?
fly in peta-o pros
fly out peta-o apo
fog i omikhli
foggy: it's foggy ekhi omikhli
folk dancing i thimotiki khori
folk music i thimotiki moosiki
follow akolooTHo
follow me akolootha meh
food to fa-yito
food poisoning trofiki
thilitiriasi
food shop/store to bakaliko
foot* to pothi

on foot meh ta pothia
football (game) to pothosfero
(ball) i bala
football match o pothosferikos
agonas
for ya
do you have something for ...?
(headache/diarrhoea etc) ekheteh
kati ya ...?

•••••• DIALOGUES ••••••

who's the moussaka for? ya pion
ineh o moosakas?
that's for me ya mena
and this one? ki afto etho?
that's for her afto ineh ya ekini

where do I get the bus for
Akropolis? apo poo THa paro to
leoforio ya tin Akropoli?
the bus for Acropolis leaves from
Stathiou Street to leoforio ya tin
Akropoli fevyi apo tin Otho
Stathioo

how long have you been here for?
poso kero iseh etho pera?
I've been here for two days, how
about you? vriskomeh etho pera
etho keh thio meres, esi?
I've been here for a week
vriskomeh etho pera etho keh
mia vthomatha

forehead to metopo
foreign xenos
foreigner (man/woman) o xenos/i
xeni
forest to thasos
forget xekhno
I forget xekhno

I've forgotten xekhasa
fork (for eating) to pirooni
(in road) i thiaklathosi
form (document) i etisi
formal (dress) episimos
fortnight to theka-penTHimero
fortunately eftikhos
forward: could you forward my
mail? boriteh na moo
stileteh ta gramata moo?
forwarding address i thi-
efTHinsi apostolis
foundation cream krema
prosopoo ya makiyaz
fountain i piyi
foyer to foyer
fracture to kataGma
free elefTHeros
(no charge) thorean
is it free of charge? ineh
thorean?
freeway i eTHniki othos
freezer i katapsixi
French (adj) Galikos
(language) ta Galika
French fries i tiganites patates
frequent sikhnos
how frequent is the bus to
Corinth? kaTHeh poteh ekhi
leoforio ya tin KorinTHO?
fresh (weather, breeze) throseros
(fruit etc) freskos
fresh orange o freskos khimos
portokali
Friday i Paraskevi
fridge to psiyio
fried tiganismenos
fried egg to tiganito avgo
friend (male/female) o filos/i fili

friendly filikos
from apo
when does the next train from
Patras arrive? poteh ftani to
epomeno treno apo tin
Patra?
from Monday to Friday apo
theftera os Paraskevi
from next Thursday apo tin ali
Pempti

•••••• DIALOGUE ••••••

where are you from? apo poo
iseh?
I'm from Slough imeh apo to
Sla-oo

front to mbrostino meros
in front mbrosta
in front of the hotel mbrosta
apo to xenothokhio
at the front sto mbrostino
meros
frost i pagonia, o pa-yetos
frozen pagomenos
frozen food i katepsiymeni
trofi
fruit ta froota
fruit juice o khimos frooton
fry tiGanizo
frying pan to tiGani
full yematos
it's full of ... ineh yemato
meh ...
I'm full khortasa
full board fool pansion
fun: it was fun kala itan,
kanameh kefi
funeral i kithia
funny (strange) paraxenos

(amusing) **astios**
furniture ta **epipla**
further para**pera**
  it's further down the road **i**neh
  akoma parak**a**to

•••••• DIALOGUE ••••••

  how much further is it to Piraeus?
  poso ineh akomi mekhri ton
  Pirea?
  about 5 kilometres **yi**ro sta
  pendeh khili**o**metra

fuse i asf**a**lia
  the lights have fused
  ka-**i**kaneh ta f**o**ta
fuse box to koot**i** meh tis
  asf**a**li-es
fuse wire to s**i**rma asfal**i**as
future to m**e**lon
  in future sto m**e**lon

G

gallon* ena gal**o**ni
game (cards etc) to pekhn**i**thi
  (match) o ag**o**nas
  (meat) to kin**i**yi
garage (for fuel) to venzin**a**thiko
  (for repairs) to sinery**i**o
  (for parking) to gar**a**z

Greek garages are usually open
from approx. 8 a.m. to 8 p.m.;
the address of those which are
open at night and at weekends
is usually on the door of the
garage office. There will always
be at least one petrol pump per →

district open at the weekend but
it's best to carry a full petrol can
at all times.
see **petrol**

garden o k**i**pos
garlic to sk**o**rtho
gas to g**a**zi
gas cylinder (camping gas) i fi**a**li
  g**a**zi
gasoline i venz**i**ni
  see **petrol**
gas permeable lenses i imiskl**i**ri
  f**a**ki ep**a**fis
gas station to venzin**a**thiko
gate i avl**o**porta
  (at airport) i **e**xothos
gay (adj) omofil**o**filos
gay bar to gay bar
gears i takh**i**tita
gearbox to kiv**o**tio takh**i**titon
gear lever o lev**i**-es takh**i**t**i**ton
general yen**i**kos
gents (toilet) i too-al**e**ta ton
  anthron
genuine (antique etc)
  afTHend**i**kos
German (adj) Yermanik**o**s
  (language) ta Yermanik**a**
German measles i er**i**THra
Germany i Yerman**i**a
get (fetch) p**e**rno
  will you get me another one,
  please? THa moo p**a**ris al**o**
  ena, parakal**o**?
  how do I get to ...? pos bor**o**
  na p**a**o sto ...?
  do you know where I can get

them? **mipos xereteh poo boro na vro tetia?**

•••••• DIALOGUE ••••••

can I get you a drink? **na seh keraso kanena poto?**
no, I'll get this one, what would you like? **okhi, ego kernao afti ti fora; ti THa iTHeles?**
a glass of red wine **ena potiri kokino krasi**

get back (return) **epistrefo**
get in (arrive) **ftano**
get off kateveno
  where do I get off? **poo THa katevo?**
get on (to train etc) **aneveno**
get out (of car etc) **vyeno**
get up (in the morning) **sikonomeh**
gift to thoro

It is customary to give gifts to people on their name days, birthdays, at Christmas and on New Year's Eve, and when you want to thank someone for a favour.

gift shop katastima thoron, ithi thoron
gin to tzin
  a gin and tonic, please **ena tzin meh tonik, parakalo**
girl to koritsi
girlfriend i filenatha
give thino
  can you give me some change? **boriteh na moo**

thoseteh psila?
I gave it to him **to ethosa seh afton**
will you give this to ...? **to thinis afto ston ...?**

•••••• DIALOGUE ••••••

how much do you want for this? **posa THelis ya afto?**
10,000 drachmas **theka khiliathes thrakhmes**
I'll give you 7,000 drachmas **soo thino efta khiliathes**

give back epistrefo, thino piso
glad efkharistimenos
glass (material) **to yali**
  (tumbler, wine glass) **to potiri**
  a glass of wine **ena potiri krasi**
glasses ta yalia
gloves ta Gandia
glue i kola
go pao
  we'd like to go to the ... **theloomeh na pameh sto ...**
  where are you going? **poo pateh?**
  where does this bus go? **poo pa-i afto to leoforio?**
  let's go! **pameh**
  she's gone (left) **efiyeh**
  where has he gone? **poo piyeh aftos?**
  I went there last week **piga eki tin perasmeni evthomatha**
  hamburger to go **khamboorger ya to spiti**
go away fevGo

go away! fiyeh!
go back (return) epistrefo
go down (the stairs etc) kateveno
go in beno
go out (in the evening) v-yeno
  do you want to go out tonight?
  theleteh na pateh exo
  apopseh?
go through thiaskhizo, pao
  thia mesoo
go up (the stairs etc) aneveno
goat i katsika
goat's cheese to katsikisio tiri
God o THeos
goggles i maska
gold o khrisos
golf to golf
golf course to yipetho golf
good kalos
  good! kala!
  it's no good (product etc) afto
  then ineh kalo
  (not worth trying) then ofeli
goodbye ya khara, adio
good evening kalispera
Good Friday i Megali Paraskevi

Good Friday is a public holiday
in Greece. Post offices, banks
and some shops close at noon,
but supermarkets and public
transport are not greatly
affected.

good morning kalimera
good night kalinikhta
goose i khina
got: we've got to ... prepi na ...
  have you got any ...? ekheteh

kaTHoloo ...?
government i kivernisi
gradually siga-siga
grammar i Gramatiki
gram(me) ena gramario
granddaughter i egoni
grandfather o papoos
grandmother i ya-ya
grandson o egonos
grapefruit to grapefruit
grapefruit juice o khimos
  grapefruit
grapes ta stafilia
grass to khortari, to grasithi
grateful evGnomon
gravy o zomos too kreatos
great (excellent) poli kalo
  that's great! iperokha!
  it's a great success ineh
  meGali epitikhia
Great Britain i Megali Vretania
Greece i Elatha
greedy akhortagos
Greek (adj) Elinikos
  (language) ta Elinika
  (man) o Elinas
  (woman) i Elinitha
  the Greeks i Elines
Greek coffee Elinikos kafes
Greek-Cypriot (adj) Elinokiprios
Greek Orthodox Elinikos
  OrTHothoxos
green prasinos
green card (car insurance) i
  asfalia ya othiyisi sto
  exoteriko
greengrocer's o manavis
grey grizos
grill i psistaria

grilled psitos sti skhara
grocer's to bakaliko
ground to ethafos
  on the ground sto ethafos
ground floor to iso-yio
group to groop
guarantee i engi-isi
  is it guaranteed? ineh engi-
  imeno?
guest (man/woman) o
  filoxenoomenos/i
  filoxenoomeni
  see hospitality
guesthouse i pansion

> It is difficult to find guesthouses
> in less touristy areas of Greece,
> but local people may offer you
> private rooms (thomatia) and
> food. Between November and
> early April, private rooms are
> closed to keep hotels in
> business.

guide o/i xenaGos
guidebook o tooristikos
  othiGos
guided tour i xenayisi
guitar i kiTHara
gum (in mouth) to oolo
gun (pistol) to pistoli
  (rifle) to oplo
gym to yimnastirio

H

hair ta malia
hairbrush i voortsa ya malia, i
  khtena

haircut (man's) to koorema
  (woman's) to kopsimo
hairdresser's to komotirio
  (men's) to koorio
hairdryer to pistolaki
hair gel o afros malion
hairgrips ta piastrakia malion
hair spray to spray ya ta malia
half misos
  half an hour misi ora
  half a litre miso litro
  about half that peripoo to
  miso apo afto
half board demi-pansion
half-bottle miso bookali
half fare miso isitirio
half price misotimis
ham to zambon
hamburger to khamboorger
hammer to sfiri
hand to kheri
handbag i tsanda
handbrake to khirofreno
handkerchief to mandili
  (paper) to khartomandilo
handle to kherooli
hand luggage to sakvooa-yaz
hang-gliding i anemoporia
hangover o ponokefalos
  I've got a hangover ekho
  ponokefalo
happen simveni
  what's happening? ti simveni?
  what has happened? ti sinevi?
happy eftikhismenos
  I'm not happy about this then
  imeh efkharistimenos meh
  afto
harbour to limani

hard skliros
  (difficult) thiskolos
hard-boiled egg to sfikhto avgo
hard lenses i skliri faki
hardly meta vias
  hardly ever s-khethon poteh
hardware shop ta ithi
  kingalerias
hat to kapelo
hate miso
have* ekho
  can I have a ...? boro na ekho
  ena ...?
  do you have ...? ekheteh ...?
  what'll you have? ti THa
  piiteh?
  I have to leave now prepi na
  piyeno tora
  do I have to ...? prepi na ...?
  can we have some ...?
  boroomeh na ekhoomeh
  merika ...?
hayfever aler-yia sti yiri
hazelnuts to foondooki
he* aftos
  is he here? ineh etho?
head to kefali
headache o ponokefalos
headlights i provolis
headphones ta akoostika
health food shop katastima iyi-
  inon trofon
healthy iyi-is
hear akoo-o
•••••• DIALOGUE ••••••
  can you hear me? meh akoos?
  I can't hear you, could you repeat
  that? then seh akoo-o, boris na
  to epanalavis?

hearing aid ta akoostika
heart i karthia
heart attack i karthiaki
  prosvoli
heat i zesti
heater i THermansi
  (radiator) to kalorifer
heating i THermansi
heavy varis
heel (of foot) i fterna
  (of shoe) to takooni
  could you heel these? boriteh
  na moo valeteh kenooryia
  takoonia safta?
heelbar o tsagaris
height to ipsos
helicopter to elikoptero
hello ya sas
  (familiar) ya soo
  (answer on phone) embros, neh,
  parakalo
helmet (for motorcycle) to kranos
help i vo-ITHia
  (verb) vo-ITHo
  help! vo-ITHia!
  can you help me? boriteh na
  meh vo-ITHiseteh?
  thank you very much for your
  help efkharisto ya ti vo-iTHia
  sas
helpful exipiretikos
hepatitis i ipatititha
her*: I haven't seen her then tin
  ekho thi
  to her saftin
  with her mazi tis
  for her yaftin
  that's her afti ineh
  that's her towel afti ineh i

petseta tis
herbal tea tsa-i too voonoo
herbs ta votana
here etho
  here is/are ... na ...
  here you are (offering) oristeh
hers* thiko tis
  that's hers afto ineh thiko tis
hey! eh!
hi! (hello) ya soo
hide (something) krivo
  (oneself) krivomeh
high psilos
highchair to kareklaki moroo
highway i eTHniki othos
hill o lofos
him*: I haven't seen him then
  ton ekho thi
  to him safton
  with him mazi too
  for him yafton
  that's him aftos ineh
hip o Gofos
hire niki-azo
  for hire eniki-azonteh
  where can I hire a bike? poo
  boro na niki-aso ena
  pothilato?
  see rent
his*: it's his car ineh to
  aftokinito too
  that's his ineh thiko too
hit khtipao
hitch-hike kano otostop
hobby to khobi
hold kratao
hole i tripa
holiday i thiakopes

on holiday imeh seh
thiakopes
Holy Week i Megali
Evthomatha
home to spiti
  at home (in my house etc) sto
  spiti
  (in my country) stin patritha
  moo
  we go home tomorrow piyeno
  stin patritha moo avrio
honest timios
honey to meli
honeymoon o minas too
  melitos
hood (US) to kapo
hope elpizo
  I hope so etsi elpizo
  I hope not elpizo pos okhi
hopefully meh kali tikhi
horn (of car) to klaxon
horrible friktos
horse to alogo
horse riding i ipasia
hospital to nosokomio
hospitality i filoxenia
  thank you for your hospitality
  sas efkharisto ya ti filoxenia
  sas

If you are invited for a meal, it
is customary to bring a present
of sweets or flowers for your
host. You will be treated very
courteously – in some places
(especially small villages)
hospitality is still a matter of
honour. For this reason avoid
→

offending your hosts by being unfriendly and unwilling to eat what you are served. As few Greeks are vegetarians, it is wise to warn your host in advance if you cannot eat certain foods.

hot zestos
(spicy) kafteros, kaftos
I'm hot zestenomeh
it's hot today kani poli zesti simera
hotel to xenothokhio

There are five hotel categories: classes A to E, A allegedly being the best and E the most basic. All except the highest category have to keep within set price limits. Categories assigned to establishments should not be regarded as absolutely rigid: some of the low-ranking places will also have more expensive rooms including en suite facilities and vice versa. You need your passport or ID for registration.

hotel room: in my hotel room sto thomatio too xenothokhioo
hour i ora
house to spiti
house wine to krasi too maGazioo
see **wine**
hovercraft to hovercraft, o

a-erolisTHitiras
how pos
how many? posi?
how do you do? khero poli

•••••• DIALOGUES ••••••

how are you? pos iseh?
fine, thanks, and you? poli kala, efkharisto; ki esi?

how much is it? poso kani afto?
5000 drachmas pendeh khiliathes thrakhmes
I'll take it THa to paro

humid iGros
humour to khioomor

Avoid jokes about politicians and political parties, Macedonia and the relationship between Greece and Turkey. It's not a good idea to joke or flirt with women you meet in villages as this could cause offence.

hungry pinasmenos
are you hungry? pinas?
hurry (verb) viazomeh
I'm in a hurry viazomeh
there's no hurry then iparkhi via
hurry up! viasoo!
hurt travmatizomeh
it really hurts pragmatika pona-i poli
husband o siziGos
hydrofoil to iptameno thelfini

I

I eGo
ice o paGos
  with ice meh paGo
  no ice, thanks khoris paGo,
  efkharisto
ice cream to paGoto
ice-cream cone to paGoto
  khonaki
iced coffee to frapeh
ice lolly to paGoto xilaki
idea i ithea
idiot o vlakas
if an
ignition i miza
ill arostos
  I feel ill imeh arostos
illness i arostia
imitation (leather etc) i
  apomimisi
immediately amesos
important spootheos
  it's very important ineh poli
  simandiko
  it's not important then ineh
  spootheo
impossible athinaton
impressive endiposiakos
improve veltiono
  I want to improve my Greek
  THelo na kaliterepso ta
  Elinika moo
in: it's in the centre ineh sto
  kendro
  in my car mesa sto aftokinito
  moo
  in Athens stin ATHina
  in two days from now seh

thio meres apo tora
  in May sto Ma-io
  in English sta Anglika
  in Greek sta Elinika
  is he in? ineh eki?
  in five minutes seh pendeh
  lepta
inch* i intsa
include perilamvano
  does that include meals? afto
  perilamvani keh fayito?
  is that included in the price?
  perilamvaneteh stin timi?
inconvenient akatalilos, avolos
incredible apiTHanos
Indian (adj) Inthikos
indicator to flas, o thiktis
indigestion i thispepsia
indoor pool i esoteriki pisina
indoors mesa
inexpensive ftinos
  see cheap
inner tube (for tyre) i sabrela
infection i molinsi
infectious kolitikos
inflammation i anaflexi
informal anepisimos
information i plirofori-es
  do you have any information
  about ...? ekheteh tipoteh
  plirofori-es skhetika meh ...?
information desk i plirofori-es
injection i enesi
injured travmatismenos
  she's been injured khtipiseh
in-laws ta peTHerika
innocent aTHo-os
insect to endomo
insect bite to tsibima endomoo

do you have anything for
insect bites? ekheteh tipoteh
ya tsibimata apo endoma?
insect repellent to AUTAN®
inside mesa
  inside the hotel mesa sto
  xenothokhio
  let's sit inside as katsoomeh
  mesa
insist epimeno
  I insist epimeno
insomnia i a-ipnia
instant coffee to Neskafeh
instead andi
  give me that one instead
  thosteh moo afto sti THesi
  too aloo
  instead of ... sti THesi too ...
insulin i insoolini
insurance i asfalia
intelligent exipnos
interested: I'm interested in ...
  enthiaferomeh poli ya ...
interesting enthiaferon
  that's very interesting ineh
  poli enthiaferon
international thi-ethnis
interpret thi-erminevo
interpreter o/i thi-ermineas
intersection to stavrothromi
interval (at theatre) to thi-alima
into mesa
  I'm not into ... then moo aresi
introduce sistino
  may I introduce ...? boro na
  sas sistiso ton ...?
invitation i prosklisi
invite proskalo
Ionian Sea to I-onio pelagos

Ireland i Irlanthia
Irish Irlanthos
  I'm Irish (man/woman) imeh
  Irlanthos/Irlantheza
iron (for ironing) to ilektriko
  sithero
  can you iron these for me?
  boriteh na moo ta
  sitheroseteh?
is* inch
island to nisi
it afto
  it is ... ineh ...
  Is it ...? ineh ...?
  where is it? poo ineh?
  it's him ineh aftos
  it was ... itan ...
Italian (adj) Italos
  (language) ta Italika
Italy i Italia
itch: it itches meh tro-i

J

jack (for car) o Grilos
jacket to sakaki
jar to vazaki
jam i marmelatha
jammed: it's jammed ineh
  frakarismeno
January o I-anooarios
jaw to saGoni
jazz i tzaz
jealous ziliaris
jeans ta tzins
jellyfish i tsookhtra
jersey to fanelaki
jetty o molos
Jewish Evra-ikos

jeweller's to khrisokho-io
jewellery ta kosmimata
job i thoolia
jogging to jogging
  to go jogging pao ya jogging
joke to astio
journey to taxithi
  have a good journey! kalo
  taxithi!
jug i kanata
  a jug of water mia kanata
  nero
juice o khimos
July o I-oolios
jump pithao
jumper to poolover
jump leads ta kalothia batarias
junction i thiastavrosi
June o I-oonios
just (only) monon
  just two mono thio
  just for me mono ya mena
  just here akrivos etho
  not just now okhi tora
  we've just arrived molis
  ftasameh

K

keep krato
  keep the change krata ta
  resta
  can I keep it? boro na to
  kratiso?
  please keep it kratisteh to,
  sas parakalo
ketchup to ketsap
kettle i booyota, o vrastiras
key to klithi

the key for room 201, please
to klithi ya to 201 (thiakosia
ena), parakalo
key ring to brelok
kidneys ta nefra
kill skotono
kilo* ena kilo
kilometre* ena khiliometro
  how many kilometres is it
  to ...? posa khiliometra ineh
  mekhri to ...?
kind (generous) evyenikos
  that's very kind ineh poli
  evyeniko

•••••• DIALOGUE ••••••

which kind do you want? ti ithos
THeleteh?
I want this/that kind THelo afto/
ekino to ithos

king o vasilias
kiosk to periptero
kiss to fili
  (verb) filao

It is customary to greet friends
and relatives by kissing them on
both cheeks. The exception to
this is when men greet each
other when they generally shake
hands instead. Foreign visitors
are expected to accept the
same kind of greeting, although
you wouldn't necessarily be
expected to reciprocate – in fact
it could cause offence if a
foreign visitor were to kiss
someone's wife in greeting.

kitchen i koozina
kitchenette i koozinoola
Kleenex® ta khartomandila
knee to Gonato
knickers i kilota
knife to makheri
knitwear plekta rookha
knock khtipo
knock down khtipo
  he's been knocked down
  khtipiTHikeh
knock over (object) anapotho-
  yirizo
  (pedestrian) khtipo
know (somebody) Gnorizo
  (something, a place) xero
  I don't know then xero
  I didn't know that then to
  ixera
  do you know where I can
  find ...? mipos xereteh poo
  boro na vro ...?

L

label i etiketa
ladies' (toilets) i too-aleta ton
  yinekon
ladies' wear yinekia ithi
lady i kiria
lager i bira
  see beer
lake i limni
lamb (meat) to arni
lamp i lamba
lane (on motorway) i loritha
  (small road) i parothos
language i Glosa
language course maTHimata

xenis glosas
large meGalos
last telefteos
  last week i perasmeni
  evthomatha
  last Friday tin perasmeni
  Paraskevi
  last night kh-THes vrathi
  what time is the last train to
  Salonika? ti ora ineh to
  telefteo treno ya tin
  THesaloniki?
late arGa
  sorry I'm late meh
  sinkhoriteh poo aryisa
  the train was late to treno
  ikheh kaTHisterisi
  we must go – we'll be late
  prepi na piyenoomeh – THa
  aryisoomeh
  it's getting late nikhtoni
later arGotera
  I'll come back later THa yiriso
  argotera
  see you later adio, THa ta
  xanapoomeh
  later on argotera
latest o pi-o prosfatos
  by Wednesday at the latest tin
  Tetarti to argotero
laugh yelo
launderette to plindirio
  rookhon
laundromat to plindirio
  rookhon
laundry (clothes) i booGatha, ta
  aplita
  (place) to kaTHaristirio
lavatory i too-aleta

law o nomos

lawn to Grasithi

lawyer o/i thikiGoros

laxative to kaTHartiko

lazy tebelis

lead (electrical) o agogos
(verb) othiGo
where does this lead to? poo
othiyi afto?

leaf to filo

leaflet to thiafimistiko

leak i thiaro-i
(verb) stazo
the roof leaks i steyi stazi

learn maTHeno

least: not in the least katholoo
at least toolakhiston

leather to therma

leave (bag etc) afino
(go away) fevGo
(forget) xekhnao
I am leaving tomorrow fevgo
avrio
he left yesterday efiyeh
kh-THes
may I leave this here? boro
nafiso afto etho?
I left my coat in the bar afisa
tin tsanda moo sto bar
when does the bus for Athens
leave? poteh fevyi to
leoforio ya tin ATHina?

leeks ta prasa

left aristera
on the left pros ta aristera
to the left pros ta aristera
turn left stripseh aristera
there's none left then emineh
tipoteh

left-handed aristerokhiras

left luggage (office) o khoros
filaxis aposkevon

leg to pothi

lemon to lemoni

lemonade i lemonatha

lemon tea tsai meh lemoni

lend thanizo
will you lend me your ... ?
THa moo thanisis to thiko
soo ...?

lens (of camera) o fakos

lesbian i lesvia

less liGotero
less than liGotero apo
less expensive liGotero
akrivo

lesson to maTHima

let (allow) epitrepo
will you let me know? THa
moo to pis?
I'll let you know THa soo po
let's go for something to eat
pameh na fameh kati

let off katevazo
will you let me off at ...? THa
meh katevaseteh sto ...?

letter to Grama
do you have any letters for
me? ekho kanena grama?

letterbox to gramatokivotio

Letterboxes in Greece are
usually bright yellow. If you are
confronted with two slots,
'esoteriko' is for domestic mail
and 'exoteriko' is for overseas.

---

lettuce to marooli

lever o levi-**es**

library i vivlio**THi**ki

licence i **a**thi-a

lid to kap**a**ki

lie (tell untruth) l**e**o psemata

lie down xapl**o**no

life i zo-**i**

lifebelt i z**o**ni asfal**i**as

lifeguard o navagos**o**stis

life jacket to sos**i**vio

lift (in building) to asans**e**r

  could you give me a lift?
bor**i**teh na meh pat**e**h?

  would you like a lift? **TH**elet**e**h
na sas p**a**o?

light to fos

  (not heavy) elafr**o**s

  do you have a light? (for
cigarette) **e**khis fot**i**a?

  light green anikht**o** pr**a**sino

light bulb i l**a**mba, o gl**o**mbos

  I need a new light bulb
khri**a**zomeh m**i**a ken**oo**rya
l**a**mba

lighter (cigarette) o anapt**i**ras

lightning i astr**a**pi

like (verb) moo ar**e**si

  I like it moo ar**e**si aft**o**

  I like going for walks moo
ar**e**si na piy**e**no per**i**pato

  I like you moo ar**e**sis

  I don't like it then moo ar**e**si
aft**o**

  do you like it? soo ar**e**si aft**o**?

  I'd like to go swimming **TH**a
iTH**e**la na p**a**o ya kol**i**mbi

  I'd like a beer **TH**a **i**TH**e**la m**i**a
b**i**ra

  would you like a drink? **TH**a

  iTH**e**les **e**na pot**o**?

  would you like to go for a
walk? **TH**a **i**TH**e**les na p**a**meh
m**i**a v**o**lta?

  what's it like? meh ti mi**a**zi?

  I want one like this **TH**elo **e**na
san ki aft**o**

lime to moskhol**e**mono

lime cordial to lime

line (on paper) i gram**i**

  (phone) i tilefonik**i** gram**i**

  could you give me an outside
line? **TH**a moo th**o**seteh
gram**i**?

lips ta kh**i**lia

lip salve to v**oo**tiro kak**a**o

lipstick to kray**o**n

liqueur to lik**e**r

listen ak**oo**-o

litre* **e**na l**i**tro

  a litre of white wine **e**na l**i**tro
aspro kras**i**

little mikr**o**s

  just a little, thanks l**i**go m**o**no,
efkharist**o**

  a little milk l**i**go g**a**la

  a little bit more l**i**go ak**o**mi

live zo

  we live together siz**oo**meh

•••••• DIALOGUE ••••••

  where do you live? poo m**e**nis?

  I live in London m**e**no sto
L**o**nthino

lively thrast**i**rios

liver to sik**o**ti

loaf i fradz**o**la

lobby (in hotel) to sal**o**ni

lobster o astak**o**s

local dopios
  can you recommend a local
  wine/restaurant? boriteh na
  mas sistiseteh ena dopio
  krasi/estiatorio?
  see wine
lock i klitharia
  (verb) klithono
  it's locked ineh klithomeno
lock in klithono mesa
lock out klithono apo exo
  I've locked myself out
  klithoTHika apexo
locker (for luggage etc) i THiritha
lollipop to glifidzoori
London to LonTHino
long makris
  how long will it take to fix it?
  poso kero THa pari ya na to
  ftiaxeteh?
  how long does it take? posi
  ora kani?
  a long time polis keros, poli
  ora
  one day/two days longer mia
  mera/thio meres parapano
long distance call to iperastiko
  tilefonima
look: I'm just looking, thanks
  efkharisto, vlepo mono
  you don't look well then
  feneseh kala
  look out! prosexe!
  can I have a look? boro na tho?
look after prosekho, frondizo
look at kitazo
look for psakhno
  I'm looking for ... psakhno ya
look forward to perimeno meh

khara
  I'm looking forward to it to
  perimeno pos keh pos
loose (handle etc) khalaros
lorry to fortigo
lose khano
  I've lost my way ekho khaTHi
  I'm lost, I want to get to ...
  ekho khaTHi, THelo na pao
  sto ...
  I've lost my (hand)bag ekhasa
  tin tsanda moo
lost property (office) to grafio
  apolesTHendon
lot: a lot, lots pola
  not a lot okhi pola
  a lot of people poli anTHropi
  a lot bigger poli megalitero
  I like it a lot moo aresi poli
lotion i losion
loud thinatos
lounge to saloni
love i agapi
  (verb) agapo
  I love Greece latrevo tin
  Elatha
lovely oreos
low khamilos
luck i tikhi
  good luck! kali tikhi!
luggage i aposkeves
luggage trolley to karotsaki ya
  tis aposkeves
lump (on body) to priximo
lunch to yevma
lungs o pnevmonas
luxurious (hotel, furnishings)
  politelis
luxury politelias

M

Macedonia i Makethonia
machine i mikhani
mad (insane) trelos
  (angry) trelos apo THimo
magazine to periothiko
maid (in hotel) i servitora
maiden name to patronimo
mail ta gramata, to
  takhithromio
  (verb) takhithromo
  is there any mail for me? ekho
  kanena grama?
  see post
mailbox to gramatokivotio
  see letterbox
main kirios
main course to kirio piato
Mainland Greece i Ipirotiki
  Elatha
main post office kendriko
  takhithromio
main road (in town) o kendrikos
  thromos
  (in country) o aftokinito-
  thromos
main switch o kendrikos
  thiakoptis
make (brand name) i marka
  (verb) kano
  I make it 500 drachmas
  ipoloyizo oti kani pedakosi-
  es thrakhmes
  what is it made of? apo ti
  ineh ftiagmeno?
make-up to make-up
man o andras
manager o thi-efTHindis, o

manager
  can I see the manager? boro
  na tho ton thi-efTHindi?
manageress i thi-efTHindria

---

manners

It is bad manners to refuse
someone else's offer to pay for
your share in a meal, or their
offer to pay for the wine; the
equivalent of the two-finger
gesture is a five-finger or a
raised middle finger gesture;
avoid these, unless you want to
get in trouble.

---

manual to aftokinito meh
  kanonikes takhitites
many pola
  not many liga, okhi pola
map o khartis
March o Martios
margarine i marGarini
market i aGora
marmalade i marmelatha
married: I'm married (said by a
  man/woman) imeh
  pandremenos/pandremeni
  are you married? (said to a man/
  woman) isteh pandremenos/
  pandremeni?
mascara i maskara
match (football etc) to mats, o
  agonas
matches ta spirta
material (fabric) to ifasma
matter: it doesn't matter then
  pirazi
  what's the matter? ti simveni?

mattress to stroma
May o Ma-ios
may: may I have another one?
  THa iTHela ki alo ena?
  may I come in? boro na bo?
  may I see it? boro na to tho?
  may I sit here? boro na
  kaTHiso etho?
maybe isos
mayonnaise i ma-yoneza
me* emena
  that's for me afto ineh ya
  mena
  send it to me stilteh to seh
  mena
  me too ki eGo episis
meal to fa-yito

•••••• DIALOGUE ••••••

  did you enjoy your meal? sas
  areseh to fayito?
  it was excellent, thank you itan
  poli nostimo, efkharisto

mean: what do you mean? ti
eno-iteh?

•••••• DIALOGUE ••••••

  what does this word mean? ti
  simeni afti i lexi?
  it means ... in English simeni ... sta
  Anglika

measles i ilara
meat to kreas
mechanic o mikhanikos
medicine to farmako
Mediterranean i Meso-yios
medium (adj: size) metrios
medium-dry imixiro krasi
medium-rare misopsimeno

medium-sized metrio
  meyeTHos
meet sinandao
  nice to meet you kharika poo
  sas gnorisa
  where shall I meet you? poo
  THa sas sinandiso?
meeting i sinandisi
meeting place to meros
  sinandisis
melon to peponi
men i anthres
mend thiorTHono
  could you mend this for me?
  boriteh na moo to
  ftiaxeteh?
menswear ta anthrika ithi
mention anafero
  don't mention it parakalo
menu to menoo
  may I see the menu, please?
  boro na tho to menoo,
  parakalo?
  see Menu Reader
message to minima
  are there any messages for
  me? iparkhi kanena minima
  ya mena?
  I want to leave a message
  for ... thelo nafiso ena
  minima ya ...
metal to metalo
metre* to metro
microwave (oven) o foornos
  mikrokimaton, to
  microwave
midday to mesimeri
  at midday to mesimeri
middle: in the middle sti mesi

in the middle of the night arga
ti nikhta
the middle one to meseo
midnight ta mesanikhta
at midnight ta mesanikhta
might: I might THa boroosa
I might not then THa boroosa
I might want to stay another
day bori na THelo na mino
akomi mia mera
migraine i imikrania
mild (weather) eTHrios
(taste) elafros
mile* ena mili
milk to Gala
milkshake to milkshake
millimetre* ena khiliosto
minced meat o kimas
mind: never mind then pirazi
I've changed my mind alaxa
gnomi

•••••• DIALOGUE ••••••

do you mind if I open the window?
seh pirazi an anixo to
paraTHiro?
no, I don't mind okhi, then meh
pirazi

mine*: it's mine ineh thiko moo
mineral water to emfialomeno
nero
mint (sweet) i menda
minute to lepto
in a minute seh ena lepto
just a minute ena lepto
mirror o kaTHreftis
Miss thespinis
miss khano
I missed the bus ekhasa to

leoforio
missing lipi
one of my ... is missing lipi
ena ...
there's a suitcase missing lipi
mia valitsa
mist i katakhnia
mistake to laTHos
I think there's a mistake
nomizo oti iparkhi ena
laTHos etho
sorry, I've made a mistake meh
sinkhoriteh, ekana laTHos
misunderstanding i parexiyisi
mix-up: sorry, there's been a
mix-up meh sinkhoriteh,
iparkhi ena berthema
modern modernos
modern art gallery i galeri
modernas tekhnis
Modern Greek ta Nea Elinika
moisturizer i ithatiki krema
moment: I won't be a moment
mia stigmi parakalo
monastery to monastiri
Monday i theftera
money ta lefta
month o minas
monument to mnimio
moon to fengari
moped to mikhanaki
more* perisoteros
can I have some more water,
please? akomi ligo nero,
parakalo
more expensive/interesting pio
akrivo/enthiaferon
more than 50 perisotero apo
peninda

more than that pio poli ap
afto
a lot more poli perisotero

•••••• DIALOGUE ••••••

would you like some more? THa
THelateh ligo akomi?
no, no more for me, thanks okhi,
okhi alo ya mena, efkharisto
how about you? ki esis?
I don't want any more, thanks then
THelo alo, efkharisto

morning to pro-i
this morning simera to pro-i
in the morning to pro-i
mosquito to koonoopi
mosquito repellent to fithaki ya
ta koonoopia
most: I like this one most of all
afto moo aresi pio poli apo
ola
most of the time siniTHos
most tourists i perisoteri
tooristes
mostly kirios
mother i mitera
motorbike i motosikleta
motorboat i varka meh
mikhani
motorway i eTHniki othos
mountain to voono
in the mountains pano sta
voona
mountaineering i orivasia
mouse to pondiki
moustache to moostaki
mouth to stoma
mouth ulcer pliyi sto stoma
move metakino

he's moved to another room
piyeh seh alo thomatio
could you move your car?
boriteh na metakiniseteh to
aftokinito sas?
could you move up a little?
boriteh na metakiniTHiteh
ligo?
where has it moved to? poo
metaferTHikeh?
movie to film
movie theater o kinimato-
grafos, to sinema
Mr kiri-eh
Mrs kiria
Ms thespinis
much poli
much better/worse poli
kalitera/khirotera
much hotter poli pio zesta
not much okhi poli
not very much okhi para
poli
I don't want very much then
THelo para poli
mud i laspi
mug (for drinking) i koopa
I've been mugged meh
listepsan
mum i mama
mumps i parotititha
museum to moosio

There is usually an admission
charge for both state-run and
private museums, archaeo-
logical sites and art galleries.
Entrance to all state-run sites
→

and museums is free to everyone on Sundays and public holidays. Opening hours vary considerably (and often change) and you should find these out before you go in order to avoid disappointment. Some small museums and sites may close for a long lunch. Churches and monasteries are usually open to visitors when there is no service. Visitors are requested to be properly dressed (long trousers for men; long sleeves, long skirt and no trousers for women).

mushrooms ta manit**a**ria
music i moosik**i**
musician o/i moosik**o**s
Muslim (adj) Moosoolmanik**o**s
mussels ta m**i**thia
must: I must ... pr**e**pi na ...
  I mustn't drink alcohol then pr**e**pi na pi**o** alko-**o**l
mustard i moost**a**rtha
my* o/i/to ... moo
myself: I'll do it myself THa to k**a**no o **i**thios
  by myself ap**o** m**o**nos moo

N

nail (finger) to n**i**khi
  (metal) to karf**i**
nailbrush i v**oo**rtsa ya ta n**i**khia
nail varnish to man**o**
name to **o**noma
  my name's John meh l**e**neh John

what's your name? pos seh l**e**neh?
what is the name of this street? pos l**e**neh aft**o** to thr**o**mo?

It is not uncommon to hear Greeks address or greet each other formally by their profession: 'kalim**e**ra yatr**eh**' ('good morning doctor'). First names are only used between friends and relatives. In formal situations '**ki**rios' (Mr) '**ki**ri-eh' (Mr) or '**ki**ria' (Mrs/Miss/Ms) + surname are used. It is possible, however, to use '**ki**ri-eh/**ki**ria' + first name in semi-formal relationships, e.g. to a neighbour who is older than you, or a shopkeeper you know well.

napkin i pets**e**ta
nappy i p**a**na
narrow (street) sten**o**s
nasty (person) ap**e**sios
  (weather, accident) **a**skhimos
national eTHnik**o**s
nationality i eTHnik**o**tita
natural fisik**o**s
nausea i naft**i**a
navy (blue) ble mar**e**n
near kond**a**
  is it near the city centre? ineh kond**a** sto k**e**ndro tis p**o**lis?
  do you go near the Acropolis? pern**a**teh ap**o** tin Akr**o**poli?
  where is the nearest ...? poo **i**neh to plisi-**e**stero ...?

nearby eth**o** konda
nearly skheth**on**
necessary apar**e**titos,
  anang**e**os
neck o l**e**mos
necklace to koli-**e**
necktie i Grav**a**ta
need: I need ... khri**a**zomeh ...
  do I need to pay? khri**a**zeteh
  na plir**o**so?
needle i vel**o**na
negative (film) to arnitik**o**
neither: neither (one) of them
  kanen**a**s ap**o** aft**oos**
  neither ... nor ... **oo**teh ...
  ooteh ...
nephew o anips**i**os
net (in sport) to th**i**khti
network map o kh**a**rtis othik**oo**
  thikt**i**oo
never pot**eh**

•••••• D I A L O G U E ••••••

have you ever been to Athens?
ekheteh pa-i pot**eh** stin
ATH**i**na?
no, never, I've never been there
okhi, pot**eh**, then **e**kho pa-i
pot**eh** eki

new neos, ken**oo**ryos
news (radio, TV etc) ta n**e**a
newsagent's to prakt**o**rio
  efimer**i**thon
newspaper i efim**e**ritha
newspaper kiosk to per**i**ptero
  meh efimer**i**thes
New Year to neo **e**tos

New Year's Eve and Day are
traditionally family celeb-
rations, although nowadays
many Greeks celebrate both by
going out to expensive dinner
dances. It is traditional to have
fireworks at midnight and cut
the cake with the lucky coin in
it.

Happy New Year!
eftikh**i**smenos o ken**oo**ryos
khr**o**nos!
New Year's Eve i protokhroni**a**
New Zealand i Nea Zilanth**i**a
New Zealander: I'm a New
  Zealander (man/woman) **i**meh
  Neozilanth**o**s/
  Neozilanth**e**za
next ep**o**menos
  the next turning on the left i
  ep**o**meni strof**i** sta arister**a**
  the next street on the left o
  ep**o**menos thr**o**mos sta
  arister**a**
  at the next stop stin ep**o**meni
  st**a**si
  next week tin **a**li evtho-
  m**a**tha
  next to thipl**a** ap**o**
nice (food) n**o**stimos
  (looks, view etc) or**e**os
  (person) kal**o**s
niece i anips**i**a
night i n**i**khta
  at night to vr**a**thi
  good night kalin**i**khta

do you have a single room for one
night? ekheteh ena mono
thomatio ya mia nikhta?
yes, madam malista, kiria moo
how much is it per night? poso
kani ti mia nikhta?
it's 5000 drachmas for one night
ineh pendeh khiliathes
thrakhmes ya mia nikhta
thank you, I'll take it efkharisto,
THa to kliso

nightclub to nait-klab
nightdress to nikhtiko
night porter o nikhterinos
THiroros
no okhi
  I've no change then ekho
  psila
  there's no … left then eminet
  kaTHoloo …
  no way! apokli-eteh!
  oh no! (upset) okh!, o okhi!
nobody kanenas
  there's nobody there then
  ineh kanis eki
noise i fasaria
noisy: it's too noisy ekhi poli
  fasaria
non-alcoholic khoris alko-ol
none kanis
nonsmoking compartment o
  khoros ya mi kapnizondes
noon to mesimeri
no-one kanenas
nor: nor do I ooteh kego
normal fisiolo-yikos
north o voras

in the north sta vori-a
north of Athens vori-a tis
  ATHinas
northeast o vorio-anatolikos
northwest o vorio-thitikos
northern vorios
Northern Ireland i Vorios
  Irlanthia
Norway i Norviyia
Norwegian (adj) Norviyikos
nose i miti
nosebleed i emorayia sti miti
not* then
  no, I'm not hungry okhi, then
  pina-o
  I don't want any, thank you
  efkharisto, then THelo
  it's not necessary then ineh
  aparetito
  I didn't know that then to
  ixera
  not that one – this one okhi
  afto – to alo
note (banknote) to khartonomisma
notebook to blokaki, to
  simiomatario
notepaper (for letters) to kharti
  alilografias
nothing tipoteh
  nothing for me, thanks tipoteh
  ya mena, efkharisto
  nothing else tipoteh alo
novel to miTHistorima
November o No-emvrios
now tora
number* o ariTHmos
  I've got the wrong number
  pira laTHos noomero

what is your phone number?
pio **i**neh to tilefono soo?
number plate i pinaki**th**a
nurse (man/woman) o
nosoko**mos/i** nosoko**ma**
nursery slope i p**i**sta
ekma**TH**isis
nut (for bolt) to paxima**th**i
nuts to kari**th**i

O

o'clock* i o**ra**
occupied (toilet) katilimenos
October o Okt**o**vrios
odd (strange) para**x**enos
of* too
off (lights) klist**o**
it's just off Omonia Square li**g**o
pio eki a**po** tin Om**o**ni-a
we're off tomorrow
fevgoomeh **a**vrio
offensive (language, behaviour)
prosvlitikos
office (place of work) to Gra**f**io
officer (said to policeman)
astin**o**meh
often sikh**na**
not often okhi sikh**na**
how often are the buses?
ka**TH**eh p**o**teh **e**khi
leofor**i**a?
oil (for car) ta l**a**thia
(for salad) to l**a**thi
ointment i alif**i**
OK end**a**xi
are you OK? iseh kal**a**?
is that OK with you? iseh
efkharistimenos **e**tsi?

is it OK to ...? pira**zi** na ...?
that's OK thanks (it doesn't
matter) **i**neh end**a**xi,
efkharist**o**
I'm OK (nothing for me) tipoteh
ya m**e**na
(I feel OK) imeh mia khara
is this train OK for ...? afto
ineh to treno ya ...?
I said I'm sorry, OK? soo ipa
sign**o**mi, end**a**xi?
old (person) **y**eros
(thing) palios

•••••• DIALOGUE ••••••

how old are you? poso khronon
iseh?
I'm twenty-five imeh ikosi-pendeh
khronon
and you? ki esi?

old-fashioned demod**eh**
old town (old part of town) i palia
p**o**li
in the old town stin palia p**o**li
olive oil to ele**o**latho
olives i eli-es
omelette i omeleta
on pano
(lights) anikht**o**
on the street/beach sto
thro**mo/stin paralia
is it on this road? ineh safto
to thro**mo?
on the plane m**e**sa sto
a-eropl**a**no
on Saturday to S**a**vato
on television stin tileorasi
I haven't got it on me then to
ekho ma**zi** moo

this one's on me (drink) ego
kernao afti ti for**a**
the light wasn't on to fos then
itan anikht**o**
what's on tonight? ti pezi
simera?
once (one time) mia for**a**
at once (immediately) am**e**sos
one* enas, mia, ena
the white one to **a**spro
one-way ticket: a one-way ticket
to ... **e**na apl**o** ya ...
onion to kremithi
only m**o**no
only one m**o**no ena
it's only 6 o'clock ineh m**o**no
exi i **o**ra
I've only just got here m**o**lis
eftasa
on/off switch o thiak**o**ptis
open (adj) anikt**o**s
(verb: door, shop) an**i**go
when do you open? p**o**teh
aniyeteh?
I can't get it open then bor**o**
na to an**i**xo
in the open air stin **i**peTHro
opening times **o**res litooryias
open ticket isit**i**rio meh anikht**i**
epistrof**i**
opera i **o**pera
operation (medical) i enkh**i**risi
operator (telephone: man/woman) o
tilefon**i**tis/i tilefon**i**tria

The number for the inter-
national operator is 161.

opposite: the opposite direction

stin and**i**THeti katefTH**i**nsi
the bar opposite to bar
apenandi
opposite my hotel apenandi
ap**o** to xenothokhio moo
optician o optik**o**s
or i
orange (fruit) to portok**a**li
(colour) portokal**i**
orange juice i portokal**a**tha
orchestra i orkh**i**stra
order: can we order now? (in
restaurant) bor**oo**meh na
paragiloomeh tor**a**?
I've already ordered, thanks
ekho ithi paragili,
efkharist**o**
I didn't order this then
paragila aft**o**
out of order then litoory**i**
ordinary kanonik**o**s
other **a**los, **a**li, **a**lo
the other one to **a**lo
the other day tis pro-**a**les
I'm waiting for the others
perimeno toos **a**loos
do you have any others?
ekheteh tipoteh **a**la?
otherwise thiaforetik**a**
our* o/i/to ... mas
ours* thik**o**s mas
out: he's out then ineh etho
three kilometres out of town
tria khiliometra exo apo tin
poli
outdoors exo
outside ... exo ...
can we sit outside?
borr**oo**meh na

kaTHisoomeh exo?
oven o foornos
over: over here etho
  over there eki, eki pera
  over 500 pano apo
  pendakosia
  it's over teliosa
overcharge: you've overcharged
  me meh khreosateh
  parapano
overcoat to palto
overlook: I'd like a room
  overlooking the courtyard THa
  iTHela ena thomatio meh
  THea stin avli
overnight (travel) oloniktio
overtake prosperno
owe: how much do I owe you?
  poso sas khrostao?
own: my own ... thiko moo ...
  are you on your own? iseh
  monos soo?
  I'm on my own imeh monos
  moo
owner (man/woman) o ithioktitis/
  i ithioktitria

P

pack (verb) ftiakhno tis valitses
  a pack of ... ena paketo ...
package (parcel) to paketo
package holiday i orGanomeni
  ekthromi
packed lunch to etimo
  mesimeriano
packet: a packet of cigarettes
  ena paketo tsigara
padlock to looketo, i klitharia

page (of book) i selitha
  could you page Mr ...? boriteh
  na fonaxeteh ton kirio ...?
pain o ponos
  I have a pain here
  esTHanomeh ena pono etho
painful othiniros
painkillers to pafsipono
paint i boya
painting o pinakas zoGrafikis
pair: a pair of ... ena zevGari ...
Pakistani (adj) Pakistanikos
palace to palati
pale khlomos
  pale blue galazios
pan to tapsi
panties to slip, i kilotes
pants (underwear: men's) to
  sovrako
  (women's) to slip, i kilotes
  (US: trousers) to pandaloni
pantyhose to kalson
paper to kharti
  (newspaper) i efimeriTHa
  a piece of paper ena komati
  kharti
paper handkerchiefs ta
  khartomandila
parcel to thema
pardon (me)? (didn't understand/
  hear) pardon!, siGnomi?
parents: my parents i Gonis moo
parents-in-law ta peTHerika
park to parko
  (verb) parkaro
  can I park here? boro na
  parkaro etho?
parking lot to parking
part to meros

partner (boyfriend, girlfriend) o
    filos, i fili
party (group) i omatha
    (celebration) to parti
pass (in mountains) to perasma
passenger o/i epivatis
passport to thiavatirio
past: in the past sto parelTHon
    just past the information office
    amesos meta to grafio
    pliroforion
path to monopati
pattern to s-khethio
pavement to pezothromio
    on the pavement sto
    pezothromio
pavement café kafenio sto
    thromo
pay plirono
    can I pay, please? boro na
    pliroso, parakalo?
    it's already paid for ineh ithi
    pliromeno

•••••• DIALOGUE ••••••

who's paying? pios THa plirosi?
I'll pay ego THa pliroso
no, you paid last time, I'll pay okhi,
    esi pliroses tin teleftea fora, ego
    THa pliroso

payphone to tilefono meh
    kermata
peaceful irinikos
peach to rothakino
peanuts fistikia arapika
pear to akhlathi
peas ta bizelia
peculiar (taste, custom)
    paraxenos

pedestrian crossing i thiavasi
    pezon
pedestrian precinct o pezo-
    thromos
peg (for washing) i kremastra, to
    mandalaki
    (for tent) to palooki
pen to stilo
pencil to molivi
penfriend (male/female) o filos
    thi' alilografias/i fili thi'
    alilografias
penicillin i penikilini
penknife o soo-yias
pensioner o/i sindaxiookhos
people i anTHropi
    the other people in the hotel i
    ali anTHropi sto xeno-
    thokhio
    too many people ipervolika
    poli anTHropi
pepper (spice) to piperi
    (vegetable) i piperia
peppermint (sweet) i menda
per: per night tin vrathia
    how much per day? poso tin
    imera?
per cent tis ekato
perfect telios
perfume to aroma
perhaps isos
    perhaps not isos okhi
period (time, menstruation) i
    periothos
perm i permanand
permit i athia
person to atomo
personal stereo to walkman®
petrol i venzini

Petrol is either 3-star 'apl**i**'
(regular), 4-star '**soo**per'
(super) or unleaded 'am**o**livthi'.
Most petrol stations are staffed,
not self-service.
see **garage**

petrol can ena thokh**i**o
venz**i**nis
petrol station to venzin**a**thiko
pharmacy to farmak**i**o
see **chemist's**
phone to tilefono
(verb) p**e**rno til**e**fono,
tilefon**o**

Phone, telegraph, fax, and telex
facilities are provided by OTE
(Greek Telecommunications).
In the largest towns, there is
sometimes an OTE branch
which opens 24 hours, but most
are likely to be open from 7 a.m.
to 10 or 11 p.m. Local calls are
relatively straightforward – in
many hotel lobbies or cafés
you'll find red payphones which
presently take a 10-drachma
coin. Long-distance and
international calls can be made
from local branches of the OTE
and from street kiosks
(per**i**ptero) which have a
telephone meter (o metr**i**tis) –
you pay after having made the
call. It is, however, preferable to
make international calls from
an OTE branch as a per**i**ptero
→

can be unreliable and the line
may be bad. Reverse charge
calls can only be made from
branches of the OTE. Phonecards are sold from newspaper
or tobacco kiosks. All public
phones in Athens now take
phonecards instead of coins.
see **speak**

phone book o tilefonik**o**s
katalo**G**os
phonecard i tilek**a**rta
phone number o ari**THM**os
tilef**o**noo
photo i foto**G**raf**i**a
excuse me, could you take a
photo of us? meh
sinkhor**i**teh, **TH**a boro**o**sateh
na mas p**a**reteh m**i**a
fotograf**i**a?
phrase book to vivl**i**o
thialo**G**on
piano to pi**a**no
pickpocket o portof**o**las
**pick up: will you be there to pick
me up?** **TH**a **i**seh ek**i** na meh
par**i**s?
picnic to pikn**i**k
picture i ik**o**na
pie i p**i**ta
(meat) i kreat**o**pita
(fruit) i froot**o**pita
piece to kom**a**ti
a piece of ... ena kom**a**ti ...
pill to kh**a**pi
I'm on the pill p**e**rno
antisilipt**i**ka kh**a**pia

pillow to maxilari
pillow case i maxilaroTHiki
pin i karfitsa
pineapple o ananas
pineapple juice o khimos
  anana
pink roz
pipe (for smoking) i pipa, to
  tsibooki
  (for water) o solinas
pipe cleaners kaTHaristis
  pipas
Piraeus o Pireas
pistachio nuts fistiki-a Eyinis
pity: it's a pity ineh krima
pizza i pitsa
place to meros
  is this place taken? ineh
  piasmeni afti i THesi?
  at your place sti THesi soo
  at his place sti THesi too
plain (not patterned)
  monokhromo
plane to a-eroplano
  by plane meh to
  a-eroplano
plant to fito
plaster cast o yipsos
plasters to lefkoplast
plastic plastikos
  (credit cards) i pistotiki karta
plastic bag i plastiki sakoola
plate to piato
plate-smashing spasimo
  pi-aton
platform i platforma
  which platform is for Patras,
  please? pia platforma ya tin
  Patra, parakalo?

play (in theatre) to THeatriko
  erGo
  (verb) pezo
playground to yipetho
pleasant efkharistos
please parakalo
  yes please neh, parakalo
  could you please ...? THa
  boroosateh, parakalo,
  na ...?
  please don't stamata, seh
  parakalo
  pleased to meet you kharika
  poli
pleasure: i efkharistisi
  my pleasure efkharistisi
  moo
plenty: plenty of ... poli/pola ...
  there's plenty of time iparkhi
  arketi ora
  that's plenty, thanks
  efkharisto, arki
pliers i pensa
plug (electrical) i briza
  (for car) to boozi
  (in sink) i tapa
plumber o ithravlikos
p.m.* meta mesimvrias
poached egg to avgo poseh
pocket i tsepi
point: two point five thio koma
  pendeh
  there's no point then iparkhi
  logos
points (in car) i platines
poisonous thilitiriothis
police i astinomia
  call the police! kalesteh tin
  astinomia!

There is a separate tourist police force called 'Tooristiki Astinomia' which should be able to deal with any problems you may have. You should phone 171 for the tourist police.

policeman o astifilakas
police station to astinomiko tmima
policewoman i astinomikos
polish to verniki
polite evGenikos
polluted molismenos
pony to poni
pool (for swimming) i pisina
poor (not rich) ftokhos
  (quality) kakos
pop music i moosiki pop
pop singer o traGoothistis pop,
  i traGoothistria pop
population o pliTHismos
pork to khirino
port (for boats) to limani
  (drink) i mavrothafni
porter (in hotel) o akh-THoforos
portrait to portreto
posh (restaurant) akrivos
  (people) kiriles
possible thinatos
  is it possible to ...? ineh thinaton na ...?
  as ... as possible oso to thinaton ...
post (mail) ta Gramata
  (verb) takhithromo
  could you post this for me? boriteh na moo to

takhithromiseteh?
postbox to gramatokivotio
postcard i kartpostal
postcode o takhithromikos kothikos
poster (for room) to poster
  (in street) i afisa
post office to takhithromio

Post office hours are approximately 8 a.m. to 2.30 p.m. Monday to Friday. Some post offices in the larger cities may be open until 9 p.m. from Monday to Friday for postal services only. You may be asked to open a heavy envelope or registered letter in order to show its contents. Stamps can also be bought from street kiosks, but the proprietors are entitled to a 10 per cent commission and never seem to know the current international rates.

poste restante post restand
pots and pans (cooking implements) katsaroles keh tigania
potato i patata
potato chips ta tsips
pottery ta keramika
pound* (money) i lira
  (weight) i libra
power cut i thiakopi revmatos
power point o revmatothotis
practise: I want to practise my Greek THelo na exaskiso ta

Elinika moo
prawns i Garithes
  (larger) i karavitha
prefer: I prefer ... protimo ...
pregnant engios
prescription (for chemist) i
  sindayi
present (gift) to thoro
president (of country) o pro-
  ethros
pretty (beautiful) omorfos,
  oreos
  (quite) arketa
  it's pretty expensive ineh
  arketa akrivo
price i timi
priest o papas
prime minister o proTHi-
  poorgos
printed matter ta endipa
priority (in driving) i protereotita
prison i filaki
private ithiotikos
private bathroom to ithiotiko
  banio
probably piTHanon
problem to provlima
  no problem! kanena
  provlima!
program(me) to proGrama
promise: I promise iposkhomeh
pronounce: how is this
  pronounced? pos to proferis
  afto?
properly (repaired, locked etc) opos
  prepi
protection factor (of suntan lotion)
  o vaTHmos prostasias
Protestant o thiamartiromenos

public convenience i kinokhristi
  tooaleta
public holiday i thimosia aryia
pudding (dessert) to glikisma
pull travao
pullover to poolover
puncture to foo-it
purple mov
purse (for money) to portofoli
  (US: handbag) i tsanda
push sprokhno
pushchair to karotsaki
put vazo
  where can I put ...? poo boro
  na valo ...?
  could you put us up for the
  night? boriteh na mas
  filoxeniseteh ya ena vrathi?
pyjamas i pitzames

Q

quality i piotita
quarantine i karantina
quarter to tetarto
quayside: on the quayside stin
  provlita
question i erotisi
queue i oora
quick GriGora
  that was quick afto itan
  GriGoro
  what's the quickest way there?
  pios ineh o pio GriGoros
  thromos?
  fancy a quick drink? ekhis
  orexi ya ena poto sta
  GriGora?
quickly GriGora

quiet (place, hotel) isikhos
  quiet! siopi!
quince to kithoni
quite (fairly) arketa
  (very) telios
  that's quite right poli sosta
  quite a lot arketa

R

rabbit o lagos
race (for runners, cars) i koorsa
racket i raketa
radiator (in room) to kalorifer
  (of car) to psiyio aftokinitoo
radio to rathiofono
  on the radio sto rathiofono
rail: by rail sithirothromikos
railway o sithirothromos
rain i vrokhi
  in the rain mes tin vrokhi
  it's raining vrekhi
raincoat i kabardina, to
  athiavrokho
rape o viasmos
rare (steak) okhi poli psimeno
rash (on skin) to exanTHima
raspberry to vatomooro
rat o arooreos
rate (for changing money) i timi
  sinalagmatos
rather: it's rather good ineh
  malon kalo
  I'd rather ... THa protimoosa
  na ...
razor (dry) to xirafaki
  (electric) i xiristiki mikhani
razor blades to xirafaki
read thiavazo

ready etimos
  are you ready? (to man/woman)
  iseh etimos/etimi?
  I'm not ready yet then imeh
  etimos akomi

•••••• DIALOGUE ••••••

  when will it be ready? poteh THa
  ineh etimo?
  it should be ready in a couple of
  days THa prepi na ineh etimo
  seh mia-thio meres

real pragmatikos
really pragmatika
  that's really great afto ineh
  pragmatika spootheo
really! (surprise, doubt) psemata!
really? (interest) aliTHia?
rearview mirror o kaTHreftis
  aftokinitoo
reasonable (prices etc) loyikos
receipt i apothixi
recently prosfata
reception (in hotel) i resepsion
  (for guests) i thexiosi
  at reception stin paralavi
reception desk to grafio
  ipothokhis
receptionist i/o resepsionist
recognize anaGnorizo
recommend: could you
  recommend ...? boriteh na
  moo sistiseteh ...?
record (music) o thiskos
red kokinos
red wine to kokino krasi
refund i epistrofi khrimaton
  can I have a refund? moo
  epistrefondeh khrimata?

region i periokhi
registered: by registered mail
sistimeno
registration number o ariTHmos
kikloforias
relative o/i singenis
religion i THriskia
remember: I don't remember
then THimameh
I remember THimameh
do you remember? THimaseh?
rent (for apartment etc) to enikio
(verb) niki-azo
to/for rent eniki-azonteh

•••••• DIALOGUE ••••••

I'd like to rent a car THa iTHela na
nikiaso ena aftokinito
for how long? ya poso kero?
two days ya thio meres
this is our range afti ineh i lista
mas
I'll take the ... THa paro to ...
is that with unlimited mileage?
ineh meh aperioristo ariTHmo
khiliometron?
it is neh, ineh
can I see your licence please? boro
na tho tin athi-a sas, parakalo?
and your passport keh to
thiavatirio sas
is insurance included?
simperilamvaneteh i asfalia?
yes, but you pay the first 3,000
drachmas neh, ala esis THa
pliroseteh tis protes tris
khiliathes thrakhmes
can you leave a deposit of 1,000
drachmas? boriteh na afiseteh ya

engi-isi khili-es thrakhmes?

rented car to enikiasmeno
aftokinito
repair i episkevi
can you repair it? boriteh na
to episkevaseteh?
repeat epanalamvano
could you repeat that? boriteh
na to epanalaveteh?
reservation (train, bus) to klisimo
THesis

•••••• DIALOGUE ••••••

I have a reservation ekho kani
mia kratisi
yes sir, what name please?
malista, kiri-eh; seh ti onoma,
parakalo?

reserve krato

•••••• DIALOGUE ••••••

can I reserve a table for tonight?
boro na kliso ena trapezi ya
apopseh?
yes madam, for how many
people? malista, kiria moo; ya
posa atoma?
for two ya thio
and for what time? keh ya ti ora?
for eight o'clock ya tis okhto
and could I have your name
please? to onoma sas,
parakalo?
see alphabet page vi for
spelling

rest: I need a rest khriazomeh
xekoorasi
the rest of the group to

ipolipo groop
restaurant to estiatorio

There are two basic types of restaurants: the 'estiatorio' and the taverna. Distinctions between the two are slight but restaurants can be more formal and more expensive than tavernas. The latter may be found more often in the old parts of towns – they may have a more limited choice of dishes and may not display a menu. The best strategy is to go where the Greeks go.

---

rest room i too-aleta
  see toilet
retired: I'm retired imeh seh sindaxi
return: a return to ... ena isitirio met epistrofis ya to ...
reverse charge call to tilefonima kolekt
reverse gear i opisTHen
revolting apesios
Rhodes i Rothos
rib to plevro
rice to rizi
rich (person) ploosios
  (food) varis
ridiculous yelios
right (correct) sostos
  (not left) thexia
  you were right ikhes thikio
  that's right sosta
  this can't be right afto then bori na ineh sosto

right! entaxi!
  is this the right road for ...? ineh aftos o sostos thromos ya ...?
  on the right sta thexia
  turn right stripseh thexia
right-hand drive meh thexio timoni
ring (on finger) to thaktilithi
  I'll ring you THa soo tilefoniso
ring back THa seh paro piso
ripe (fruit) orimos
rip-off: it's a rip-off ineh listia
rip-off prices astronomikes times
risky ripsokinthinos
river to potami
road (country) o thromos
  (in town) i othos
  is this the road for ...? ineh aftos o thromos ya ...?
  down the road parakato
road accident to aftokinitistiko thistikhima
road map o othikos khartis
roadsign i pinakitha
rob: I've been robbed meh listepsan
rock o vrakhos
  (music) i rok moosiki
  on the rocks (with ice) meh pagakia
roll (bread) to psomaki
roof i orofi, i steyi
  (flat) i taratsa
roof rack i s-khara aftokinitoo
room to thomatio
  (space) to meros

in my room sto thomatio
moo

•••••• DIALOGUE ••••••

do you have any rooms? ekheteh
kaTHoloo thomatia?

for how many people? ya posa
atoma?

for one/for two ya ena/ya thio

yes, we have some vacancies neh,
ekhoomeh elefTHera thomatia

for how many nights will it be? ya
posa vrathia to THeleteh?

just for one night mono ya ena
vrathi

how much is it? poso kani?

... drachmas with bathroom and ...
drachmas without bathroom ...
thrakhmes meh mbanio keh ...
thrakhmes khoris mbanio

can I see a room with bathroom?
boro na tho ena thomatio meh
mbanio?

OK, I'll take it entaxi, THa to paro

room service to servis
thomatioo

rope to skhini

rosé (wine) to rozeh

roughly (approximately) pano-
kato

round: it's my round ineh i sira
moo

roundabout (for traffic) o
kikloforiakos komvos, i
platia

round trip ticket: a round trip
ticket to ... ena isitirio met
epistrofis ya to ...

route i poria

what's the best route for ...?
pios ineh o kaliteros
thromos ya ...?

rubber (material) lastikho
(eraser) i svistra, i goma

rubber band to lastikhaki

rubbish (waste) ta skoopithia
(poor quality goods) kaki piotita

rubbish! (nonsense) trikhes!

rucksack to sakithio

rude a-yenis

ruins ta eripia, i arkheotites

rum to roomi
rum and coke ena roomi meh
koka kola

run (person) trekho
how often do the buses run?
poso sikh-na pernoon ta
leoforia?
I've run out of money moo
teliosan ta khrimata

rush hour ora ekhmis

S

sad lipimenos

saddle i sela

safe (not in danger) asfalis
(not dangerous) akinthinos,
avlavis

safety pin i paramana

sail to pani

sailboard to windsurf

sailboarding to windsurf

salad i salata

salad dressing to lathoxitho

sale: for sale politeh

salmon o solomos

Salonika i THcsaloniki

salt to alati
same: the same o ithios
  the same as this to ithio opos
  afto
  the same again, please to
  ithio xana, parakalo
  it's all the same to me to ithio
  moo kani
sand i amos
sandals ta santhalia
sandwich to sandwich
sanitary napkins i servi-etes
sanitary towels i servi-etes
sardines i sartheles
Saturday to Savato
sauce i saltsa
saucepan i katsarola
saucer to piataki
sauna i sa-oona
sausage to lookaniko
say: how do you say ... in Greek?
  pos to leneh ... sta Elinika?
  what did he say? ti ipeh?
  I said ... ipa ...
  he said ... ipeh ...
  could you say that again?
  boriteh na to xanapiteh?,
  boriteh na to epanalaveteh?
scarf (for neck) to kaskol
  (for head) to mandili
scenery to topio
schedule (US) to proGrama
scheduled flight i
  programatismeni ptisi
school to skholio
scissors: a pair of scissors to
  psalithi
scotch to skots whisky
Scotch tape® to sellotape®

Scotland i Skotia
Scottish Skotsezikos
  I'm Scottish (man/woman) imeh
  Skotsezos/Skotseza
scrambled eggs ta khtipita
  avga
scratch i gratzoonia
screw i vitha
screwdriver to katsavithi
scuba diving i anapnefstiki
  siskevi katathiti
sea i THalasa
  by the sea konda sti THalasa
seafood ta THalasina
seafood restaurant i psaro-
  taverna
seafront i paralia
  on the seafront stin paralia
seagull o Glaros
search psakh-no
seashell i akhivaTHa
seasick: I feel seasick
  esthanomeh naftia
  I get seasick meh piani i
  THalasa
seaside: by the seaside konda
  stin paralia
seat i THesi
  is this anyone's seat? ineh
  kanenos afti i THesi?
seat belt i zoni asfalias
sea urchin o akhinos
seaweed ta fikia
secluded apomeros
second (of time) to theftero-
  lepto
  (adj) thefteros
  just a second! mia stigmi!
second class (travel) thefteri

THesi

second floor o thefteros orofos

(US) o tritos orofos

second-hand apo thefteros kheri

see vlepo, kitazo

can I see? boro na tho?

have you seen ...? ekhis thi ...?

see you! ta xanalemeh!

I see (I understand) katalava

I saw him this morning ton itha simera to pro-i

self-catering apartment to anexartito thiamerisma

self-service self-servis

sell poolo

do you sell ...? poolateh ...?

Sellotape® to sellotape®

send stelno

I want to send this to England thelo na stilo afto stin Anglia

senior citizen o/i sindaxiookhos

separate (adj) khoristos

separated: I'm separated imeh khorismenos/khorismeni

separately (pay, travel) xekhorista

September o Septemvrios

septic siptikos

serious sovaros

service charge (in restaurant) to filothorima

service station to venzinathiko

serviette i hartopetseta, i petseta

set menu to tabl-dot

several arketi

sew ravo

could you sew this back on? boriteh na to rapseteh pali sti THesi too?

sex to sex

shade: in the shade sti skia

shake: let's shake hands as thosoomeh ta kheria

shallow (water) rikha nera

shame: what a shame! ti krima!

shampoo to samboo-an

a shampoo and set ena loosimo meh mizampli

share (verb: room, table etc) mirazomeh

sharp (knife etc) kofteros

(taste, pain) thinatos

shattered (very tired) exandlimenos

shaver i xiristiki mikhani

shaving foam o afros xirismatos

shaving point i priza xiristikis mikhanis

she* afti

is she here? ineh etho?

sheet (for bed) to sendoni

shelf to rafi

shellfish ta ostraka

sherry to seri

ship to plio

by ship meh plio

shirt to pookamiso

shit! skata!

shock to sok

I got an electric shock from the ... ilektristika meh ...

shock-absorber to amortiser

shocking (behaviour, prices) exofrenik**os**

shoe to pap**oo**tsi
a pair of shoes ena zevgari pap**oo**tsia

shoelaces ta korth**o**nia papootsi**on**

shoe polish to vern**i**ki papootsi**on**

shoe repairer o tsangar**is**

shop to maGaz**i**

> Shops are usually open Monday to Friday from 8 a.m. to 1.30 p.m. and from 5 p.m. to 8.30 p.m. (on Saturdays they open only in the morning); however, some may open all day, especially in tourist areas.

shopping: I'm going shopping p**ao** ya ps**o**nia

shopping centre to emborik**o** k**e**ndro

shop window i vitr**i**na

shore i akt**i**

short (person) kond**os**
(time) l**i**Gos
(journey) s**i**ndomos

shortcut o s**i**ndomos thr**o**mos

shorts to s**o**rts

should: what should I do? ti pr**e**pi na k**a**no?
he shouldn't be long then pr**e**pi na ar**yi**si
you should have told me epr**e**peh na moo to **i**khes pi

shoulder o **o**mos

shout (verb) fon**a**zo

show (in theatre) to **e**rgo
could you show me? bor**i**teh na moo th**i**xeteh?

shower (in bathroom) to doos
(rain) i b**o**ra
with shower meh doos

shower gel to afrol**oo**tro

shut (verb) kl**i**no
when do you shut? p**o**teh kl**i**neteh?
when do they shut? p**o**teh kl**i**noon?
they're shut **i**neh klist**a**
I've shut myself out klist**i**ka ap**e**xo
shut up! sk**a**seh!

shutter (on camera) to thiafr**a**Gma
(on window) to ex**o**filo, to pandz**oo**ri

shy dr**o**palos

sick (ill) ar**o**stos
I'm going to be sick (vomit) **e**kho t**a**si pros emet**o**
see ill

side i pl**e**vra
the other side of town i **a**li **a**kri tis p**o**lis

side lights ta khamil**a** f**o**ta

side salad i sal**a**ta ya garnit**oo**ra

side street to throm**a**ki

sidewalk to pezothr**o**mio

sight: the sights of ... ta axioTH**e**ata too ...

sightseeing: we're going sightseeing p**a**meh na th**oo**meh ta axioTH**e**ata

sightseeing tour i xenayisi sta
  axioTHeata
sign (roadsign etc) to sima
signal: he didn't give a signal
  then ekaneh sima
signature i ipografi
signpost i pinakitha, i tabela
silence i siopi
silk to metaxi
silly ano-itos
silver to asimi
silver foil to aloominokharto
similar omios
simple (easy) aplos
since: since yesterday apo
  kh-THes
  since I got here apo toteh
  poo irTHa etho
sing traGootho
singer (man/woman) o traGoo-
  thistis/i traGoothistria
single monos
  a single to ... ena aplo ya ...
  I'm single imeh elefTHeros/
  elefTHeri
single bed to mono krevati
single room to mono thomatio
sink (in kitchen) o nerokhitis
sister i athelfi
sister-in-law (brother's wife) i nifi
  (wife's sister) i kooniatha
sit: can I sit here? boro na
  kaTHiso etho?
  is anyone sitting here?
  kaTHeteh kanis etho?
sit down kaTHomeh
  sit down! katseh kato!
site to axioTHeato
  (archaeological) arkheoloyikos

khoros
size to meh-yeTHos
skin to therma
skindiving i katathisis
skinny kokaliaris
skirt i foosta
sky o ooranos
sleep (verb) kimameh
  did you sleep well? kimi-
  THikes kala?
  I need a good sleep
  khriazomeh ena kalo ipno
sleeper (on train) i kooketa
sleeping bag to sleeping bag
sleeping car i klinamaxa, i
  kooketa
sleeping pill to ipnotiko khapi
sleepy: I'm feeling sleepy
  nistazo
sleeve to maniki
slide (photographic) to slide
slip (under dress) to misofori
slippery Glisteros
slow arGos
  slow down! pio arga
slowly siGa-siGa
  could you say it slowly?
  boriteh na to piteh arga-
  arga?
  very slowly poli arga
small mikros
smell: it smells (smells bad)
  vroma-i
smile (verb) khamo-yelo
smoke o kapnos
  do you mind if I smoke? sas
  pirazi an kapniso?
  I don't smoke then kapnizo
  do you smoke? kapnizeteh?

snack: I'd just like a snack THa
iTHela na fao kati prokhiyo
snake to fithi
sneeze to ftarnisma
snorkel o anapnefstiras
snow to khioni
so: it's so good ineh poli kalo
not so fast okhi toso GriGora
so am I keh ego to ithio
so do I keh ego episis
so-so etsi ki etsi
soaking solution (for contact
lenses) igro sindirisis fakon
epafis
soap to sapooni
soap powder to aporipandiko
sober xemeTHistos
socks i kaltses
socket (electrical) i priza
soda (water) i sotha
sofa o kanapes
soft (material etc) apalos
soft-boiled egg to melato avgo
soft drink to anapsiktiko
soft lenses i malaki faki
sole i sola
could you put new soles on
these? boriteh na moo
valeteh kenooryi-es soles
safta?
some: can I have some water/
rolls? moo thineteh ligo
nero?/liga psomakia?
can I have some? boro na
paro ligo?
somebody, someone kapios
something kati
something to drink kati na
pi-iteh

sometimes merikes fores
somewhere kapoo
son o yos
song to traGoothi
son-in-law o Gambros
soon sindoma
I'll be back soon THa yiriso
sindoma
as soon as possible oso to
thinaton grigorotera
sore: it's sore ineh
ereTHismeno
sore throat pona-i o lemos
moo
sorry: (I'm) sorry signomi
sorry? (didn't understand/hear)
pardon?, signomi?
sort: what sort of ...? ti ithos ...?
soup i soopa
sour (taste) xinos
south notos
south of noti-a
in the south sto noto
to the south noti-a
South Africa i Noti-os Afriki
South African (adj) Notio-
afrikanos
I'm South African (man/woman)
imeh Notio-afrikanos/Notio-
afrikana
southeast notio-anatolikos
southwest notio-thitikos
souvenir to enTHimio
Spain i Ispania
Spanish (adj) ispanikos
(language) ta ispanika
spanner to klithi
spare part ta andalaktika
spare tyre i rezerva

spark plug to boozi
speak: do you speak English?
milateh Anglika?
I don't speak ... then milo ...

•••••• DIALOGUE ••••••

can I speak to Costas? boro na
miliso ston Kosta, parakalo?
who's calling? pios ton zita-i?
it's Patricia i Patricia
I'm sorry, he's not in, can I take a
message? lipameh, then ineh
etho, boro na too thoso kapio
minima?
no thanks, I'll call back later okhi,
efkharisto, THa xanaparo
argotera
please tell him I called parakalo,
piteh too pos tilefonisa

speciality i spesialiteh
spectacles ta yali-a
speed i takhitita
speed limit to orio takhititas
speedometer to konder
spell: how do you spell it? pos
to grafeteh?
see alphabet page vi
spend xothevo
spider i arakhni
spin-dryer to stegnotirio
splinter i agitha
spoke (in wheel) i aktina
spoon to kootali
sport to spor
sprain: I've sprained my ...
straboolixa to ...
spring (season) i anixi
(in seat etc) to elatirio
square (in town) i platia

stairs ta skalopatia, i skales
stale (bread, taste) bayatikos
stall: the engine keeps stalling i
mikhani sinekhos stamata
stamp to Gramatosimo
see post office

•••••• DIALOGUE ••••••

a stamp for England, please ena
gramatosimo ya Anglia,
parakalo
what are you sending? ti THa
stileteh?
this postcard afti tin karta

star to asteri
(in film) o/i star
start i arkhi, to xekinima
(verb) arkhizo
when does it start? poteh
arkhizi?
the car won't start to
aftokinito then xekina
starter (of car) i miza
(food) to proto piato
starters ta orektika
starving: I'm starving peTHeno
tis pinas
state (in country) i politia
the States (USA) i Inomenes
Politi-es
station o staTHmos
statue to agalma
stay: where are you staying?
poo meneteh?
I'm staying at ... meno sto ...
I'd like to stay another two
nights THa iTHela na mino
ales thio nikhtes
steak i brizola

steal klevo
my bag has been stolen
klepsaneh tin tsanda moo
steep (hill) apotomos
steering to timoni
step: on the steps sta
skalopati-a
stereo to stereofoniko
singrotima
sterling i lira sterlina
steward (on plane) o
a-erosinothos
stewardess i a-erosinothos
sticking plaster to lefkoplast
still: I'm still waiting akoma
perimeno
is he still there? ineh akoma
eki?
keep still! stasoo akinitos!
sting: I've been stung by ... meh
tsibiseh ...
stockings i na-ilon kaltses
stomach to stomakhi
stomach ache o ponos sto
stomakhi, o stomakhoponos
stone (rock) i petra
stop stamatao
please, stop here (to taxi driver
etc) parakalo, stamatisteh
etho
do you stop near ...?
stamatateh konda ...?
stop doing that! stamata na to
kanis afto!
stopover i stasi
storm i THi-ela
straight: it's straight ahead ineh
olo efrHia
a straight whisky ena sketo

whisky
straightaway amesos
strange (odd) paraxenos
stranger (man/woman) o xenos/i
xeni
I'm a stranger here imeh
xenos etho
strap to loori
strawberry i fraoola
stream to rema, to potamaki
street o thromos
on the street sto thromo
streetmap o othikos khartis
string (cord) o spangos
(guitar etc) i khorthi
strong thinatos
stuck frakarismenos
the key's stuck koliseh to
klithi
student o fititis, i fititria
stupid vlakas
suburb ta pro-astia
subway (US: railway) o ipo-yios
suddenly xafnika
suede to kastori
sugar i zakhari
suit (man's) to koostoomi
(woman's) to ta-yer
it doesn't suit me (jacket etc)
then moo pa-i
it suits you soo pa-i
suitcase i valitsa
summer to kalokeri
in the summer to kalokeri
sun o ilios
in the sun ston ilio
out of the sun sti skia
sunbathe kano ilioTHerapia
sunblock (cream) to andiliako

sunburn to **k**apsimo apo ton
  ilio
sunburnt kamenos apo ton ilio
Sunday i Kiriaki
sunglasses ta yalia ilioo
sun lounger i shez long
sunny: it's sunny ekhi liakatha
sun roof (in car) i tzamenia
  skepi
sunset i thisi too ilioo
sunshade i ombrela ilioo
sunshine i liakatha
sunstroke i ili-asi
suntan to **m**avrisma
suntan lotion to lathi
  mavrismatos
suntanned iliokamenos
suntan oil to lathi
  mavrismatos
super kataplik**t**ikos
supermarket to supermarket
supper to thipno
supplement (extra charge)
  epipleon, to prosTHeto
sure: are you sure? iseh
  sigooros?
  sure! veveos!
surname to epiTHeto
swearword i vrisia
sweater to poolover
sweatshirt i fanela
Sweden i Soo-ithia
Swedish (adj) Soo-ithikos
sweet (taste) Glikos
  (dessert) to Gliko
sweets i karameles
swelling to priximo
swim kolimbao
  I'm going for a swim pao ya

kolibi
  let's go for a swim pameh ya
  kolibi
swimming costume to ma-yo
swimming pool i pisina
swimming trunks to ma-yo
switch o thiakoptis
switch off (engine) svino
  (TV, lights) klino
switch on (engine) anavo
  (TV, lights) anigo
swollen prismenos

T

table to trapezi
  a table for two ena trapezi ya
  thio
tablecloth to trapezomandilo
table tennis to ping-pong
table wine to epitrapezio krasi
tailback (of traffic) i oora
tailor o raftis
take (lead) perno
  (accept) thekhomeh
  can you take me to the airport?
  boriteh na meh pateh sto
  a-erothromio?
  do you take credit cards?
  thekhesteh pistotikes
  kartes?
  fine, I'll take it entaxi THa to
  paro
  can I take this? (leaflet etc)
  boro na paro afto?
  how long does it take? posi
  ora THa pari?
  it takes three hours perni tris
  ores

is this seat taken? ineh
piasmeni i THesi?
hamburger to take away
khamboorger ya to spiti
can you take a little off here?
(to hairdresser) boriteh na
pareteh ligo apo etho?
talcum powder i poothra talk
talk (verb) milo
tall psilos
tampons ta tampax®, ta tabon
tan to mavrisma
  to get a tan mavrizo
tank (of car) to depozito
tap i vrisi
tape (cassette) i kaseta
  (sticky) i tenia
tape measure to metro
tape recorder to magnitofono
taste i yefsi
  can I taste it? boro na to
  thokimaso?
taxi to taxi
  will you get me a taxi? THa
  moo kaleseteh ena taxi?
  where can I find a taxi? poo
  boro na vro ena taxi?

•••••• DIALOGUE ••••••

to the airport/to the Hilton Hotel
please sto a-erothromio/sto
xenothokhio Khilton, parakalo
how much will it be? poso THa
stikhisi?
1,500 drachmas khili-es
pendakosi-es thrakmes
that's fine, right here, thanks
entaxi, etho pera ineh,
efkharisto

taxi-driver o taxidzis

Greek taxis, especially Athenian
ones, are among the least
expensive in Western Europe.
Within city or town limits, use
of the meter is mandatory if one
is present. Double tariff applies
between 1 and 6 a.m., and
outside city or town limits at any
time of the day and there are
also surcharges for entering a
ferry harbour or airport and for
large items of luggage. In rural
areas, taxis sometimes have no
meters and you have to agree a
price. Taxi-drivers very often
charge you much more than they
should. It's a good idea to check
the official price list usually
displayed in airports for the fare
from an airport to a city centre.
You should be wary of
unlicenced taxi-drivers outside
major railway stations.

taxi rank o staTHmos taxi
tea to tsa-i
  tea for one/two please tsa-i ya
  enan/thio parakalo
teabags ta fakelakia tsa-i
teach: could you teach me?
  boris na meh maTHis?
teacher (man/woman) o
  thaskalos/i thaskala
team i omatha
teaspoon to kootalaki
tea towel i petseta koozinas
teenager o neos, i nea

telegram to tileGrafima

telephone to tilefono
  see phone

television i tileorasi

tell: could you tell him ...?
  boriteh na too piteh ...?

temperature (weather) i
  THermokrasia
  (fever) o piretos

temple (church) o na-os

tennis to tennis

tennis ball i bala too tennis

tennis court to yipetho tennis

tennis racket i raketa tennis

tent i skini

term (at university, school)
  i s-kholiki periothos

terminus (rail) to terma

terrible foveros

terrific exeretikos

than* apo
  smaller than mikroteros apo

thanks, thank you efkharisto
  thank you very much
  efkharisto para poli
  thanks for the lift efkharisto
  poo meh pirateh
  no thanks okhi efkharisto

•••••• DIALOGUE ••••••

  thanks efkharisto
  that's OK, don't mention it
  parakalo, then kani tipoteh

that ekinos, ekini, ekino
  that one ekino
  I hope that ... elpizo oti ...
  that's nice ti orea!
  is that ...? afto ineh ...?
  that's it (that's right) akrivos

the* o, i, to; (pl) i, i, ta

theatre to THeatro

their* o/i/to ... toos

theirs* thiki toos

them* toos, tis, ta
  for them ya ekinoos
  with them maftoos
  I gave it to them to ethosa
  saftoos
  who? – them pi-i? – afti

then (at that time) toteh
  (after that) katopin

there eki
  over there eki pera
  up there eki pano
  is there ...? iparkhi ...?
  are there ...? iparkhoon ...?
  there is ... iparkhi ...
  there are ... iparkhoon ...
  there you are (giving something)
  oristeh

thermometer to THermometro

thermos flask to THermos

these afti, aftes, afta
  can I have these? boro na
  ekho afta?

Thessaly i THesalia

they* afti, aftes, afta

thick pakhis
  (stupid) khazos

thief (man/woman) o kleftis/i
  kleftra

thigh to booti

thin leptos
  (person) athinatos

thing to praGma
  my things ta pragmata moo

think skeptomeh
  (believe) nomizo

I think so etsi nomizo

I don't think so then nomizo

I'll think about it THa to skepto

third party insurance asfalia ya khrisi apo tritoos

thirsty: I'm thirsty thipso

this aftos, afti, afto

this one afto etho

this is my wife apo etho i yineka moo

is this …? ineh …?

those ekini, ekines, ekina

which ones? – those pi-a? – afta

Thrace i THraki

thread i klosti

throat o lemos

throat pastilles pastili-es lemoo

through thiamesoo

does it go through …? (train, bus) perna-i apo to …?

throw (verb) rikhno

throw away (verb) peto

thumb o andikhiras

thunderstorm i kateyitha, i THi-ela

Thursday i Pempti

ticket to isitirio

•••••• DIALOGUE ••••••

a return to Athens ena isitirio epistrofis ya tin AThina

coming back when? poteh ineh i epistrofi?

today/next Tuesday simera/tin epomeni Triti

that will be 2,000 drachmas thio khiliathes thrakhmes, parakalo

ticket office (bus, rail) i THiritha

tide i paliri-a

tie (necktie) i Gravata

tight (clothes etc) stenos

it's too tight ineh poli steno

tights to kalson

till mekhri

time* o khronos

(occasion) i fora

what's the time? ti ora ineh?

this time afti ti fora

last time tin perasmeni fora

next time tin epomeni fora

four times teseris fores

timetable to proGrama

tin (can) i konserva

tinfoil to asimokharto

tin-opener to anikhtiri

tiny mikroskopikos

tip (to waiter etc) to filothorima

There are no specific rules on how large a tip you should leave in a restaurant and tipping is not regarded as essential. In most restaurants and tavernas a service charge is included. Look for the word 'to filothorima' το φιλοδώρημα on the menu which indicates whether the service charge is included. You are expected to tip cinema- or theatre-attendants. It is not usual to tip taxi-drivers; they usually round up the fare if the amount of change is small and often claim that they have no change!

tired koorasmenos
I'm tired imeh koorasmenos
tissues ta khartomandila
to: to Salonica/London ya tin
THesaloniki/to Lonthino
to Greece/England ya tin
Elatha/Anglia
to the post office sto
takhithromio
toast (bread) to tost
today simera
toe to thakhtilo too pothioo
together mazi
we're together (in shop etc)
imasteh mazi
can we pay together?
boroomeh na plirosoomeh
mazi?
toilet i too-aleta
where is the toilet? poo ineh i
too-aleta?
I have to go to the toilet prepi
na pao stin too-aleta

> Public toilets are rare in Greece,
> especially in less touristy places,
> but are sometimes found in
> parks or squares. You will have
> to take advantage of toilets in
> restaurants and bars or toilets
> at railway/bus stations and in
> museums etc. Throughout
> Greece you place used paper in
> the adjacent wastebaskets, not
> in the bowl.

toilet paper kharti iyias
tomato i domata
tomato juice to domatozoomo,

o domatokhimos
tomato ketchup to ketsap
tomorrow avrio
tomorrow morning avrio to
pro-i
the day after tomorrow
methavrio
toner (cosmetic) to tonotiko
tongue i Glosa
tonic (water) to tonik
tonight apopseh
tonsillitis i amiGthalititha
too (excessively) poli
(also) episis
too hot poli kafto
too much para poli
me too kego episis
tooth to thondi
toothache o ponothondos
toothbrush i othondovoortsa
toothpaste i othondokrema
top: on top of ... pano apo ...
at the top stin korifi
top floor to retire
topless yimnostiTHi
torch o fakos
total to sinolo
tour i peri-iyisi, i xenayisi
is there a tour of ...? iparkhi
peri-iyisi ya ...?
tour guide o/i xenagos
tourist (man/woman) o tooristas/i
tooristria
tourist information office Grafio
Pliroforion E-OT
tour operator to taxithiotiko
grafio
towards pros
towel i petseta

town i poli
  in town stin poli
  just out of town akrivos exo
  apo tin poli
town centre to kendro tis polis
town hall to thimarkhio
toy to pekh-nithi
track (US) i platforma
  see platform
tracksuit i aTHlitiki forma
traditional parathosiakos
traffic i kikloforia
traffic jam i kikloforiaki
  simforisi
traffic lights ta fanaria tis
  trokheas
trailer (for carrying tent etc) i
  rimoolka
  (US: caravan) to trokhospito
trailer park topoTHesia ya
  trokhospita
train to treno
  by train meh treno

•••••• DIALOGUE ••••••

is this the train for ...? afto ineh to
treno ya ...?
sure neh
no, you want that platform there
okhi, THa pateh seh ekini tin
platforma eki

trainers (shoes) ta aTHlitika
  papootsia
train station o sithiro-
  thromikos staTHmos
tram to tram
translate metafrazo
  could you translate that?
  boriteh na metafraseteh

afto?
translation i metafrasi
translator o/i metafrastis
trashcan o skoopithodenekes
travel taxithevo
  we're travelling around
  taxithevoomeh triyiro
travel agent's to taxithiotiko
  Grafio
traveller's cheque i taxithiotiki
  epitayi
tray o thiskos
tree to thendro
tremendous tromeros
trendy modernos
trim: just a trim please (to
  hairdresser) ligo konditera,
  parakalo
trip (excursion) to taxithi
  I'd like to go on a trip to ... THa
  iTHela na pao ena taxithi
  stin ...
trolley to trolley, to karotsaki
trolleybus to trolley
  see bus
trouble o belas
  I'm having trouble with ... ekho
  provlimata meh ...
  sorry to trouble you meh
  sinkhoriteh poo sas vazo
  seh mbela
trousers to pandaloni
true aliTHinos
  that's not true then ineh
  aliTHia
trunk (US: of car) to port-bagaz
trunks (swimming) to mayo
try prospaTHo, thokimazo
  can I have a try? boro na

thokimaso?
try on provaro
  can I try it on? boro na to
  thokimaso pano moo?
T-shirt to bloozaki
Tuesday i Triti
tuna o tonos
tunnel i siraga
Turkey i Toorkia
Turkish (adj) Toorkikos
Turkish coffee Toorkikos kafes,
  Elinikos kafes
    see coffee
Turkish-Cypriot (adj) Toorkiko-
  Kipriakos
turn: turn left/right stripseh
  aristera/thexia
  where do I turn off? poo
  strivo?
turn off: can you turn the heating
  off? boris na klisis ti
  THermansi/to kalorifer?
turn on: can you turn the heating
  on? boris na anixis ti
  THermansi/to kalorifer?
turning (in road) i strofi
TV i tileorasi
tweezers to tsimbithaki
twice thio fores
  twice as much ta thipla
twin beds thio krevatia
twin room to thomatio meh
  thio krevatia
twist: I've twisted my ankle
  stramboolixa ton astragalo
  moo
type to ithos
  a different type of ... ena alo
  ithos apo ...

typical kharaktiristikos
tyre to lastikho

U

ugly askhimos
UK to Inomeno Vasili-o
ulcer to elkos
umbrella i ombrela
uncle o THios
unconscious anesTHitos
under apo kato
  (less than) ligotero apo
underdone (meat) misop-
  simenos
underground (railway) o ipo-yios
underpants to sovrako, to slip
understand: I understand
  katalaveno
  I don't understand then
  katalaveno
  do you understand?
  katalavenis?
unemployed anerGos
United States i Inomenes
  Politi-es
university to panepistimio
unleaded petrol i amolivthi
  venzini
unlimited mileage aperiorista
  khiliometra
unlock xeklithono
unpack aniGo tis valitses
until mekhri
unusual asiniTHistos
up pano
  (upwards) pros ta pano
  up there eki pano
  he's not up yet (not out of bed)

then sikoTHikeh akomi
what's up? (what's wrong?) ti
yineteh?
upmarket (restaurant etc) akrivos
upset stomach o
stomakhoponos
upside down ta pano kato
upstairs pano
urgent epiGon
us* mas
with us meh mas
for us ya mas
USA i IPA
use khrisimopi-o
may I use ...? boro na
khrisimopi-iso ...?
useful khrisimos
usual siniTHismenos
the usual (drink etc) to
siniTHismeno

V

vacancy: do you have any
vacancies? (hotel) ekheteh
elefTHera thomatia?
vacation i thiakopes
see holiday
vaccination o emvoliasmos
vacuum cleaner i ilektriki
skoopa
valid (ticket etc) engiros
how long is it valid for? ya
poso is-khi-i?
valley i kilatha
valuable (adj) politimos
can I leave my valuables here?
boro na afiso ta timalfi moo
etho?

value i axia
van to trokhospito
vanilla i vanilia
a vanilla ice cream ena
pagoto vanilia
vary: it varies metavaleteh
vase to vazo
veal to moskhari
vegetables ta lakhanika
vegetarian o/i khortofaGos
vending machine o aftomatos
politis
very poli
very little for me poli ligo ya
mena
I like it very much moo aresi
para poli
vest (under shirt) to fanelaki
via thia mesoo
video (film) i video-tenia
(video recorder) to video
view i THea
villa i vila
village to khorio
vinegar to xithi
vineyard to ambeli
visa i viza
visit (verb) episkeptomeh
I'd like to visit ... THa iTHela na
episkefto ...
vital: it's vital that ... ineh vasiko
na ...
vodka i votka
voice i foni
volleyball to volley-ball, i
khirosferisi
voltage i tasis
see electricity
vomit (verb) kano emeto

W

waist i mesi

waistcoat to yileko

wait perimeno
 wait for me perimeneh mch!
 don't wait for me mi meh
 perimenis
 can I wait until my wife gets
 here? boro na paragilo otan
 elTHi i yineka moo?
 can you do it while I wait? na
 perimeno na to kaneteh?
 could you wait here for me?
 boriteh na meh
 perimeneteh na yiriso?

waiter o servitoros
 waiter! garson!

waitress i garsona, i servitora
 waitress! garson!

wake: can you wake me up at
 5.30? boriteh na meh
 xipniseteh stis pendeh keh
 misi?

wake-up call tilefonima ya
 xipnima

Wales i Oo-alia

walk: is it a long walk? ineh
 poli perpatima?
 it's only a short walk ekhi ligo
 perpatima
 I'll walk THa perpatiso
 I'm going for a walk pao ena
 peripato

Walkman® to walkman®

wall o tikhos

wallet to portofoli

wander: I like just wandering
 around moo aresi na

khazevo triyiro

want: I want a … THelo ena …
 I don't want any … then
 THelo …
 I want to go home THelo na
 pao spiti moo
 I don't want to then THelo
 he wants to … THeli na …
 what do you want? ti THelis?

ward (in hospital) o THalamos

warm zestos
 I'm so warm zestenomeh
 arketa

was*: I was … imoon …
 he/she/it was … itan …

wash (verb) pleno
 (oneself) plenomeh
 can you wash these? boriteh
 na plineteh afta?

washer (for bolt etc) i rothela

washhand basin o niptiras

washing (clothes) i booGatha

washing machine to plindirio

washing powder i skoni
 plindirioo, to aporipandiko

washing-up liquid to sapooni
 piaton

wasp i sfinga

watch (wristwatch) to rolo-i
 will you watch my things for
 me? boriteh na prosekheteh
 ta pragmata moo?
 watch out! prosekheh!

watch strap to looraki roloyioo

water to nero
 may I have some water? moo
 thineteh ligo nero?

waterproof (adj) athi-avrokhos

waterskiing to THalasio ski

wave (in sea) to **kima**
way: could you tell me the way
to ...? **boriteh na moo piteh
pos** THa **pa-o sto ..?**
it's this way **apo etho ineh**
it's that way **apo eki ineh**
is it a long way to ...? **ineh
makri-a** ya to ...?
no way! **apokli-eteh!**

•••••• DIALOGUE ••••••

could you tell me the way to?
**boriteh na moo thixeteh to
thromo ya ...?**
go straight on until you reach the
traffic lights **piyeneteh olo isia
mekhri na ftaseteh sta fanaria**
turn left **stripsteh aristera**
take the first on the right **parteh
ton proto thromo sta thexia**
see **where**

we* **emis**
weak **athinatos**
weather **o keros**

•••••• DIALOGUE ••••••

what's the weather forecast? **ti
ipeh to theltio keroo?**
it's going to be fine **THa ineh
kalos keros**
it's going to rain **THa vrexi**
it'll brighten up later **THa anixi o
keros argotera**

wedding **o Gamos**
wedding ring **i vera**
Wednesday **i Tetarti**
week **i evthomatha**
a week (from) today **seh mia
evthomatha apo simera**

a week (from) tomorrow **seh
mia evthomatha apo avrio**
weekend **to Savatokiriako**
at the weekend **to
Savatokiriako**
weight **to varos**
weird **paraxenos**
weirdo **o trelaras**
welcome: welcome to ... **kalos
ilTHateh sto ...**
you're welcome (don't mention
it) **parakalo**
well: I don't feel well then
esTHanomeh kala
she's not well **ekini then ineh
kala**
you speak English very well
milateh poli kala Anglika
well done! **bravo**
this one as well **ki afto episis**
well well! (surprise) **ya thes!**

•••••• DIALOGUE ••••••

how are you? **ti kanis?**
very well, thanks **poli kala,
efkharisto**
and you? **ki esi?**

well-done (meat) **kalopsimenos**
Welsh **Oo-alos**
I'm Welsh (man/woman) **imeh
Oo-alos/Oo-ali**
were*: we were **imasteh**
you were **isasteh/isteh**
they were **itan**
west **thitikos**
in the west **sta thitika**
West Indian (adj) **apo tis
thitikes Inthi-es**
wet **vregmenos**

what? ti?
  what's that? ti ineh ekino?
  what should I do? ti prepi na
  kano?
  what a view! ti THea!
  what bus do I take? ti leoforio
  prepi na paro?
wheel i rotha
wheelchair i anapiriki
  poliTHrona
when? poteh?
  when we get back otan
  yirisoomeh
  when's the train/ferry? poteh
  fevyi to treno/to karavi?
where? poo?
  I don't know where it is then
  xero poo ineh

• • • • • • DIALOGUE • • • • • •

  where is the cathedral? poo ineh o
  kaTHethrikos naos?
  it's over there ineh eki pera
  could you show me where it is on
  the map? boriteh na moo
  thixeteh sto kharti poo ineh?
  it's just here ineh akrivos etho
  see way

which: which bus? pio
  leoforio?

• • • • • • DIALOGUE • • • • • •

  which one? pio?
  that one ekino
  this one? afto?
  no, that one okhi, ekino

while: while I'm here oso imeh
  etho
whisky to whisky

white aspros
white wine to aspro krasi
who? pios?
  who is it? pios ineh?
  the man who ... o anTHropos
  poo ...
whole: the whole week oli tin
  evthomatha
  the whole lot ola
whose: whose is this? pianoo
  ineh afto?
why? yati?
  why not? yati okhi?
wide platis
wife: my wife i sizigos moo
will: will you do it for me? THa
  moo to kanis afto?
wind o anemos
window to paraTHiro
  near the window konda sto
  paraTHiro
  in the window (of shop) sti
  vitrina
window seat i THesi sto
  paraTHiro
windscreen to parbriz
windscreen wiper o
  ialokaTHaristiras
windsurfing to windsurfing
windy: it's so windy ekhi poli
  a-era
wine to krasi
  can we have some more
  wine? boroomeh na
  ekhoomeh ligo krasi
  akoma?

ENGLISH ❖ GREEK |Wi

Both estatoria and tavernas will
usually offer you a choice of
bottled wines, and some
(mainly tavernas) may have
their own house variety, kept in
barrels and served out in metal
jugs. If you want house wine, ask
for 'khima krasi/retsina'.
Retsina – pine-resinated wine,
a slightly acquired taste – is
invariably better straight from
the barrel. Not as many tavernas
keep it as once did, but always
ask whether they have wine
'varelisio' or 'khima' – both
mean, in effect, 'from the
barrel'.

women
Many women travel by them-
selves about Greece without
being harassed or feeling
intimidated. Most of the hassle
you are likely to get is from a
small minority of Greeks who
migrate to the main resorts and
towns in summer in pursuit of
'fun-loving' tourists. In remote
mountains and inland areas,
you may feel more un-
comfortable travelling alone.
The intensely traditional Greeks
may have trouble understanding
why you are unaccompanied,
and might not welcome your
presence in their exclusively
male 'kafenia' – often the only
place where you can get a drink.
Because of the machismo of the
majority of Greek men, foreign
women should be careful when
dealing with approaches; flirting
can often lead to unpleasant
misunderstandings.

wine list o kataloGos ton
   krasion
winter o khimonas
   in the winter ton khimona
winter holiday i khimerines
   thiakopes
wire to sirma
   (electric) to ilektriko
   kalothio
wish: best wishes poles
   efkhes
with meh
   I'm staying with ... meno
   meh ...
without khoris
witness o/i martiras
   will you be a witness for me?
   THa iseh martiras moo?
woman i yineka

wonderful THavmasios
won't*: it won't start then THa
   xekinisi
wood (material) to xilo
woods (forest) to thasos
wool to mali
word i lexi
work i thoolia
   it's not working then thoolevi
   I work in ... ergazomeh seh ...
world o kosmos

worry: I'm worried stenokhori-
emeh

worry beads to kombolo-i

worse: it's worse ineh
khirotera

worst o khiroteros

worth: is it worth a visit? axizi
mia episkepsi?

would: would you give this to ...?
boriteh na thoseteh afto
ston ...?

wrap: could you wrap it up?
boriteh na to tilixeteh?

wrapping paper to kharti
peritiliGmatos
(for presents) kharti ya thora

wrist o karpos

write Grafo
could you write it down?
boriteh na moo to
grapseteh?
how do you write it? pos to
grafeteh?

writing paper to kharti
aliloGrafias

wrong: it's the wrong key afto
ineh laTHos klithi
the bill's wrong o
logariasmos ineh laTHos
sorry, wrong number signomi,
laTHos noomero
sorry, wrong room signomi,
laTHos thomatio
there's something wrong with
... iparkhi kapio laTHos
meh ...
what's wrong? ti simveni?

X

X-ray i aktinoGrafia

Y

yacht to yot

yard* i yartha
(courtyard, backyard) i avli

year o khronos

yellow kitrinos

yes neh

yesterday kh-THes

yesterday morning kh-THes to
pro-i
the day before yesterday
prokh-THes

yet akomi

• • • • • • DIALOGUE • • • • • •

has it arrived yet? akomi then
eftaseh?
no, not yet okhi, okhi akomi
you'll have to wait a little longer yet
THa prepi na perimeneteh akomi
ligo

yoghurt to ya-oorti

you* (fam) esi
(pl or polite) esis
I'll see you later THa seh tho
arGotera
this is for you afto ineh ya sas
with you mazi sas

young neos

your* (fam) o/i/to ... soo
(pl or polite) o/i/to ... sas
your camera i fotografiki
mikhani soo/sas

yours (fam) thiko soo

(pl or polite) thik**o** sas
youth hostel o xen**o**nas neon

Z

zero mith**e**n
zip to fermoo-**ar**
  could you put a new zip in?
  bor**i**teh na v**a**leteh **e**na
  ken**oor**-yio fermoo-**ar**?
zip code o takhithromik**o**s
  kothik**o**s
zoo o zo-oloyik**o**s k**i**pos

Greek-English

A

αγάπη (η) [agapi (i)] love

αγαπημένος [agapimenos] favourite

αγαπώ [agapo] love (verb)

αγγίζω [angizo] touch (verb)

ΑΓΓΛΙΑ Αγγλία (η) [Anglia (i)] England

Αγγλίδα (η) [Anglitha (i)] Englishwoman

ΑΓΓΛΙΚΑ Αγγλικά (τα) [Anglika (ta)] English

ΛΓΓΛΙΚΟΣ Αγγλικός [Anglikos] English

Άγγλος (ο) [Anglos (o)] Englishman

αγελάδα (η) [ayelatha (i)] cow

αγενής [ayenis] rude

άγκυρα (η) [angira (i)] anchor

αγκώνας (ο) [angonas (o)] elbow

ΑΓΝΟ ΠΑΡΘΕΝΟ ΜΑΛΛΙ αγνό παρθένο μαλλί pure new wool

ΑΓΟΡΑ αγορά (η) [agora (i)] market

αγοράζω [agorazo] buy (verb)

αγόρι (το) [agori (to)] boy

άγριος [agrios] wild, fierce

αγρόκτημα (το) [agroktima (to)] farm

αγρότης (ο) [agrotis (o)] farmer

αγώνας (ο) [agonas (o)] fight, struggle; game

άδεια (η) [athia (i)] licence; permission

άδεια οδηγήσεως (η) [athia othiyiseos (i)] driving licence

άδειος [athios] empty, vacant

αδελφή (η) [athelfi (i)] sister

ΑΔΕΛΦΟΙ αδελφοί brothers

αδελφός (ο) [athelfos (o)] brother

ΑΔΙΕΞΟΔΟ αδιέξοδο cul-de-sac, dead end

αδύνατος [athinatos] impossible; weak

A.E. public limited company

ΑΕΡΑΝΤΛΙΑ αεραντλία (η) air pump

αέρας (ο) [aeras (o)] air; wind; choke

ΑΕΡΟΔΡΟΜΙΟ αεροδρόμιο (το) [aerothromio (to)] airport

ΑΕΡΟΛΙΜΗΝ αερολιμήν (ο) [aerolimin (o)] airport

αεροπλάνο (το) [aeroplano (to)] plane

αεροπορική εταιρεία (η) [aeroporiki eteria (i)] airline

ΑΕΡΟΠΟΡΙΚΩΣ αεροπορικώς [aeroporikos] by air; by air mail

ΑΕΡΟΣΥΝΟΔΟΣ αεροσυνοδός (ο/η) [aerosinothos (o/i)] steward, stewardess

ΑΘΗΝΑ Αθήνα (η) [ATHina (i)] Athens

αθλητής (ο) [aTHlitis (o)] athlete

ΑΘΛΗΤΙΚΑ αθλητικά (τα) [aTHlitika (ta)] sports shop

αθλητικά παπούτσια (τα) [aTHlitika papootsia (ta)] trainers

Α Β Γ Δ Ε Ζ Η Θ Ι Κ Λ Μ Ν Ξ Ο Π Ρ Σ Τ Υ Φ Χ Ψ Ω

ΑΘΛΗΤΙΚΕΣ
ΕΓΚΑΤΑΣΤΑΣΕΙΣ
αθλητικές εγκαταστάσεις
sporting facilities
αθλητική φόρμα (η) [aτΗlitiki
forma (i)] tracksuit
ΑΘΛΗΤΙΚΟ ΚΕΝΤΡΟ
αθλητικό κέντρο (το)
[aτΗlitiko kendro (to)] sports
centre
αθώος [aτΗoos] innocent
ΑΙΓΑΙΟ Αιγαίο (το) [E-yeo
(to)] Aegean
ΑΙΘΟΥΣΑ ΤΡΑΝΖΙΤ
αίθουσα τράνζιτ transit
lounge
αίμα (το) [ema (to)] blood
αιμορραγώ [emorago] bleed
αισθάνομαι [esτΗanomeh] feel
(verb)
ΑΙΤΗΣΗ αίτηση (η) [etisi (i)]
application form;
application
αιτία (η) [etia (i)] cause;
reason
εξ αιτίας ... [exetias ...]
because of ...
αιώνας (ο) [eonas (o)] century
ΑΚΑΤΑΛΛΗΛΟ
ακατάλληλο adults only
Α΄ ΚΑΤΗΓΟΡΙΑΣ Α΄
κατηγορίας first class
ακολουθώ [akolooτΗo] follow
ακόμα, ακόμη [akoma, akomi]
still; yet; even; also
ακουστικά (τα) [akoostika (ta)]
hearing aid; headphones
ΑΚΟΥΣΤΙΚΟ ακουστικό
(το) [akoostiko (to)] receiver

ακούω [akoo-o] hear; listen
άκρη (η) [akri (i)] edge; end;
tip
ΑΚΡΙΒΕΣ ΑΝΤΙΤΙΜΟ
ΜΟΝΟ ακριβές αντίτιμο
μόνο exact fare only
ακριβός [akrivos] expensive
ακροατήριο (το) [akroatirio
(to)] audience
ΑΚΡΥΛΙΚΟ ακρυλικό
[akriliko] acrylic
ΑΚΤΗ ακτή (η) [akti (i)]
beach; coast, shore
ακυρώνω [akirono] cancel
ΑΛΒΑΝΙΑ Αλβανία (η)
[Alvania (i)] Albania
αληθινός [aliτΗinos] true; real
αλλά [alla] but
ΑΛΛΑΓΗ ΛΑΔΙΩΝ αλλαγή
λαδιών oil change
αλλάζω [allazo] change (verb)
αλλάζω ρούχα [allazo rookha]
change one's clothes
ΑΛΛΕΡΓΙΑ αλλεργία (η)
[alleryia (i)] allergy
ΑΛΛΕΡΓΙΑ ΣΤΗ ΓΥΡΗ
αλλεργία στη γύρη [alleryia
sti yiri] hay fever
αλλεργικός σε [alleryikos seh]
allergic to
άλλη [ali] other; else
άλλη μία [ali mia] another
άλλο [alo] other; else; another
όχι άλλο [okhi alo] no more
άλλο ένα [alo ena] another
άλλος [alos] other; else
άλλος ένας [alos enas] another
αλλού [aloo] elsewhere
αλμυρός [almiros] salty

άλογο (το) [alogo (to)] horse

ΑΛΟΙΦΗ αλοιφή (η) [alifi (i)] ointment

αλουμινόχαρτο (το) [aloominokharto (to)] aluminium foil

ΑΛΣΟΣ άλσος (το) [alsos (to)] wooded park, grove

αλτ! [alt!] stop!

αλυσίδα (η) [alisitha (i)] chain

ΑΜΑΞΑ άμαξα (η) [amaxa (i)] coach, car (on train)

ΑΜΑΞΙ αμάξι (το) [amaxi (to)] car (on train)

ΑΜΑΞΟΣΤΟΙΧΙΑ αμαξοστοιχία (η) [amaxostikhia (i)] train

Αμερικανίδα (η) [Amerikanitha (i)] American (woman)

Αμερικανικός [Amerikanikos] American (adj)

Αμερικανός (ο) [Amerikanos (o)] American (man)

ΑΜΕΡΙΚΗ Αμερική (η) [Ameriki (i)] America

ΑΜΕΣΟΣ ΔΡΑΣΙΣ άμεσος δράσις emergencies

αμέσως [amesos] immediately

αμμόλοφοι (οι) [amolofi (i)] sand dunes

άμμος (η) [amos (i)] sand

αμορτισέρ (το) [amortiser (to)] shock-absorber

αμπέλι (το) [ambeli (to)] vineyard

αμπέρ (το) [amper (to)] amp

ΑΜΠΟΥΛΕΣ αμπούλες ampoules

αν [an] if

ΑΝΑΒΡΑΖΟΝΤΑ ΔΙΣΚΙΑ αναβράζοντα δισκία effervescent tablets

ανάβω [anavo] light (verb)

αναγκαίος [anangeos] necessary

ανάγκη [anangi] need

αναγνωρίζω [anagnorizo] recognize, acknowledge, admit

ανακατεύω [anakatevo] mix (verb)

ΑΝΑΚΟΙΝΩΣΗ ανακοίνωση (η) [anakinosi (i)] announcement

ΑΝΑΚΛΗΣΙΣ ανάκλησις (η) [anaklisis (i)] withdrawal

ΑΝΑΛΗΨΗ ανάληψη withdrawal(s) (of money)

αναμείνατε στο ακουστικό [anaminateh sto akoostiko] hold the line please

ανάμεσα [anamesa] among; between

αναπαύομαι [anapavomeh] rest, relax

ανάπαυση (η) [anapafsi (i)] rest

αναπαυτικός [anapaftikos] comfortable

αναπηρική πολυθρόνα (η) [anapiriki politHrona (i)] wheelchair

ανάπηρος [anapiros] disabled

αναπνέω [anapneo] breathe

αναποδογυρίζω [anapothoyirizo] knock over

αναπτήρας (ο) [anaptiras (o)] lighter

A B Γ Δ E Z H Θ I K Λ M N Ξ O Π P Σ T Y Φ X Ψ Ω

αναπτύσσω [anaptiso] develop;
explain

ανατολή (η) [anatoli (i)] east;
dawn

ανατολή του ήλιου (η) [anatoli
too ilioo (i)] sunrise

ΑΝΑΧΩΡΕΙ
ΚΑΘΗΜΕΡΙΝΑ ΓΙΑ ...
αναχωρεί καθημερινά γιά ...
departs daily to ...

ΑΝΑΧΩΡΗΣΕΙΣ
αναχωρήσεις departures

ΑΝΑΧΩΡΗΣΗ αναχώρηση
(η) [anakhorisi (i)] departure

ΑΝΑΨΥΚΤΗΡΙΟ
αναψυκτήριο refreshments

άνδρας (ο) [anthras (o)] man

ΑΝΔΡΙΚΑ ανδρικά (τα)
[anthrika (ta)] menswear

ΑΝΔΡΙΚΑ ΕΙΔΗ ΚΑΙ
ΑΞΕΣΟΥΑΡ ανδρικά είδη
και αξεσουάρ men's
fashions and accessories

ΑΝΔΡΙΚΑ ΕΝΔΥΜΑΤΑ
ανδρικά ενδύματα [anthrika
enthimata] menswear

ΑΝΔΡΙΚΑ ΕΣΩΡΟΥΧΑ
ανδρικά εσώρουχα [anthrika
esorookha] men's underwear

ΑΝΔΡΙΚΑΙ ΚΟΜΜΩΣΕΙΣ
ανδρικαί κομμώσεις
[anthrikeh komosis] men's
hairdresser

ΑΝΔΡΙΚΑ ΥΠΟΔΗΜΑΤΑ
ανδρικά υποδήματα [anthrika
ipothimata] men's footwear

ΑΝΔΡΙΚΑ ΥΠΟΚΑΜΙΣΑ
ανδρικά υποκάμισα [anthrika
ipokamisa] men's shirts

ΑΝΔΡΩΝ ανδρών gents'
(toilet), men's room

ανεβαίνω [aneveno] get in
(car); get up; go up

ΑΝΕΛΚΥΣΤΗΡΑΣ
ανελκυστήρας (ο)
[anelkistiras (o)] lift, elevator

ΑΝΕΜΙΣΤΗΡΑΣ
ανεμιστήρας (ο) [anemistiras
(o)] fan

άνεμος (ο) [anemos (o)] wind

ΑΝΕΞΑΡΤΗΤΟ
ΔΙΑΜΕΡΙΣΜΑ
ανεξάρτητο διαμέρισμα (το)
[anexartito thiamerisma (to)]
self-catering apartment

ανεξάρτητος [anexartitos]
independent

άνεργος [anergos] unemployed

ανήκω [aniko] belong

ανησυχώ [anisikho] be
anxious, be worried

ανησυχώ για [anisikho ya]
worry about

ανηψιά (η) [anipsia (i)] niece

ανηψιός (ο) [anipsios (o)]
nephew

ΑΝΘΟΠΩΛΕΙΟ ανθοπωλείο
(το) [anTHopolio (to)] florist's

άνθρωποι (οι) [anTHropi (i)]
people

αν και [an keh] although

ΑΝΟΔΟΣ άνοδος (η)
[anothos (i)] ascent, way up

ανοίγω [anigo] open (verb);
switch on

ανοίγω τις βαλίτσες [anigo tis
valitses] unpack

ΑΝΟΙΚΤΑ ανοικτά [anikta]

open

ΑΝΟΙΚΤΟ ΑΠΟ ... ΩΣ ...
ανοικτό από ... ως ... [anikto
apo ... os ...] open from ... to ...

ΑΝΟΙΚΤΟΝ ανοικτόν
[anikton] open (adj)

ανοικτός [aniktos] open (adj);
on (light)

άνοιξη (η) [anixi (i)] spring
(season)

ανοιχτήρι (το) [anikhtiri (to)]
tin opener; corkscrew

ΑΝΟΙΧΤΟ ανοιχτό [anikhto]
open; light (colour)

ΑΝΤΑΛΛΑΚΤΙΚΑ
ανταλλακτικά (τα) spare
parts

ΑΝΤΑΛΛΑΚΤΙΚΑ
ΑΥΤΟΚΙΝΗΤΩΝ
ανταλλακτικά αυτοκινήτων
(τα) auto spares

ανταλλάσω [adalaso]
exchange (verb)

άντε! [adeh!] come on!

αντέχω [adekho] endure,
tolerate

αντί [adi] instead of

ΑΝΤΙΒΙΟΤΙΚΟ αντιβιοτικό
(το) [adiviotiko (to)] antibiotic

ΑΝΤΙ-ΙΣΤΑΜΙΝΙΚΟ
ΦΑΡΜΑΚΟ αντι-
ισταμινικό φάρμακο (το)
[adi-istaminiko farmako (to)]
antihistamine

αντίκα (η) [adika (i)] antique

ΑΝΤΙΚΕΣ αντίκες [adikes]
antiques

αντίο [adio] goodbye

αντιπαθητικός [adipaтИitikos]

obnoxious

ΑΝΤΙΠΡΟΣΩΠΕΙΑ
ΑΥΤΟΚΙΝΗΤΩΝ
αντιπροσωπεία
αυτοκινήτων (η) [adiprosopia
aftokiniton (i)] car dealer

ΑΝΤΙΠΡΟΣΩΠΟΣ
αντιπρόσωπος (ο)
[adiprosopos (o)] agent

αντιπυρετικό [adipiretiko] anti-
fever

ΑΝΤΙΣΗΠΤΙΚΟ
αντισηπτικό (το) [adisiptiko
(to)] antiseptic

ΑΝΤΙΣΥΛΛΗΠΤΙΚΟ
αντισυλληπτικό (το)
[adisiliptiko (to)]
contraceptive

ΑΝΤΙΣΥΛΛΗΠΤΙΚΟ ΧΑΠΙ
αντισυλληπτικό χάπι (το)
[adisiliptiko khapi (to)]
contraceptive pill

ΑΝΤΙΤΙΜΟ (ΔΙΑΔΡΟΜΗΣ)
αντίτιμο (διαδρομής) (το)
[aditimo (thiathromis) (to)]
fare

ΑΝΤΙΦΛΕΓΜΩΔΕΣ
αντιφλεγμώδες anti-
inflammation

αντλία (η) [adlia (i)] pump

ΑΝΤΛΙΑ ΒΕΝΖΙΝΗΣ
αντλία βενζίνης petrol/gas
pump

ΑΝΤΛΙΑ ΝΤΙΖΕΛ αντλία
ντίζελ diesel pump

ΑΝΩ άνω [ano] up

ΑΞΕΣΟΥΑΡ
ΑΥΤΟΚΙΝΗΤΩΝ
αξεσουάρ αυτοκινήτων (τα)

auto accessories

άξονας (ο) [**a**xonas (ο)] axle

ΑΠΑΓΟΡΕΥΕΤΑΙ
απαγορεύεται it is
prohibited

ΑΠΑΓΟΡΕΥΕΤΑΙ Η
ΕΙΣΟΔΟΣ απαγορεύεται η
είσοδος no entry, no
admission

ΑΠΑΓΟΡΕΥΕΤΑΙ Η
ΚΑΤΑΠΟΣΙΣ
απαγορεύεται η κατάποσις
do not swallow

ΑΠΑΓΟΡΕΥΕΤΑΙ Η
ΚΑΤΑΣΚΗΝΩΣΗ
απαγορεύεται η
κατασκήνωση no camping

ΑΠΑΓΟΡΕΥΕΤΑΙ Η
ΚΟΛΥΜΒΗΣΗ
απαγορεύεται η κολύμβηση
no swimming

ΑΠΑΓΟΡΕΥΕΤΑΙ Η ΛΗΨΙΣ
ΔΙΑ ΤΟΥ ΣΤΟΜΑΤΟΣ
απαγορεύεται η λήψις διά
του στόματος not to be
taken orally

ΑΠΑΓΟΡΕΥΕΤΑΙ Η
ΣΤΑΘΜΕΥΣΗ
απαγορεύεται η στάθμευση
no parking

ΑΠΑΓΟΡΕΥΕΤΑΙ Η ΣΤΑΣΗ
απαγορεύεται η στάση no
waiting, no stopping

ΑΠΑΓΟΡΕΥΕΤΑΙ Η
ΧΟΡΗΓΗΣΗ ΑΝΕΥ
ΣΥΝΤΑΓΗΣ ΙΑΤΡΟΥ
απαγορεύεται η χορήγηση
άνευ συνταγής ιατρού
available on prescription

only

ΑΠΑΓΟΡΕΥΕΤΑΙ Ο
ΓΥΜΝΙΣΜΟΣ
απαγορεύεται ο γυμνισμός
nudism prohibited

ΑΠΑΓΟΡΕΥΟΝΤΑΙ ΟΙ
ΚΑΤΑΔΥΣΕΙΣ
απαγορεύονται οι
καταδύσεις no diving

ΑΠΑΓΟΡΕΥΕΤΑΙ ΤΟ
ΚΑΜΠΙΝΓΚ
απαγορεύεται το κάμπινγκ
no camping

ΑΠΑΓΟΡΕΥΕΤΑΙ ΤΟ
ΚΑΠΝΙΖΕΙΝ
απαγορεύεται το καπνίζειν
no smoking

ΑΠΑΓΟΡΕΥΕΤΑΙ ΤΟ
ΚΑΠΝΙΣΜΑ
απαγορεύεται το κάπνισμα
no smoking

ΑΠΑΓΟΡΕΥΕΤΑΙ ΤΟ
ΚΥΝΗΓΙ απαγορεύεται το
κυνήγι no hunting

ΑΠΑΓΟΡΕΥΕΤΑΙ ΤΟ
ΠΡΟΣΠΕΡΑΣΜΑ
απαγορεύεται το
προσπέρασμα no
overtaking, no passing

ΑΠΑΓΟΡΕΥΕΤΑΙ ΤΟ
ΨΑΡΕΜΑ απαγορεύεται
το ψάρεμα no fishing

ΑΠΑΓΟΡΕΥΜΕΝΗ
ΠΕΡΙΟΧΗ απαγορευμένη
περιοχή restricted area

απαγορευμένος
[apagorevm**e**nos] forbidden

απαίσιος [ap**e**sios] appalling

απαιτώ [apet**o**] demand (verb)

απαλός [apalos] soft

απαντάω [apadao] answer (verb)

απάντηση (η) [apadisi (i)] answer

απένταρος [apedaros] broke

απίθανος [apiTHanos] incredible

ΑΠΛΗ ΒΕΝΖΙΝΗ απλή βενζίνη (η) [apli venzini (i)] two-star petrol/gas

ΑΠΛΗ ΔΙΑΔΡΟΜΗ απλή διαδρομή (η) [apli thiathromi (i)] single/one-way fare

ΑΠΛΟ ΕΙΣΙΤΗΡΙΟ απλό εισιτήριο (το) [aplo isitirio (to)] single/one-way ticket

απλός [aplos] simple

απλώνω [aplono] stretch (verb)

από [apo] from; since; than
από το ... στο ... [apo to ... sto ...] from ... to ...
από κάτω [apo kato] below, under
από πάνω [apo pano] over, above

αποβιβάζομαι [apovivazomeh] land (verb)

απογειώνομαι [apoyionomeh] take off (verb)

απόγευμα (το) [apoyevma (to)] afternoon
το απόγευμα [to apoyevma] in the afternoon

ΑΠΟΓΕΥΜΑΤΙΝΗ ΠΑΡΑΣΤΑΣΗ απογευματινή παράσταση (η) [apoyevmatini parastasi (i)] matinee

απογοητευμένος [apogoitevmenos] disappointed

ΑΠΟΔΕΙΞΗ απόδειξη (η) [apothixi (i)] receipt, evidence

ΑΠΟ ΔΕΥΤΕΡΟ ΧΕΡΙ από δεύτερο χέρι [apo theftero kheri] second-hand

ΑΠΟΛΥΜΑΝΤΙΚΟ απολυμαντικό (το) [apolimadiko (to)] disinfectant

ΑΠΟΣΚΕΥΕΣ αποσκευές (οι) [aposkeves (i)] luggage, baggage

ΑΠΟΣΜΗΤΙΚΟ αποσμητικό (το) [aposmitiko (to)] deodorant

ΑΠΟΣΤΟΛΕΑΣ αποστολέας [apostoleas] sender

απότομος [apotomos] steep

απότομος βράχος (ο) [apotomos vrakhos (o)] cliff

αποφασίζω [apofasizo] decide

απόψε [apopseh] tonight

ΑΠΡΙΛΙΟΣ Απρίλιος (ο) [Aprilios (o)] April

Α΄ ΠΡΟΒΟΛΗΣ α΄ προβολής major cinema/ movie theater

απρόσμενος [aprosmenos] surprising

ΑΠΩΛΕΣΘΕΝΤΑ ΑΝΤΙΚΕΙΜΕΝΑ απωλεσθέντα αντικείμενα [apolesTHeda adikimena] lost property

αράχνη (η) [arakhni (i)] spider

αργά [arga] late, slowly

αργίες (οι) [aryies (i)] public

holidays

αργός [argos] slow

αργότερα [argotera] later

αργώ [argo] arrive late; go
slowly

ΑΡΙΘΜΟΣ αριθμός (ο)
[ariTHmos (o)] number

ΑΡΙΘΜΟΣ ΘΕΣΕΩΣ
αριθμός θέσεως [ariTHmos
THeseos] seat number

αριστερά [aristera] left

αριστερόχειρας
[aristerokhiras] left-handed

αρκετά [arketa] enough; quite

αρκετοί [arketi] several

αρνητικό (το) [arnitiko (to)]
negative

αρουραίος (ο) [arooreos (o)] rat

αρραβωνιασμένος
[aravoniasmenos] engaged (to
be married)

αρραβωνιαστικιά (η)
[aravoniastikia (i)] fiancée

αρραβωνιαστικός (ο)
[aravoniastikos (o)] fiancé

αρρενωπός [arenopos] manly;
macho

αρρώστια (η) [arostia (i)]
disease

άρρωστος [arostos] ill, sick

ΑΡΤΟΠΟΙΕΙΟ αρτοποιείο
(το) [artopi-io (to)] bakery

αρχαιολογία (η) [arkheoloyia
(i)] archaeology

αρχαίος [arkheos] ancient

αρχαιότητες (οι) [arkheotites
(i)] ruins

αρχάρια (η) [arkharia (i)]
beginner

αρχάριος (ο) [arkharios (o)]
beginner

αρχή (η) [arkhi (i)] beginning

αρχίζω [arkhizo] begin

αρχιτέκτων (ο/η) [arkhitekton
(o/i)] architect

άρωμα (το) [aroma (to)]
perfume

ΑΣΑΝΣΕΡ ασανσέρ (το)
[asanser (to)] lift, elevator

ασετόν (το) [aseton (to)] nail
varnish remover

ΑΣΗΜΕΝΙΟΣ ασημένιος
[asimenios] silver

ΑΣΗΜΙΚΑ ασημικά (τα)
[asimika (ta)] silver(ware)

ΑΣΘΕΝΟΦΟΡΟ
ασθενοφόρο (το)
[asTHenoforo (to)] ambulance

ΑΣΘΜΑ άσθμα (το) [asTHma
(to)] asthma

ΑΣΠΙΡΙΝΗ ασπιρίνη (η)
[aspirini (i)] aspirin

άσπρος [aspros] white

άστατος [astatos] changeable

αστείο (το) [astio (to)] joke

αστείος [astios] funny,
amusing

αστέρι (το) [asteri (to)] star

αστράγαλος (ο) [astragalos (o)]
ankle

ΑΣΤΥΝΟΜΙΑ αστυνομία
(η) [astinomia (i)] police

ΑΣΤΥΝΟΜΙΚΟ ΤΜΗΜΑ
αστυνομικό τμήμα (το)
[astinomiko tmima (to)] police
station

αστυφύλακας (ο) [astifilakas
(o)] policeman

αστυνομικός (η) [astinomikos (i)] policewoman

ΑΣΦΑΛΕΙΑ ασφάλεια (η) [asfalia (i)] fuse; insurance

ΑΣΦΑΛΕΙΑΙ ασφάλειαι [asfali-eh] insurance

ασφαλής [asfalis] safe

άσχημα [askhima] badly

άσχημος [askhimos] ugly

ατζέντα (η) [atzenda (i)] address book

ατμόπλοιο (το) [atmoplio (to)] steamer

άτομο (το) [atomo (to)] person

ΑΥΓΟΥΣΤΟΣ Αύγουστος (ο) [Avgoostos (o)] August

αυθεντικός [afтнedikos] genuine

αύριο [avrio] tomorrow

Αυστραλέζα (η) [Afstraleza (i)] Australian (woman)

Αυστραλέζικος [Afstralezikos] Australian (adj)

ΑΥΣΤΡΑΛΙΑ Αυστραλία (η) [Afstralia (i)] Australia

Αυστραλός (ο) [Afstralos (o)] Australian (man)

αυτά, αυτές [afta, aftes] these; they; them

αυτή [afti] she; this (one)

αυτής [aftis] of her

αυτί (το) [afti (to)] ear

αυτό [afto] it; this
  αυτό εδώ [afto etho] this one

αυτοί [afti] these; they

ΑΥΤΟΚΙΝΗΤΟ αυτοκίνητο (το) [aftokinito (to)] car

αυτόματος [aftomatos] automatic (adj)

αυτό που [afto poo] what

αυτός [aftos] he; this (one)

αυτός ο ίδιος [aftos o ithios] himself

αυτού [aftoo] of him, of it

αυτούς [aftoos] them

ΑΥΤ/ΤΟ αυτ/το car

αυτών [afton] of them

αφεντικό (το) [afediko (to)] boss

ΑΦΕΤΗΡΙΑ αφετηρία (η) [afetiria (i)] terminus

αφήνω [afino] leave (verb)

ΑΦΙΞΕΙΣ αφίξεις arrivals

ΑΦΙΞΗ άφιξη (η) [afixi (i)] arrival

αφίσα (η) [afisa (i)] poster

ΑΦΟΙ. αφοί. bros.

ΑΦΟΡΟΛΟΓΗΤΑ αφορολόγητα (τα) [aforoloyita (ta)] duty-free

αφροδίσιο νόσημα (το) [afrothisio nosima (to)] VD

ΑΦΡΟΣ ΞΥΡΙΣΜΑΤΟΣ αφρός ξυρίσματος (ο) [afros xirismatos (o)] shaving foam

αφρός (ο) [afros (o)] surf

αχθοφόρος (ο) [akhтнoforos (o)] doorman

αχινός (ο) [akhinos (o)] sea urchin

Β

ΒΑΓΟΝΙ βαγόνι (το) [vagoni (to)] coach, car (train)

ΒΑΓΚΟΝ-ΛΙ βαγκόν-λι [vagon-li] sleeper, sleeping car

βάζο (το) [v**a**zo (to)] vase
βάζω [v**a**zo] put
ΒΑΘΙΑ ΝΕΡΑ βαθιά νερά
deep water
βάθος: στο βάθος [sto v**a**THos]
in the background; at the
bottom
βαθύς [vaTH**i**s] deep
βαλβίδα (η) [valv**i**tha (i)] valve
βαλίτσα (η) [val**i**tsa (i)] bag,
suitcase
ΒΑΜΒΑΚΕΡΟ βαμβακερό
(το) [vamvak**e**ro (to)] cotton
βαρετός [var**e**tos] boring
ΒΑΡΚΑ βάρκα (η) [v**a**rka (i)]
small boat; dinghy
βάρκα με κουπιά [v**a**rka meh
koop**i**a] rowing boat
βάρκα με μηχανή [v**a**rka meh
mikhan**i**] motorboat
ΒΑΡΟΣ βάρος (το) [v**a**ros (to)]
weight
βαρύς [var**i**s] heavy; rich (food)
βασιλιάς (ο) [vasil**i**as (o)] king
βασίλισσα (η) [vas**i**lisa (i)]
queen
ΒΑΦΗ βαφή (η) [vaf**i** (i)] hair
dye
βάφω [v**a**fo] paint; tint (verb)
βγάζω φωτογραφία [vg**a**zo
fotograf**i**a] photograph (verb)
βγαίνω [vg**e**no] go out
ΒΓΑΛΤΕ ΤΗΝ ΚΑΡΤΑ
βγάλτε την κάρτα remove
the card
βέβαια [v**e**veh-a] of course
βελόνα (η) [vel**o**na (i)] needle
βελτιώνω [velt**i**ono] improve
ΒΕΝΖΙΝΑΔΙΚΟ

βενζινάδικο (το)
[venzin**a**thiko (to)] petrol
station, gas station
ΒΕΝΖΙΝΗ βενζίνη (η)
[venz**i**ni (i)] petrol, gas(oline)
βεντιλατέρ (το) [vendilat**e**r
(to)] fan belt
ΒΕΡΝΙΚΙ ΠΑΠΟΥΤΣΙΩΝ
βερνίκι παπουτσιών (το)
[vern**i**ki papootsi**o**n (to)] shoe
polish
ΒΗΧΑΣ βήχας (ο) [v**i**khas (o)]
cough
βήχω [v**i**kho] cough (verb)
βιάζομαι [vi**a**zomeh] hurry
(verb)
βιάσου! [vi**a**soo!] hurry up!
βιασμός (ο) [viasm**o**s (o)] rape
βιβλίο (το) [vivl**i**o (to)] book
βιβλίο διαλόγων [vivl**i**o
thial**o**gon] phrase book
ΒΙΒΛΙΟΘΗΚΗ βιβλιοθήκη
(η) [vivlioTH**i**ki (i)] library
ΒΙΒΛΙΟΠΩΛΕΙΟ
βιβλιοπωλείο (το) [vivliopol**i**o
(to)] bookshop, bookstore
ΒΙΔΑ βίδα (η) [v**i**tha (i)]
screw
ΒΙΖΑ βίζα (η) [v**i**za (i)] visa
βίλλα (η) [v**i**la (i)] villa
βίντεο (το) [v**i**deo (to)] video
ΒΙΤΑΜΙΝΕΣ βιταμίνες (οι)
[vitam**i**nes (i)] vitamins
Β΄ ΚΑΤΗΓΟΡΙΑΣ
Β΄ κατηγορίας second class
βλάβη (η) [vl**a**vi (i)]
breakdown (car)
βλάκας (ο) [vl**a**kas (o)] idiot;
stupid

βλέπω [vlepo] see
βοήθεια (η) [voiThia (i)] help
βοηθώ [vo-iTHo] help (verb)
βόμβα (η) [vomva (i)] bomb
Βόρειος Ιρλανδία (η) [vorios
  Irlanthia (i)] Northern Ireland
ΒΟΥΛΓΑΡΙΑ Βουλγαρία (η)
  [voolgaria (i)] Bulgaria
Βουλγαρικός [voolgarikos]
  Bulgarian (adj)
βουλιάζω [vooliazo] sink (verb)
ΒΟΥΛΚΑΝΙΖΑΤΕΡ
  βουλκανιζατέρ
  [voolkanizater] tyre repairs
βουνό (το) [voono (to)]
  mountain
βούρτσα (η) [voortsa (i)] brush
βουτάω [vootao] dive (verb)
Β´ ΠΡΟΒΟΛΗΣ β´ προβολής
  local cinema/movie theater
βράδυ (το) [vrathi (to)] evening
  το βράδυ [to vrathi] in the
  evening
βραδυά (η) [vrathia (i)]
  evening
ΒΡΑΔΥΝΗ ΠΑΡΛΣΤΑΣΗ
  βραδυνή παράσταση
  evening performance
βράζω [vrazo] boil (verb)
βράχια (τα) [vrakhia (ta)]
  rocks; cliffs
βραχιόλι (το) [vrakhioli (to)]
  bracelet
βράχος (ο) [vrakhos (o)] rock
ΒΡΕΤΑΝΝΙΑ Βρεταννία (η)
  [vretania (i)] Britain
Βρεταννίδα (η) [vretanitha (i)]
  Briton (woman)
Βρεταννικός [vretanikos]
  British
Βρεταννός (ο) [vretanos (o)]
  Briton (man)
βρέχει [vrekhi] it's raining
βρίσκω [vrisko] find (verb)
βροντή (η) [vrodi (i)] thunder
βροχή (η) [vrokhi (i)] rain
βρύση (η) [vrisi (i)] tap, faucet
βρώμικος [vromikos] dirty
βυζαίνω [vizeno] breastfeed
βυθός (ο) [viTHos (o)] bottom
  (of sea)

Γ

γάιδαρος (ο) [gaitharos (o)]
  donkey
ΓΑΛΑΚΤΟΠΩΛΕΙΟ
  γαλακτοπωλείο (το)
  [galaktopolio (to)] shop/take-
  away café selling dairy
  products
ΓΑΛΑΚΤΩΜΑ
  ΚΑΘΑΡΙΣΜΟΥ
  γαλάκτωμα καθαρισμού (το)
  [galaktoma kaTHarismoo (to)]
  cleansing lotion
ΓΑΛΛΙΑ Γαλλία (η) [Galia
  (i)] France
Γαλλικός [Galikos] French
  (adj)
γάμος (ο) [gamos (o)] wedding
γαμπρός (ο) [gambros (o)]
  bridegroom; son-in-law;
  brother-in-law
γάντια (τα) [gadia (ta)] gloves
γάτα (η) [gata (i)] cat
γειά σου! [yia soo!] hello!;
  bless you!; cheers!

A
B
Γ
Δ
E
Z
H
Θ
I
K
Λ
M
N
Ξ
O
Π
P
Σ
T
Y
Φ
X
Ψ
Ω

γείτονας (ο) [yitonas (ο)] neighbour

γελοίο [yelio] ridiculous

γελώ [yelo] laugh (verb)

γεμάτος [yematos] full

γεμίζω [yemizo] fill (verb)

γενέθλια (τα) [yeneTHlia (ta)] birthday

γένια (τα) [yenia (ta)] beard

γενναίος [yeneos] brave

ΓΕΡΜΑΝΙΑ Γερμανία (η) [Yermania (i)] Germany

Γερμανικός [Yermanikos] German (adj)

γέρος [yeros] old (person)

ΓΕΥΜΑ γεύμα (το) [yevma (to)] meal

γεύση (η) [yefsi (i)] flavour; taste

ΓΕΦΥΡΑ γέφυρα (η) [yefira (i)] bridge

ΓΗΠΕΔΟ γήπεδο (το) [yipetho (to)] football pitch

ΓΗΠΕΔΟ ΤΕΝΝΙΣ γήπεδο τέννις [yipetho tenis] tennis court

για [ya] for

για μένα [ya mena] for me

γιαγιά (η) [yaya (i)] grandmother

ΓΙΑ ΕΞΩΤΕΡΙΚΗ ΧΡΗΣΗ ΜΟΝΟΝ για εξωτερική χρήση μόνον for external use only

ΓΙΑ ΕΣΩΤΕΡΙΚΗ ΧΡΗΣΗ ΜΟΝΟΝ για εσωτερική χρήση μόνον for internal use only

γιακάς (ο) [yakas (ο)] collar

γιατί; [yati?] why?

ΓΙΑ ΤΟ ΣΠΙΤΙ για το σπίτι [ya to spiti] to take away, to go (food)

ΓΙΑΤΡΟΣ γιατρός (ο/η) [yatros (ο/i)] doctor

γίνομαι [yinomeh] become; happen

τι γίνεται; [ti yineteh?] what's happening?

ΓΙΟΡΤΗ ΚΡΑΣΙΟΥ γιορτή κρασιού (η) [yorti krasioo (i)] wine festival

γιός (ο) [yos (ο)] son

γιώτ (το) [yot (to)] yacht

γκάζι (το) [gazi (to)] gas; accelerator

ΓΚΑΛΕΡΙ γκαλερί (η) [galeri (i)] art gallery

ΓΚΑΡΑΖ γκαράζ (το) [garaz (to)] garage (for parking/repairs)

ΓΚΑΡΝΤΑΡΟΜΠΑ γκαρνταρόμπα (η) [gardaroba (i)] cloakroom (for coats)

Γ΄ ΚΑΤΗΓΟΡΙΑΣ Γ΄ κατηγορίας third class

γκολφ (το) [golf (to)] golf

γκρίζος [grizos] grey

γκρουπ (το) [groop (to)] group

γλάρος (ο) [glaros (ο)] seagull

ΓΛΙΦΙΤΖΟΥΡΙ γλιφιτζούρι (το) [glifidzoori (to)] lollipop

ΓΛΥΚΟ γλυκό (το) [gliko (to)] sweet, candy

γλυκός [glikos] sweet (adj)

γλυστερός [glisteros] slippery

γλυστράω [glistrao] skid (verb)

γλώσσα (η) [glosa (i)] language; tongue

γνωρίζω [gnorizo] know
δεν γνωρίζω [then gnorizo] I
don't know

γόνατο (το) [gonato (to)] knee

γονείς (οι) [gonis (i)] parents

γουίντσερφ (το) [gooindserf
(to)] sailboard

ΓΟΥΝΑΡΙΚΑ γουναρικά
(τα) [goonarika (ta)] furrier

ΓΟΥΝΕΣ γούνες [goones]
furs

γουόκμαν (το) [goo-okman (to)]
personal stereo

γουρούνι (το) [goorooni (to)]
pig

γοφός (ο) [gofos (o)] hip

γραβάτα (η) [gravata (i)] tie,
necktie

γράμμα (το) [grama (to)] letter

γράμματα (τα) [gramata (ta)]
post, mail

γραμματική (η) [gramatiki (i)]
grammar

ΓΡΑΜΜΑΤΟΚΙΒΩΤΙΟ
γραμματοκιβώτιο (το)
[gramatokivotio (to)]
letterbox, mailbox

γραμματόσημο (το)
[gramatosimo (to)] stamp

ΓΡΑΜΜΕΣ ΤΡΑΙΝΟΥ
γραμμές τραίνου railway
crosses road

ΓΡΑΜΜΗ γραμμή (η) [grami
(i)] route, line

γρασίδι (το) [grasithi (to)] lawn

γραφείο (το) [grafio (to)] office

ΓΡΑΦΕΙΟ ΤΑΞΙΔΙΩΝ
γραφείο ταξιδίων [grafio
taxithion] travel agency

γραφομηχανή (η) [grafomikhani
(i)] typewriter

γράφω [grafo] write

γρήγορα [grigora] quick;
quickly

γρήγορος [grigoros] fast

ΓΡΙΠΠΗ γρίππη (η) [gripi (i)]
flu

γρύλλος (ο) [grilos (o)] jack

γυαλί (το) [yali (to)] glass
(material)

ΓΥΑΛΙΑ γυαλιά (τα) [yalia
(ta)] glasses, eyeglasses

ΓΥΑΛΙΑ ΗΛΙΟΥ γυαλιά
ηλίου [yalia ilioo] sunglasses

ΓΥΜΝΑΣΙΟ γυμνάσιο (το)
[yimnasio (to)] secondary
school

γυμνασμένος [yimnasmenos] fit
(healthy)

ΓΥΜΝΑΣΤΗΡΙΟ
γυμναστήριο (το) [yimnastirio
(to)] gym

γυμνός [yimnos] naked

γυναίκα (η) [yineka (i)]
woman; wife

ΓΥΝΑΙΚΕΙΑ γυναικεία (τα)
[yinekia (ta)] ladies' wear

ΓΥΝΑΙΚΕΙΑΙ
ΚΟΜΜΩΣΕΙΣ γυναικείαι
κομμώσεις (οι) [yinekieh
komosis (i)] ladies' salon

ΓΥΝΑΙΚΕΙΑ ΦΟΡΕΜΑΤΑ
γυναικεία φορέματα [yinekia
foremata] ladies' dresses

ΓΥΝΑΙΚΕΙΕΣ ΚΑΛΤΣΕΣ -
ΚΑΛΣΟΝ γυναικείες
κάλτσες - καλσόν [yinekies
kaltses - kalson] ladies' socks

Α
Β
Γ
Δ
Ε
Ζ
Η
Θ
Ι
Κ
Λ
Μ
Ν
Ξ
Ο
Π
Ρ
Σ
Τ
Υ
Φ
Χ
Ψ
Ω

- stockings

ΓΥΝΑΙΚΩΝ γυναικών
ladies' (toilet), ladies' room

γυρνώ [yirno] turn (verb)

γυρνώ πίσω [yirno piso]
arrive back, return; take
back

γυρνώ σπίτι [yirno spiti]
return home

Δ

δακτυλίδι (το) [thaktilithi (to)]
ring (on finger)

δανείζομαι [thanizomeh]
borrow

δανείζω [thanizo] lend

δασκάλα (η) [thaskala (i)]
instructor; teacher

δάσκαλος (ο) [thaskalos (o)]
instructor; teacher

δάσος (το) [thasos (to)] forest

δάχτυλο (το) [thakhtilo (to)]
finger

δάχτυλο του ποδιού [thakhtilo
too pothioo] toe

δε [theh] not

Δ.Ε.Η. public electricity
company

δείκτης (ο) [thiktis (o)] gauge;
index finger

ΔΕΙΠΝΟ δείπνο (το) [thipno
(to)] evening meal

δείχνω [thikhno] show (verb)

δέκα [theka] ten

δεκαεννιά [theka-enia]
nineteen

δεκαέξι [theka-exi] sixteen

δεκαεπτά [theka-epta]

seventeen

δεκαοχτώ [theka-okhto]
eighteen

δεκαπενθήμερο
[thekapenTHimero] fortnight

δεκαπέντε [thekapedeh] fifteen

ΔΕΚΑΡΙΚΟ δεκάρικο (το)
[thekariko (to)] 10-drachma
coin

δεκατέσσερα [thekatesera]
fourteen

δέκατος [thekatos] tenth

δεκατρία [thekatria] thirteen

ΔΕΚΕΜΒΡΙΟΣ Δεκέμβριος
(ο) [thekemvrios (o)]
December

δέμα (το) [thema (to)] parcel

ΔΕΜΑΤΑ δέματα parcels,
packages

δεν [then] not

δένδρο (το) [thenthro (to)] tree

ΔΕΝ ΛΕΙΤΟΥΡΓΕΙ δεν
λειτουργεί [then litooryi] out
of order

ΔΕΝ ΣΙΔΕΡΩΝΕΤΑΙ δεν
σιδερώνεται do not iron

δεξιός, δεξιά [thexios, thexia]
right (side)

δεξίωση (η) [thexiosi (i)]
reception (party)

ΔΕΡΜΑ δέρμα (το) [therma
(to)] skin; leather

ΔΕΡΜΑΤΑ δέρματα (τα)
[thermata (ta)] leather goods

ΔΕΣΠΟΙΝΙΔΑ δεσποινίδα
(η) [thespinitha (i)] young
woman; Miss; Ms

ΔΕΣΠΟΙΝΙΣ δεσποινίς
[thespinis] Miss; Ms

ΔΕΥΤΕΡΑ Δευτέρα (η)
[theftera (i)] Monday

ΔΕΥΤΕΡΗ ΘΕΣΗ δεύτερη
θέση second class

δευτερόλεπτο (το)
[thefterolepto (to)] second

δεύτερος [thefteros] second
(adj)

ΔΕΥΤΕΡΟ ΧΕΡΙ δεύτερο
χέρι [theftero kheri] second-
hand

δέχομαι [thekhomeh] accept;
receive

δηλητηρίαση (η) [thilitiriasi
(i)] poisoning

δηλητήριο (το) [thilitirio (to)]
poison

ΔΗΜΑΡΧΕΙΟ δημαρχείο
(το) [thimarkhio (to)] town
hall

ΔΗΜΟΣΙΑ ΛΟΥΤΡΑ
δημόσια λουτρά (τα)
[thimosia lootra (ta)] public
baths

δημόσιος [thimosios] public

δημοσιογράφος (ο/η)
[thimosiografos (o/i)] reporter

δημοτική μουσική (η)
[thimotiki moosiki (i)] folk
music

διαβάζω [thiavazo] read

ΔΙΑΒΑΣΗ ΠΕΖΩΝ διάβαση
πεζών (η) pedestrian
crossing

ΔΙΑΒΑΤΗΡΙΟ διαβατήριο
(το) [thiavatirio (to)] passport

διαβητικός (ο) [thiavitikos (o)]
diabetic

διαβητική (η) [thiavitiki (i)]
diabetic

ΔΙΑΔΡΟΜΗ ΜΕΤ'
ΕΠΙΣΤΡΟΦΗΣ διαδρομή
μετ' επιστροφής (η)
[thiathromi met' epistrofis (i)]
return/round trip fare

διάδρομος (ο) [thiathromos (o)]
corridor

διάθεση (η) [thiaTHesi (i)]
mood

δίαιτα (η) [thieta (i)] diet

διακοπές (οι) [thiakopes (i)]
holiday, vacation

διακοπή (η) [thiakopi (i)]
interruption; power cut

διακόπτης (ο) [thiakoptis (o)]
switch

διακόπτω [thiakopto] interrupt

διακόσια [thiakosia] two
hundred

διαλέγω [thialego] choose

ΔΙΑΛΕΙΜΜΑ διάλειμμα
(το) [thialima (to)] interval,
intermission

διάλεκτος (η) [thialektos (i)]
dialect

ΔΙΑΛΥΜΑ διάλυμα (το)
[thialima (to)] solution

διαμάντι (το) [thiamandi (to)]
diamond

Διαμαρτυρόμενος (ο)
[thiamartiromenos (o)]
Protestant

ΔΙΑΜΕΡΙΣΜΑ διαμέρισμα
(το) [thiamerisma (to)]
apartment; flat

διά μέσου [thia mesoo]
through

διαμονή (η) [thiamoni (i)]

accommodation; stay

ΔΙΑΝΥΚΤΕΡΕΥΟΝ
διανυκτερεύον open all
night

διάρκεια (η) [thi**a**rkia (i)]
duration

ΔΙΑΡΚΕΙΑ ΠΤΗΣΕΩΣ
διάρκεια πτήσεως [thi**a**rkia
pt**i**seos] flight time

διαρροή (η) [thiaro**i** (i)] leak

ΔΙΑΡΡΟΙΑ διάρροια (η)
[thi**a**ria (i)] diarrhoea

διάσημος [thi**a**simos] famous

ΔΙΑΣΤΑΥΡΩΣΗ
διασταύρωση (η) [thiast**a**vrosi
(i)] junction, crossroads,
intersection

διασχίζω [thiaskh**i**zo] go
through

ΔΙΑΤΗΡΕΙΤΑΙ ΣΕ ΨΥΓΕΙΟ
διατηρείται σε ψυγείο keep
refrigerated

διαφημιστικό (το)
[thiafimistik**o** (to)] leaflet;
advertisements (on TV);
trailer (cinema)

διαφορετικά [thiaforetik**a**]
otherwise

διαφορετικός [thiaforetik**o**s]
different

διάφραγμα (το) [thi**a**fragma
(to)] shutter (in camera)

διαχειριστής (ο) [thiakhirist**i**s
(o)] manager

διαχειρίστρια (η) [thiakhir**i**stria
(i)] manageress

διδάσκω [thith**a**sko] teach

δίδυμοι (οι) [th**i**thimi (i)] twins

ΔΙΕΥΘΥΝΣΗ διεύθυνση (η)

[thi**e**fΤΗinsi (i)] address

δικό τους [thik**o** toos] theirs

δίκαιος [thik**e**os] fair, just

δικά μας [thik**a** mas] ours

δικά μου [thik**a** moo] mine

δικά σας, δικά σου [thik**a** sas,
thik**a** soo] yours

ΔΙΚΑΣΤΗΡΙΟ δικαστήριο
(το) [thikast**i**rio (to)] law court

δικά της [thik**a** tis] hers

δικά του [thik**a** too] his, its

δικά τους [thik**a** toos] theirs

δικηγόρος (ο/η) [thikig**o**ros (o/
i)] lawyer

δική μας [thik**i** mas] ours

δική μου [thik**i** moo] mine

δική σας, δική σου [thik**i** sas,
thik**i** soo] yours

δική του [thik**i** too] his

δική τους [thik**i** toos] theirs

ΔΙΚΛΙΝΟ ΔΩΜΑΤΙΟ
δίκλινο δωμάτιο (το)
[th**i**klino thom**a**tio (to)] double
room

δικό μας [thik**o** mas] ours

δικό μου [thik**o** moo] mine

δικό σας, δικό σου [thik**o** sas,
thik**o** soo] yours

δικός μας [thik**o**s mas] ours

δικός μου [thik**o**s moo] mine

δικός σας, δικός σου [thik**o**s
sas, thik**o**s soo] yours

δικός του [thik**o**s too] his

δικός τους [thik**o**s toos] theirs

δικό της [thik**o** tis] hers

δικό του [thik**o** too] his; its

δίνω [th**i**no] give

ΔΙΟΔΙΑ διόδια (τα) [thi**o**thia
(ta)] toll

διορθώνω [thiorTHono] mend,
correct
ΔΙΠΛΗ ΤΑΡΙΦΑ διπλή
ταρίφα (η) double tariff
διπλό [thiplo] double
ΔΙΠΛΟ ΔΩΜΑΤΙΟ διπλό
δωμάτιο (το) [thiplo thomatio
(to)] double room
διπλό κρεβάτι (το) [thiplo
krevati (to)] double bed
ΔΙΣ. δις. Miss
ΔΙΣΚΑΔΙΚΟ δισκάδικο (το)
[thiskathiko (to)] record shop
ΔΙΣΚΟΙ - ΚΑΣΕΤΕΣ δίσκοι
- κασέτες [thiski - kasetes]
records - cassettes
δίσκος (ο) [thiskos (o)] record;
tray
Δ΄ ΚΑΤΗΓΟΡΙΑΣ
Δ΄ κατηγορίας fourth class
δοκιμάζω [thokimazo] taste
(verb); try (on)
ΔΟΛΛΑΡΙΟ δολλάριο (το)
[tholario (to)] dollar
δόντι (το) [thodi (to)] tooth
ΔΟΣΟΛΟΓΙΑ ΕΝΗΛΙΚΩΝ
δοσολογία ενηλίκων adult
dosage
ΔΟΣΟΛΟΓΙΑ ΠΑΙΔΩΝ
δοσολογία παίδων
children's dosage
δουλειά (η) [thoolia (i)] job;
work
δουλειές (οι) [thoolies (i)]
business
δουλεύω [thoolevo] work (verb)
δεν δουλεύει [then thoolevi]
it's not working
ΔΡΑΧΜΗ δραχμή (η)

[thrakhmi (i)] drachma
ΔΡΟΜΟΛΟΓΙΑ δρομολόγια
(τα) [thromoloyia (ta)]
timetable, (US) schedule
δρόμος (ο) [thromos (o)] road;
street
δροσερός [throseros] cool
ΔΡΧ. δρχ. drachma
δυνατός [thinatos] loud;
possible; strong
δύο [thio] two
ΔΥΟ ΠΑΡΑΣΤΑΣΕΙΣ δύο
παραστάσεις two shows
δυσάρεστος [thisarestos]
unpleasant
δύση του ήλιου (η) [thisi too
ilioo (i)] sunset
ΔΥΣΚΟΙΛΙΑ δυσκοίλια (η)
[thiskilia (i)] constipation
δύσκολος [thiskolos] difficult
ΔΥΣΠΕΨΙΑ δυσπεψία (η)
[thispepsia (i)] indigestion
δυστύχημα (το) [thistikhima
(to)] accident
δυστυχώς [thistikhos]
unfortunately
δώδεκα [thotheka] twelve
ΔΩΔΕΚΑΔΑ δωδεκάδα (η)
[thothekatha (i)] dozen
ΔΩΜΑΤΙΟ δωμάτιο (το)
[thomatio (to)] room
ΔΩΡΑ δώρα gifts
ΔΩΡΕΑΝ δωρεάν [thorean]
free (of charge)
δώρο (το) [thoro (to)] present
ΔΩΡΟ ΠΑΣΧΑ Δώρο Πάσχα
[thoro Paskha] Easter
supplement paid to taxi
drivers

A
B
Γ
Δ
E
Z
H
Θ
I
K
Λ
M
N
Ξ
O
Π
P
Σ
T
Y
Φ
X
Ψ
Ω

ΔΩΡΟ ΧΡΙΣΤΟΥΓΕΝΝΩΝ
Δώρο Χριστουγέννων [thoro ΚΗristooyenon] Christmas supplement paid to taxi drivers

Ε

Ε.Α.Σ. Athens Public Transport Corporation

εβδομάδα (η) [evthomata (i)] week

εβδομήντα [evthomida] seventy

έβδομος [evthomos] seventh

Εβραίος [Evreos] Jewish

έγγραφο (το) [engrafo (to)] document

εγγύηση (η) [egi-isi (i)] guarantee

έγινε! [eyineh!] OK, coming up!

εγκαίρως [engeros] on time

έγκαυμα από τον ήλιο (το) [engavma apo ton ilio (to)] sunburn

έγκυος [engios] pregnant

έγκυρος [engiros] valid

έγχρωμο φιλμ (το) [enkhromo film (to)] colour film

εγώ [ego] I

εγώ ο ίδιος [ego o ithios] myself

εδώ [etho] here

έθιμο (το) [eTHimo (to)] custom

ΕΘΝΙΚΗ ΟΔΟΣ εθνική οδός (η) [eΤΗniki othos (i)] motorway, highway, freeway

ΕΘΝΙΚΗ ΠΙΝΑΚΟΘΗΚΗ
Εθνική Πινακοθήκη [ΕΤΗniki PinakoΤΗiki] National Art Gallery

ΕΘΝΙΚΟΤΗΤΑ εθνικότητα (η) [eΤΗnikotita (i)] nationality

ΕΙΔΗ είδη (τα) [ithi (ta)] goods

ΕΙΔΗ ΑΥΤΟΚΙΝΗΤΟΥ είδη αυτοκινήτου auto accessories

ΕΙΔΗ ΔΩΡΩΝ είδη δώρων gifts

ΕΙΔΗ ΜΠΕΜΠΕ είδη μπεμπέ [ithi bebeh] babywear

ΕΙΔΗ ΡΟΥΧΙΣΜΟΥ είδη ρουχισμού [ithi roukhismoo] clothes

ΕΙΔΗ ΣΠΟΡ είδη σπορ [ithi spor] sports equipment, sportswear

ΕΙΔΗ ΧΑΡΤΟΠΩΛΕΙΟΥ είδη χαρτοπωλείου [ithi khartopolioo] stationery

ΕΙΔΙΚΗ ΠΡΟΣΦΟΡΑ ειδική προσφορά special price, special offer

ειδικώς [ithikos] especially

είχες [ikhes] you had

ΕΙΚΟΣΑΡΙΚΟ εικοσάρικο [ikosariko] 20-drachma coin

είκοσι [ikosi] twenty

ειλικρινής [ilikrinis] sincere

είμαι [imeh] I am

είμαστε [imasteh] we are

είναι [ineh] he/she/it is; they are

είστε [isteh] you are
ΕΙΣΑΓΩΓΗΣ εισαγωγής
imported
είσαι [iseh] you are
ΕΙΣΙΤΗΡΙΟ εισιτήριο (το)
[isitirio (to)] ticket
ΕΙΣΙΤΗΡΙΟ ΜΕ
ΕΠΙΣΤΡΟΦΗ εισιτήριο με
επιστροφή [isitirio meh
epistrofi] return/round trip
ticket
ΕΙΣΟΔΟΣ είσοδος (η)
[isothos (i)] entrance, way in
ΕΙΣΟΔΟΣ ΕΛΕΥΘΕΡΑ
είσοδος ελευθέρα
admission free
ΕΙΣΟΔΟΣ ΠΡΑΤΗΡΙΟΥ
είσοδος πρατηρίου
entrance to petrol/gas
station
ΕΙΣΠΡΑΚΤΩΡ εισπράκτωρ
(o) ticket collector
είχα [ikha] I had
είχαμε [ikhameh] we had
είχαν [ikhan] they had
είχατε [ikhateh] you had
είχε [ikheh] he/she/it had
είχες [ikhes] you had
Ε΄ ΚΑΤΗΓΟΡΙΑΣ
Ε΄ κατηγορίας fifth class
εκατό [ekato] hundred
εκατομμύριο: ένα
εκατομμύριο [ena ekatomirio]
one million
ΕΚΔΟΣΗ ΕΙΣΙΤΗΡΙΩΝ
έκδοση εισιτηρίων [ekthosi
isitirion] ticket office
εκεί [eki] there, over there
εκεί κάτω [eki kato] down

there
εκείνα, εκείνες [ekina, ekines]
those
εκείνη, εκείνο [ekini, ekino]
that
εκείνοι [ekini] those
εκείνος [ekinos] that
ΕΚΘΕΣΗ έκθεση (η) [ekτΗesi
(i)] exhibition, showroom
ΕΚΚΛΗΣΙΑ εκκλησία (η)
[eklisia (i)] church
Ε.Κ.Ο. Greek state petrol
company
εκπληκτικός [ekpliktikos]
surprising
έκπληξη (η) [ekplixi (i)]
surprise
ΕΚΠΤΩΣΕΙΣ εκπτώσεις (οι)
sales
ΕΚΤΑΚΤΗ ΑΝΑΓΚΗ
έκτακτη ανάγκη (η) [ektakti
anangi (i)] emergency
εκτός [ektos] except
έκτος [ektos] sixth
έλα! [ela!] you don't say!;
come on!, hurry up!
ΕΛ.ΑΣ. Greek police
ΕΛΑΣΤΙΚΑ ελαστικά tyres
ελαστικός [elastikos] elastic
ελατήριο (το) [elatirio (to)]
spring (in seat etc)
ελαττωματικός [elatomatikos]
faulty
ΕΛΑΤΤΩΣΑΤΕ
ΤΑΧΥΤΗΤΑ ελαττώσατε
ταχύτητα reduce speed
ελαφρός [elafros] light (not
heavy)
ελάχιστος [elakhistos]

smallest; few

ελεγκτής (ο) [elenktis (o)] inspector (bus)

ΕΛΕΓΧΟΣ έλεγχος (ο) [elenkhos (o)] check, inspection

ΕΛΕΓΧΟΣ ΑΠΟΣΚΕΥΩΝ έλεγχος αποσκευών baggage control

ΕΛΕΓΧΟΣ ΔΙΑΒΑΤΗΡΙΩΝ έλεγχος διαβατηρίων passport control

ΕΛΕΓΧΟΣ ΕΙΣΙΤΗΡΙΩΝ έλεγχος εισιτηρίων ticket inspection

ΕΛΕΓΧΟΣ ΕΠΙΒΑΤΩΝ έλεγχος επιβατών passenger control

ΕΛΕΥΘΕΡΑ ΕΙΣΟΔΟΣ ελευθέρα είσοδος [elefTHera isothos] admission free

ΕΛΕΥΘΕΡΟΝ ελεύθερον [elefTHeron] free; for hire (taxi)

ελεύθερος [elefTHeros] free; single (unmarried)

ελιά (η) [elia (i)] olive; spot (blemish)

ελικόπτερο (το) [elikoptero (to)] helicopter

ελκυστικός [elkistikos] attractive

ΕΛΛΑΔΑ Ελλάδα (η) [Elatha (i)] Greece

Έλληνας (ο) [Elinas (o)] Greek (man)

Ελληνίδα (η) [Elinitha (i)] Greek (woman)

ΕΛΛΗΝΙΚΑ Ελληνικά (τα)

[Elinika (ta)] Greek (language)

ΕΛΛΗΝΙΚΗ ΑΣΤΥΝΟΜΙΑ Ελληνική Αστυνομία (η) Greek police

ΕΛΛΗΝΙΚΗ ΡΑΔΙΟΦΩΝΙΑ Ελληνική Ραδιοφωνία Greek radio

ΕΛΛΗΝΙΚΗ ΤΗΛΕΟΡΑΣΗ Ελληνική Τηλεόραση Greek television

ΕΛΛΗΝΙΚΗΣ ΚΑΤΑΣΚΕΥΗΣ Ελληνικής κατασκευής made in Greece

ΕΛΛΗΝΙΚΟ ΠΡΟΙΟΝ Ελληνικό προιόν produce of Greece

ΕΛΛΗΝΙΚΟΣ Ελληνικός [Elinikos] Greek (adj)

Ε.Λ.Π.Α. [E.L.P.A.] Greek motoring organization

ελπίζω [elpizo] hope (verb)

ΕΛ.ΤΑ. Greek Post Office

εμάς [emas] us

εμβολιασμός (ο) [emvoliasmos (o)] vaccination

εμβόλιο (το) [emvolio (to)] vaccine

εμείς [emis] we

εμένα [emena] me

ΕΜΠΟΡΙΚΟ ΚΕΝΤΡΟ εμπορικό κέντρο (το) [emboriko kentro (to)] shopping centre

εμπρός [ebros] come in; hello (response on phone)

ένα(ν) [ena(n)] a; one

εναντίον [enadion] against

ένας [enas] a; one

ένατος [enatos] ninth

ενδιαφέρον [enthiaferon] interesting

ενενήντα [enenida] ninety

ένεση (η) [enesi (i)] injection

ενήλικη (η) [eniliki (i)] adult

ΕΝΗΛΙΚΟΣ ενήλικος (ο) [enilikos (o)] adult

ΕΝΘΥΜΙΟ ενθύμιο (το) [enTHimio (to)] souvenir

εννιά [enia] nine

εννοώ [enoo] mean (verb)

ΕΝΟΙΚΙΑΖΟΝΤΑΙ ενοικιάζονται [enikiazodeh] for hire, to rent

ΕΝΟΙΚΙΑΖΟΝΤΑΙ ΑΥΤΟΚΙΝΗΤΑ ενοικιάζονται αυτοκίνητα car rental

ΕΝΟΙΚΙΑΖΟΝΤΑΙ ΒΑΡΚΕΣ ενοικιάζονται βάρκες boats for hire

ΕΝΟΙΚΙΑΖΟΝΤΑΙ ΔΩΜΑΤΙΑ ενοικιάζονται δωμάτια rooms to let

ΕΝΟΙΚΙΑΣΗ ΑΥΤΟΚΙΝΗΤΩΝ ενοικίαση αυτοκινήτων car rental

ενοίκιο (το) [enikio (to)] rent

ενός [enos] of a

ενοχλητικός [enokhlitikos] annoying

ενοχλώ [enokhlo] disturb

εντάξει [edaxi] that's all right; OK

έντεκα [edeka] eleven

έντομο (το) [edomo (to)] insect

ΕΝΤΥΠΑ έντυπα printed matter

ενώ [eno] while

εξαιρετικός [exeretikos] terrific

εξ αιτίας [ex etias] because of

εξαρτάται [exartateh] it depends

ΕΞΑΤΜΙΣΗ εξάτμιση (η) [exatmisi (i)] exhaust

εξαφανίζομαι [exafanizomeh] disappear

ΕΞΕΤΑΣΕΙΣ εξετάσεις (οι) [exetasis (i)] check-up; exams

εξηγώ [exigo] explain

εξήντα [exida] sixty

έξι [exi] six

ΕΞΟΔΟΣ έξοδος (η) [exothos (i)] exit; gate (at airport); door

ΕΞΟΔΟΣ ΑΥΤ/ΤΩΝ έξοδος αυτ/των vehicle exit

ΕΞΟΔΟΣ ΚΙΝΔΥΝΟΥ έξοδος κινδύνου emergency exit

εξοχή (η) [exokhi (i)] countryside

έξοχος [exokhos] excellent

ΕΞΠΡΕΣ εξπρές [expres] special delivery; express

εξυπηρετώ [exipireto] serve (verb), assist

έξυπνος [exipnos] clever, intelligent

έξω! [exo!] get out!

ΕΞΩΣΤΗΣ εξώστης [exostis] circle (in cinema etc)

εξωτερικός [exoterikos]

external
στο εξωτερικό [sto exoteriko] abroad
ΕΞΩΤΕΡΙΚΟΥ εξωτερικού postage abroad
εξωφρενικός [exofrenikos] shocking
E.O.K. [E.O.K.] EEC, EU
E.O.T. [E.O.T.] National Tourist Agency
επαληθεύω [epaliTHevo] check (verb), verify
επαναλαμβάνω [epanalamvano] repeat
επαφή: έρχομαι σε επαφή [erkhomeh seh epafi] contact (verb)
E.Π.E. Ltd
επείγον [epigon] urgent
επειδή [epithi] because
επέκταση (η) [epektasi (i)] extension lead
επέτειος (η) [epetios (i)] anniversary
ΕΠΙΒΑΤΗΣ επιβάτης (ο/η) [epivatis (o/i)] passenger
επιβεβαιώνω [epiveveono] confirm
επίδεσμος (ο) [epithesmos (o)] bandage
επίθεση (η) [epiTHesi (i)] attack (noun)
επιθετικός [epiTHetikos] aggressive
ΕΠΙΘΕΤΟ επίθετο (το) [epiTHeto (to)] surname
επικίνδυνος [epikinthinos] dangerous
ΕΠΙΛΕΞΑΤΕ ΤΟΝ ΑΡΙΘΜΟ

επιλέξατε τον αριθμό dial the number
επίπεδος [epipethos] flat (even)
έπιπλα (τα) [epipla (ta)] furniture
ΕΠΙΠΛΩΜΕΝΑ ΔΩΜΑΤΙΑ επιπλωμένα δωμάτια furnished rooms
επίσης [episis] too, also
επισκέπτομαι [episkeptomeh] visit (verb)
ΕΠΙΣΚΕΥΑΖΟΝΤΑΙ ΥΠΟΔΗΜΑΤΑ επισκευάζονται υποδήματα shoe repairs
επισκευή (η) [episkevi (i)] repair
επίσκεψη (η) [episkepsi (i)] visit
επιστήμη (η) [epistimi (i)] science
ΕΠΙΣΤΟΛΕΣ επιστολές letters
επιστρέφω [epistrefo] give back; arrive back
ΕΠΙΣΤΡΕΦΩ ΣΕ 5´ επιστρέφω σε 5´ back in 5 minutes
ΕΠΙΤΑΓΗ επιταγή (η) [epitayi (i)] cheque, (US) check
επιτέλους [epiteloos] at last
επίτηδες [epitithes] deliberately
επιτρέπω [epitrepo] let (allow)
επιτρέπεται [epitrepeteh] it is permitted
επιτυχία (η) [epitikhia (i)] success

επόμενος (ο) [epomenos (o)] next

εποχή (η) [epokhi (i)] season

επτά [epta] seven

Ε.Ρ.Α. Greek radio

ΕΡΓΑ έργα roadworks

ΕΡΓΑ ΕΠΙ ΤΗΣ ΟΔΟΥ ΣΕ ΜΗΚΟΣ...ΧΙΛ. έργα επί της οδού σε μήκος...χιλ. roadworks for ... kms

εργάζομαι [ergazomeh] work (verb)

ΕΡΓΑΛΕΙΑ ΠΥΡΑΣΦΑΛΕΙΑΣ εργαλεία πυρασφάλειας fire-fighting equipment

εργαλείο (το) [ergalio (to)] tool

ΕΡΓΑΣΤΗΡΙΟ ΗΛΕΚΤΡΟΝΙΚΩΝ εργαστήριο ηλεκτρονικών electronics

εργένης (ο) [eryenis (o)] bachelor

εργοστάσιο (το) [ergostasio (to)] factory

ερυθρά (η) [eriTHra (i)] German measles

έρχομαι [erkhomeh] come

έρωτας (ο) [erotas (o)] love κάνω έρωτα [kano erota] make love

ερώτηση (η) [erotisi (i)] question

εσάς, εσείς, εσένα [esas, esis, esena] you

ΕΣΤΙΑΤΟΡΙΟ εστιατόριο (το) [estiatorio (to)] restaurant

εσύ [esi] you

Ε.Σ.Υ. National Health Service

εσώρουχα (τα) [esorookha (ta)] underwear

ΕΣΩΡΟΥΧΑ ΓΥΝΑΙΚΕΙΑ εσώρουχα γυναικεία [esorookha yinekia] ladies' underwear

ΕΣΩΤΕΡΙΚΟΥ εσωτερικού inland postage

Ε.Τ. Greek television

εταιρεία (η) [eteria (i)] company

ετικέτα (η) [etiketa (i)] label

ΕΤΟΙΜΑ ΓΥΝΑΙΚΕΙΑ έτοιμα γυναικεία ladies' clothing

ετοιμάζω [etimazo] prepare

ΕΤΟΙΜΑ ΠΑΙΔΙΚΑ έτοιμα παιδικά children's clothing

έτοιμος [etimos] ready

έτσι [etsi] so; like this

έτσι κι έτσι [etsi ki etsi] so-so

ευαίσθητος [evesTHitos] sensitive

ευγενικός [evyenikos] kind; polite

ευγνώμων [evgnomon] grateful

ΕΥΚΑΙΡΙΑ ευκαιρία (η) [efkeria (i)] bargain

ΕΥΚΑΙΡΙΕΣ ευκαιρίες bargains

εύκολος [efkolos] easy

ΕΥΡΩΠΑΪΚΟΣ Ευρωπαϊκός [Evropa-ikos] European

ΕΥΡΩΠΗ Ευρώπη (η) [Evropi (i)] Europe

ευτυχισμένος [eftikhismenos] happy

ευτυχώς [eftikhos] fortunately

ευχαριστημένος
[efkharistimenos] glad;
pleased

ευχάριστος [efkharistos]
pleasant

ευχαριστώ [efkharisto] thank
you

ΕΦΗΜΕΡΙΔΑ εφημερίδα (η)
[efimeritha (i)] newspaper

εφημεριδοπώλης (ο)
[efimerithopolis (o)]
newsagent

ΕΦΟΡΙΑ εφορία (η) tax
office

έχει [ekhi] he/she/it has

έχεις [ekhis] you have
έχεις ...; [ekhis ...?] do you
have ...?

έχετε [ekheteh] you have
έχετε ...; [ekheteh ...?] do you
have ...?

έχουμε [ekhoomeh] we have

έχουν [ekhoon] they have

έχω [ekho] I have

Z

ζακέτα (η) [zaketa (i)]
cardigan

ΖΑΧΑΡΟΠΛΑΣΤΕΙΟ
ζαχαροπλαστείο (το)
[zakharoplastio (to)] cake shop
or café selling cakes and
soft drinks

ζέστη (η) [zesti (i)] heat
κάνει ζέστη [kani zesti] it's
warm

ΖΕΣΤΟ ζεστό [zesto] hot

ΖΕΣΤΟ ΝΕΡΟ ζεστό νερό
[zesto nero] hot water

ζεστός [zestos] hot; warm

ζευγάρι (το) [zevgari (to)] pair

ζηλιάρης [ziliaris] jealous

ζημιά (η) [zimia (i)] damage

ζημιές: κάνω ζημιές [kano
zimies] break (verb)

ζητάω συγγνώμη [zitao
signomi] apologize

ζω [zo] live (verb)

ζωγραφίζω [zografizo] paint
(verb: pictures)

ζωγραφική (η) [zografiki (i)]
painting

ζωή (η) [zoi (i)] life

ζώνη (η) [zoni (i)] belt

ζώνη ασφαλείας (η) [zoni
asfalias (i)] seat belt

ζωντανός [zodanos] alive

ζώο (το) [zo-o (to)] animal

ΖΩΟΛΟΓΙΚΟΣ ΚΗΠΟΣ
ζωολογικός κήπος (ο)
[zo-oloyikos kipos (o)] zoo

Η

η [i] the

ή [i] or
ή ... ή ... [i ... i ...] either ...
or ...

ήδη [ithi] already

ήθελα: θα ήθελα [THa iTHela] I
would like

ηθοποιός (ο/η) [iTHopios (o/i)]
actor, actress

ΗΛ/ΓΕΙΟ ηλ/γειο electrical
goods

ΗΛΕΚΤΡΙΚΑ ΕΙΔΗ

ηλεκτρικά είδη [ilektrika ithi] electrical goods

ηλεκτρική σκούπα (η) [ilektriki skoopa (i)] vacuum cleaner

ηλεκτρικό ρεύμα (το) [ilektriko revma (to)] electricity

ΗΛΕΚΤΡΙΚΟΣ ηλεκτρικός (ο) [ilektrikos (o)] underground, (US) subway

ηλεκτρικό σίδερο (το) [ilektriko sithero (to)] iron (for ironing)

ηλεκτρικός [ilektrikos] electric

ΗΛΕΚΤΡΟΛΟΓΟΣ ηλεκτρολόγος (ο) [ilektrologos (o)] electrician

ηλίαση (η) [iliasi (i)] sunstroke

ηλικία (η) [ilikia (i)] age

ηλιοθεραπεία: κάνω ηλιοθεραπεία [kano ilioTHerapia] sunbathe

ηλιόλουστος [ilioloostos] sunny

ήλιος (ο) [ilios (o)] sun

ήμαστε [imasteh] we were

ημέρα (η) [imera (i)] day

ημερολόγιο (το) [imeroloyio (to)] calendar, diary

ημερομηνία (η) [imerominia (i)] date (time)

ΗΜΕΡΟΜΗΝΙΑ ΛΗΞΗΣ ημερομηνία λήξης best before

ΗΜΕΡΟΜΗΝΙΑ ΠΑΡΑΣΚΕΥΗΣ ημερομηνία παρασκευής

date of manufacture

ΗΜΙΔΙΑΤΡΟΦΗ ημιδιατροφή (η) [imithiatrofi (i)] half board

ΗΜΙΣΚΛΗΡΟΙ ΦΑΚΟΙ ΕΠΑΦΗΣ ημίσκληροι φακοί επαφής (οι) [imiskliri faki epafis (i)] gas permeable lenses

ήμουν [imoon] I was

ΗΝΩΜΕΝΕΣ ΠΟΛΙΤΕΙΕΣ ΑΜΕΡΙΚΗΣ Ηνωμένες Πολιτείες Αμερικής (οι) [Inomenes Politles Amerikis (i)] United States

Η.Π.Α. (οι) [I.P.A. (i)] USA

ηρεμώ [iremo] calm down

ΗΡΩΟΝ ηρώον (το) [iro-on (to)] war memorial

ήσουν, ήστε [isoon, isteh] you were

ΗΣΥΧΙΑ ησυχία [isikhia] quiet

ήσυχος [isikhos] quiet

ήταν [itan] he/she/it was; they were

Θ

θάλασσα (η) [THalasa (i)] sea

ΘΑΛΑΣΣΙΑ ΣΠΟΡ θαλάσσια σπορ water sports

ΘΑΛΑΣΣΙΟ ΣΚΙ θαλάσσιο σκι (το) [THalasio ski (to)] waterskiing

θάνατος (ο) [THanatos (o)] death

θα σε δω! [THa seh tho!] see you!

Α Β Γ Δ Ε Ζ Η Θ Ι Κ Λ Μ Ν Ξ Ο Π Ρ Σ Τ Υ Φ Χ Ψ Ω

θαυμάσιος [THavmasios] wonderful

θεά (η) [THea (i)] goddess

θέα (η) [THea (i)] view

ΘΕΑΤΡΙΚΟ ΕΡΓΟ θεατρικό έργο (το) [THeh-atriko ergo (to)] play (theatre)

ΘΕΑΤΡΟ θέατρο (το) [THeatro (to)] theatre

θεία (η) [THia (i)] aunt

θείος (ο) [THios (o)] uncle

θέλετε ...; [THeleteh ...?] do you want ...?

θέλω [THelo] want (verb)

θεός (ο) [THeos (o)] God

ΘΕΡΙΝΟΣ θερινός (ο) open-air cinema/movie theater

θέρμανση (η) [THermansi (i)] heating

θερμοκρασία (η) [THermokrasia (i)] temperature

θερμόμετρο (το) [THermometro (to)] thermometer

θερμός (το) [THermos (to)] Thermos® flask

ΘΕΣΕΙΣ θέσεις seats

ΘΕΣΕΙΣ ΚΑΘΗΜΕΝΩΝ θέσεις καθημένων seats

ΘΕΣΕΙΣ ΟΡΘΙΩΝ θέσεις ορθίων standing room

θέση (η) [THesi (i)] seat
κλείνω θέση [klino THesi] book a seat

ΘΕΩΡΕΙΑ θεωρεία [THeoria] boxes (in theatre)

θλιμμένος [THlimenos] depressed; sad

θορυβώδης [THorivothis] noisy

θρησκεία (η) [THriskia (i)] religion

θύελλα (η) [THiela (i)] storm; thunderstorm

θυμάμαι [THimameh] remember

θυμωμένος [THimomenos] angry

θυρωρός (ο) [THiroros (o)] doorman; caretaker

Ι

ΙΑΜΑΤΙΚΕΣ ΠΗΓΕΣ ιαματικές πηγές [iamatikes piyes] spa

ΙΑΝΟΥΑΡΙΟΣ Ιανουάριος (ο) [Ianooarios (o)] January

ιδέα (η) [ithea (i)] idea

ιδιοκτήτης (ο) [ithioktitis (o)] owner

ιδιοκτήτρια (η) [ithioktitria (i)] owner

ΙΔΙΟΚΤΗΤΟ ΠΑΡΚΙΝΓΚ ιδιόκτητο πάρκινγκ private parking

ίδιος [ithios] same

ΙΔΙΩΤΙΚΗ/ΚΡΑΤΙΚΗ ΙΔΙΟΚΤΗΣΙΑ ιδιωτική/κρατική ιδιοκτησία private/state property

ΙΔΙΩΤΙΚΗ ΠΙΝΑΚΟΘΗΚΗ ιδιωτική πινακοθήκη private art gallery

ΙΔΙΩΤΙΚΟΣ ιδιωτικός [ithiotikos] private

ΙΔΙΩΤΙΚΟΣ ΔΡΟΜΟΣ ιδιωτικός δρόμος private road

ιδρώνω [ithrono] sweat (verb)

ιλαρά (η) [ilara (i)] measles
ΙΝΣΤΙΤΟΥΤΟ
ΑΙΣΘΗΤΙΚΗΣ ινστιτούτο
αισθητικής (το) [institooto
esTHitikis (to)] beauty salon
ΙΟΥΛΙΟΣ Ιούλιος (ο)
[Ioolios (o)] July
ΙΟΥΝΙΟΣ Ιούνιος (ο)
[Ioonios (o)] June
ιππασία (η) [ipasia (i)] horse-
riding
ΙΠΠΟΔΡΟΜΟΣ ιππόδρομος
(ο) [ipothromos (o)] race
course (for horses)
Ιρλανδέζα (η) [Irlantheza (i)]
Irishwoman
ΙΡΛΑΝΔΙΑ Ιρλανδία (η)
[Irlanthia (i)] Ireland
Ιρλανδικός [Irlanthikos] Irish
Ιρλανδός (ο) [Irlanthos (o)]
Irishman
ίσια [isia] straight
ΙΣΟΓΕΙΟ ισόγειο (το) [isoyio
(to)] ground floor, (US) first
floor
ΙΣΟΠΕΔΟΣ ΔΙΑΒΑΣΙΣ
ισόπεδος διάβασις level
crossing
ΙΣΠΑΝΙΑ Ισπανία (η)
[Ispania (i)] Spain
Ισπανικός [Ispanikos] Spanish
(adj)
ιστιοπλοΐα (η) [istioploia (i)]
sailing
ιστιοπλοϊκό σκάφος (το)
[istioplo-iko skafos (to)] sailing
boat
ΙΣΤΙΟΦΟΡΟ ιστιοφόρο (το)
[istioforo (to)] sailing boat

ιστορία (η) [istoria (i)] story;
history
ίσως [isos] maybe, perhaps
ΙΤΑΛΙΑ Ιταλία (η) [Italia (i)]
Italy
Ιταλικός [Italikos] Italian (adj)
ΙΧΘΥΟΠΩΛΕΙΟ
ιχθυοπωλείο (το)
[ikhTHiopolio (to)]
fishmonger's

K

Κ. κ. Mr
ΚΑ. κα. Mrs
ΚΑΖΙΝΟ καζίνο (το) [kazino
(to)] casino
καθαρίζω [kaTHarizo] clean
ΚΑΘΑΡΙΣΤΗΡΙΟ
καθαριστήριο (το)
[kaTHaristirio (to)] laundry
and dry cleaner's
ΚΑΘΑΡΙΣΤΙΚΟ
ΔΕΡΜΑΤΟΣ καθαριστικό
δέρματος (το) [kaTHaristiko
thermatos (to)] skin cleanser
ΚΑΘΑΡΟ ΒΑΡΟΣ καθαρό
βάρος net weight
καθαρός [kaTHaros] clean (adj)
ΚΑΘΑΡΤΙΚΟ καθαρτικό
(το) [kaTHartiko (to)] laxative
κάθε [kaTHeh] every
καθεμία, καθένα, καθένας
[kaTHemia, kaTHena, kaTHenas]
each
κάθε τι [kaTHeh ti] everything
καθηγητής (ο) [kaTHiyitis (o)]
teacher, professor
καθηγήτρια (η) [kaTHiyitria (i)]

Α Β Γ Δ Ε Ζ Η Θ Ι Κ Λ Μ Ν Ξ Ο Π Ρ Σ Τ Υ Φ Χ Ψ Ω

teacher, professor

ΚΑΘΗΜΕΡΙΝΑ καθημερινά [kaTHimerina] daily

καθήστε [kaTHisteh] please sit down

ΚΑΘΟΔΟΣ κάθοδος [kaTHothos] way down, descent

καθολικός [kaTHolikos] Catholic (adj)

καθόλου [kaTHoloo] not at all; none; any

κάθομαι [kaTHomeh] sit down

καθρέφτης (ο) [kaTHreftis (o)] mirror

καθρέφτης αυτοκινήτου (ο) [kaTHreftis aftokinitoo (o)] rearview mirror

ΚΑΘΥΣΤΕΡΗΣΗ καθυστέρηση (η) [kaTHisterisi (i)] delay

καθυστερώ [kaTHistero] delay (verb); be late

και [keh] and

και εγώ επίσης [k ego episis] me too

και οι δύο [k i thio] both of them

ΚΑΙ ΛΟΙΠΑ και λοιπά etc

καινούργιο [kenooryio] brand-new

ευτυχισμένος ο καινούργιος χρόνος! [eftikhismenos o kenooryios khronos!] happy New Year!

καιρός (ο) [keros (o)] weather

καίω [keo] burn (verb)

κακός [kakos] bad

καλά [kala] well

καλά! [kala!] good!

καλάθι (το) [kalaTHi (to)] basket

καλεί [kali] it's ringing

ΚΑΛΕΣΑΤΕ καλέσατε dial

ΚΑΛΕΣΤΕ ΤΟΝ ΑΡΙΘΜΟ καλέστε τον αριθμό dial number

καλή διασκέδαση [kali thiaskethasi] have fun

καλημέρα [kalimera] good morning

καληνύχτα [kalinikhta] good night

καλησπέρα [kalispera] good afternoon; good evening

καλλιτέχνηδα (η) [kalitekhnitha (i)] artist

καλλιτέχνης (ο) [kalitekhnis (o)] artist

ΚΑΛΛΥΝΤΙΚΑ καλλυντικά (τα) [kalidika (ta)] perfume and cosmetics

ΚΑΛΟΚΑΙΡΙ καλοκαίρι (το) [kalokeri (to)] summer

καλοκαιρινές διακοπές (οι) [kalokerines thiakopes (i)] summer holidays/vacation

καλοριφέρ (το) [kalorifer (to)] radiator (heater)

καλός [kalos] good; kind

καλοψημένος [kalopsimenos] well-done (meat)

καλσόν (το) [kalson (to)] tights, pantyhose

κάλτσες (οι) [kaltses (i)] socks

καλύτερος (ο) [kaliteros (o)] the best

καλύτερος [kaliteros] better

καλύτερος από [kaliteros apo]
better than

καλώς ήλθατε! [kalos ilTHateh!]
welcome!

ΚΑΛΩΣ ΩΡΙΣΑΤΕ ΣΤΗΝ ...
καλώς ωρίσατε στην ...
welcome to ...

καμαριέρα (η) [kamariera (i)]
chambermaid

καμμία [kamia] no-one

καμμιά φορά [kamia fora]
sometimes

καμπάνα (η) [kabana (i)] bell

ΚΑΜΠΙΝΑ καμπίνα (η)
[kabina (i)] cabin (on ship)

ΚΑΜΠΙΝΓΚ κάμπινγκ (το)
[camping (to)] campsite,
caravan site, trailer park

ΚΑΜΠΙΝΕΣ καμπίνες
[kabines] changing rooms

ΚΑΝΑΔΑΣ Καναδάς (ο)
[Kanathas (o)] Canada

Καναδή (η) [Kanathi (i)]
Canadian (woman)

Καναδικός [Kanathikos]
Canadian (adj)

Καναδός (ο) [Kanathos (o)]
Canadian (man)

κανάτα (η) [kanata (i)] jug

κάνει ... [kani ...] it is ..., it
costs ...

κάνεις [kanis] you do
τι κάνεις; [ti kanis?] how are
you?, how do you do?

κανένα [kanena] nothing

κανένας [kanenas] no-one,
nobody

κάνετε [kaneteh] you do
τι κάνετε; [ti kaneteh?] how

are you?, how do you do?

κανό (το) [kano (to)] canoe

κάνω [kano] do; make

καπάκι (το) [kapaki (to)] lid,
cap (of bottle)

καπαρντίνα (η) [kapardina (i)]
raincoat

καπέλο (το) [kapelo (to)] hat,
cap

ΚΑΠΕΤΑΝΙΟΣ καπετάνιος
(ο) [kapetanios (o)] captain (of
ship)

ΚΑΠΝΙΖΟΝΤΕΣ
καπνίζοντες [kapnizodes]
smoking

καπνίζω [kapnizo] smoke (verb)

ΚΑΠΝΙΣΤΕΣ καπνιστές
[kapnistes] smokers

ΚΑΠΝΙΣΤΗΡΙΟ
καπνιστήριο (το) [kapnistirio
(to)] smoking room

ΚΑΠΝΟΠΩΛΕΙΟ
καπνοπωλείο (το)
[kapnopolio (to)]
tobacconist's

ΚΑΠΝΟΣ καπνός (ο) [kapnos
(o)] smoke; tobacco

καπό (το) [kapo (to)] bonnet
(car), (US) hood

κάποιος [kapios] somebody

κάπου [kapoo] somewhere

ΚΑΡΑΜΕΛΑ καραμέλα (η)
[karamela (i)] caramel

καρδιά (η) [karthia (i)] heart

καρδιακή προσβολή (η)
[karthiaki prosvoli (i)] heart
attack

καρέκλα (η) [karekla (i)] chair

καρμπιρατέρ (το) [karbirater

(to)] **carburettor**

καρνέ επιταγών (το) [karneh
epitagon (to)] **cheque book,**
(US) **check book**

καροτσάκι (το) [karotsaki (to)]
pram; pushchair, buggy

καρπός (ο) [karpos (o)] **wrist**

ΚΑΡΤΑ κάρτα (η) [karta (i)]
postcard; business card

κάρτα επιβιβάσεως (η) [karta
epivivaseos (i)] **boarding pass**

κάρτα επιταγών (η) [karta
epitagon (i)] **cheque card,**
(US) **check card**

ΚΑΡΤΠΟΣΤΑΛ καρτποστάλ
(η) [kartpostal (i)] **postcard**

καρφί (το) [karfi (to)] **nail** (in
wall)

καρφίτσα (η) [karfitsa (i)] **pin;
brooch**

κασκόλ (το) [kaskol (to)] **scarf**
(for neck)

ΚΑΣΣΕΤΑ κασσέτα (η)
[kaseta (i)] **cassette, tape**

κασσεττόφωνο (το)
[kasetofono (to)] **cassette
player**

καστόρι (το) [kastori (to)]
suede

κάστρο (το) [kastro (to)] **castle**

κατά [kata] **against; about**

κάταγμα (το) [katagma (to)]
fracture

καταδύσεις (οι) [katathisis (i)]
skin-diving

ΚΑΤΑΘΕΣΗ κατάθεση (η)
[kataTHesi (i)] **deposit**

καταλαβαίνω [katalaveno]
understand

δεν καταλαβαίνω [then
katalaveno] **I don't
understand**

ΚΑΤΑΛΛΗΛΟ κατάλληλο
suitable for all ages

κατάλογος (ο) [katalogos (o)]
list; menu

ΚΑΤΑΝΑΛΩΣΗ ΠΡΙΝ ...
κατανάλωση πριν ...
consume before ...

καταπίνω [katapino] **swallow**
(verb)

καταρράκτης (ο) [kataraktis
(o)] **waterfall**

ΚΑΤΑΣΚΕΥΑΖΟΝΤΑΙ
ΚΛΕΙΔΙΑ
κατασκευάζονται κλειδιά
keys cut here

κατασκήνωση (η) [kataskinosi
(i)] **camping**

ΚΑΤΑΣΤΗΜΑ
ΑΦΟΡΟΛΟΓΗΤΩΝ
κατάστημα αφορολογήτων
(το) [katastima aforoloyiton
(to)] **duty-free shop**

καταστροφή (η) [katastrofi (i)]
disaster

ΚΑΤΑΣΤΡΩΜΑ
κατάστρωμα (το) [katastroma
(to)] **deck**

κατά τη διάρκεια [kata ti
thiarkia] **while, during**

καταψύκτης (ο) [katapsiktis (o)]
freezer

κατάψυξη (η) [katapsixi (i)]
freezer compartment

κατεβαίνω [kateveno] **get off;
go down**

κατειλημμένος [katilimenos]

engaged, occupied

ΚΑΤΕΠΕΙΓΟΝ κατεπείγον [katepigon] express

κατευθείαν [kateffHian] direct

ΚΑΤΕΨΥΓΜΕΝΑ κατεψυγμένα (τα) [katepsigmena (ta)] frozen food

ΚΑΤΕΨΥΓΜΕΝΟ κατεψυγμένο [katepsigmeno] frozen (food)

ΚΑΤΕΙΛΗΜΜΕΝΟΣ κατειλημμένος [katilimenos] engaged, occupied

κάτι [kati] something

κάτι άλλο [kati alo] something else

ΚΑΤΟΛΙΣΘΗΣΕΙΣ κατολισθήσεις falling rocks

ΚΑΤΟΣΤΑΡΙΚΟ κατοστάρικο (το) [katostariko (to)] 100-drachma note/bill

κατσαβίδι (το) [katsavithi (to)] screwdriver

κατσαρόλα (η) [katsarola (i)] saucepan

κατσίκα (η) [katsika (i)] goat

ΚΑΤΩ κάτω [kato] down; downstairs

κάτω από [kato apo] under

καυτερός [kafteros] spicy, hot

καυτός [kaftos] hot (to taste)

καφέ [kafe] brown

ΚΑΦΕΚΟΠΤΕΙΟ καφεκοπτείο (το) [kafekoptio (to)] coffee shop

ΚΑΦΕΝΕΙΟ καφενείο (το) [kafenio (to)] coffee house, where Greek coffee is

served with traditional sweets

ΚΑΦΕΤΕΡΙΑ καφετέρια (η) [kafeteria (i)] café, coffee shop

κάψιμο (το) [kapsimo (to)] burn

ΚΕΛΣΙΟΥ Κελσίου [Kelsioo] centigrade

κέλυφος (το) [kelifos (to)] shell

ΚΕΝΤΗΜΑΤΑ κεντήματα (τα) [kedimata (ta)] embroidery

κεντρική θέρμανση (η) [kedriki THermansi (i)] central heating

ΚΕΝΤΡΟ κέντρο (το) [kedro (to)] centre

κέντρο της πόλης [kedro tis polis] city centre

ΚΕΡΑΜΙΚΑ κεραμικά (τα) [keramika (ta)] ceramics

κερδίζω [kerthizo] earn; win (verb)

κερί (το) [keri (to)] candle

ΚΕΡΚΥΡΑ Κέρκυρα (η) [Kerkira (i)] Corfu

ΚΕΡΜΑ κέρμα (το) [kerma (to)] coin

ΚΕΡΜΑΤΑ κέρματα [kermata] coins

ΚΕΣ. κες. Mrs

κεφάλι (το) [kefali (to)] head

κηδεία (η) [kithia (i)] funeral

ΚΗΠΟΘΕΑΤΡΟ κηποθέατρο (το) open-air theatre

ΚΗΠΟΣ κήπος (ο) [kipos (o)] garden, park

κιβώτιο ταχυτήτων (το)
[kivotio takhititon (to)]
gearbox

κιθάρα (η) [kiΤΗara (i)] guitar

ΚΙΛΟ κιλό (το) [kilo (to)] kilo

ΚΙΝΔΥΝΟΣ κίνδυνος (ο)
[kinthinos (o)] danger;
caution

ΚΙΝΔΥΝΟΣ ΠΥΡΚΑΓΙΑΣ
κίνδυνος πυρκαγιάς fire risk

κινηματογραφική μηχανή (η)
[kinimatografiki mikhani (i)]
camcorder

ΚΙΝΗΜΑΤΟΓΡΑΦΟΣ
κινηματογράφος (ο)
[kinimatografos (o)] cinema,
movie theater

κίτρινος [kitrinos] yellow

ΚΚ. κκ. Messrs

κλαίω [kleo] cry (verb)

κλάξον (το) [klaxon (to)] horn
(in car)

κλέβω [klevo] steal

κλειδαριά (η) [klitharia (i)]
lock

κλειδί (το) [klithi (to)] key;
spanner, wrench

ΚΛΕΙΔΙΑ κλειδιά keys cut
here

κλειδώνω [klithono] lock (verb)

ΚΛΕΙΝΕΤΕ ΤΗΝ ΠΟΡΤΑ
κλείνετε την πόρτα close
the door

κλείνω [klino] close (verb);
switch off

ΚΛΕΙΣΤΑ κλειστά [klista]
closed

ΚΛΕΙΣΤΟ ΑΠΟ ... ΩΣ ...
κλειστό από ... ως ... [klisto

apo ... os ...] closed from ...
to ...

ΚΛΕΙΣΤΟΝ κλειστόν
[kliston] closed

κλειστός [klistos] closed; off
(lights)

κλέφτης (ο) [kleftis (o)] thief

κλέφτρα (η) [kleftra (i)] thief

κλίμα (το) [klima (to)] climate

ΚΛΙΜΑΤΙΖΟΜΕΝΟΣ
κλιματιζόμενος
[klimatizomenos] air-
conditioned

ΚΛΙΜΑΤΙΣΜΟΣ
κλιματισμός (ο) [klimatismos
(o)] air-conditioning

κλοπή (η) [klopi (i)] theft

Κ.Λ.Π. κλπ etc

ΚΛΩΣΤΗ κλωστή (η) [klosti
(i)] thread

κόβω [kovo] cut (verb)

κοιλάδα (η) [kilatha (i)] valley

κοιμάμαι [kimameh] sleep
(verb); be asleep

ΚΟΙΜΗΤΗΡΙΟ κοιμητήριο
(το) [kimitirio (to)] cemetery

ΚΟΙΝΟΤΙΚΟ ΓΡΑΦΕΙΟ
κοινοτικό γραφείο (το)
local government office

κοκκαλιάρης [kokaliaris]
skinny

κόκκαλο (το) [kokalo (to)]
bone

κόκκινος [kokinos] red

κόλλα (η) [kola (i)] glue

κολλιέ (το) [kolie (to)]
necklace

κόλπος (ο) [kolpos (o)] vagina;
gulf

ΚΟΛΥΜΒΗΤΗΡΙΟ
κολυμβητήριο (το)
[kolimvitirio (to)] swimming
pool

κολυμπάω [kolibao] swim (verb)

κολύμπι (το) [kolibi (to)]
swimming

κολυμπώ [kolibo] swim (verb)

κολώνια (η) [kolonia (i)] eau
de toilette

κολώνια μετά το ξύρισμα
[kolonia meta to xirisma]
aftershave

κομμάτι (το) [komati (to)]
piece

ΚΟΜΜΩΣΕΙΣ κομμώσεις
(οι) [komosis (i)]
hairdresser's

ΚΟΜΜΩΤΗΡΙΟ
κομμωτήριο (το) [komotirio
(to)] hairdresser's

κομμώτρια (η) [komotria (i)]
hairdresser

κομπιουτεράκι (το) [kombi-
ooteraki (to)] calculator

κομπολόι (το) [komboloi (to)]
worry beads

κοντά [koda] near, close by

κοντέρ (το) [koder (to)]
speedometer

ΚΟΝΤΙΣΙΟΝΕΡ
κοντίσιονερ (το) [kodisioner
(to)] conditioner

κοντός [kodos] short (person)

ΚΟΡΔΟΝΙΑ ΠΑΠΟΥΤΣΙΩΝ
κορδόνια παπουτσιών (τα)
[korthonia papootsion (ta)]
shoelaces

κόρη (η) [kori (i)] daughter

κορίτσι (το) [koritsi (to)] girl

κόρνα (η) [korna (i)] horn (in
car)

κορυφή (η) [korifi (i)] top

ΚΟΣΜΗΜΑΤΑ κοσμήματα
(τα) [kosmimata (ta)]
jewellery

ΚΟΣΜΗΜΑΤΟΠΩΛΕΙΟ
κοσμηματοπωλείο (το)
[kosmimatopolio (to)]
jeweller's

κόσμος (ο) [kosmos (o)] world;
people, crowd

κοστίζει [kostizi] it costs

κόστος (το) [kostos (to)] cost

κουβάς (ο) [koovas (o)] bucket

κουβέρτα (η) [kooverta (i)]
blanket

κουδούνι (το) [koothooni (to)]
bell (for door)

ΚΟΥΖΙΝΑ κουζίνα (η)
[koozina (i)] cooker; kitchen

ΚΟΥΚΕΤΑ κουκέτα (η)
[kooketa (i)] couchette

κουκέτες (οι) [kooketes (i)]
bunk beds

κούκλα (η) [kookla (i)] doll

κουμπί (το) [koobi (to)] button

κουνέλι (το) [kooneli (to)]
rabbit

κούνια (η) [koonia (i)] cot

κουνούπι (το) [koonoopi (to)]
mosquito

κουπέ (το) [koopeh (to)]
compartment

κουρασμένος [koorasmenos]
tired

ΚΟΥΡΕΑΣ κουρέας (ο)
[kooreas (o)] barber

Α
Β
Γ
Δ
Ε
Ζ
Η
Θ
Ι
Κ
Λ
Μ
Ν
Ξ
Ο
Π
Ρ
Σ
Τ
Υ
Φ
Χ
Ψ
Ω

ΚΟΥΡΕΙΟ κουρείο (το)
[koorio (to)] barber's shop

κούρεμα (το) [koorema (to)]
haircut

κουρτίνα (η) [koortina (i)]
curtain

κουστούμι (το) [koostoomi
(to)] suit

κουτάλι (το) [kootali (to)]
spoon

ΚΟΥΤΑΛΙΕΣ ΓΛΥΚΟΥ
κουταλιές γλυκού
teaspoonfuls

ΚΟΥΤΑΛΙΕΣ ΣΟΥΠΑΣ
κουταλιές σούπας
tablespoonfuls

κουτί (το) [kooti (to)] box; can

κουφός [koofos] deaf

ΚΡΑΓΙΟΝ κραγιόν (το)
[krayon (to)] lipstick

κράμπα (η) [kramba (i)] cramp

κρανίο (το) [kranio (to)] skull

κρατάω [kratao] hold; keep

ΚΡΑΤΗΣΕΙΣ ΘΕΣΕΩΝ
κρατήσεις θέσεων
reservations; seat
reservations

κράτηση θέσης (η) [kratisi
THesis (i)] reservation

κρεβάτι (το) [krevati (to)] bed

ΚΡΕΜΑ ΠΡΟΣΩΠΟΥ
κρέμα προσώπου (η) [krema
prosopoo (i)] moisturizer

κρεμάστρα (η) [kremastra (i)]
coathanger

ΚΡΕΟΠΩΛΕΙΟ κρεοπωλείο
(το) [kreopolio (to)] butcher's

κρίμα: είναι κρίμα [ineh
krima] it's a pity

κρουαζιέρα (η) [kroo-aziera (i)]
cruise

κρύβομαι [krivomeh] hide
(oneself)

κρύβω [krivo] hide (something)

κρύο (το) [krio (to)] cold
κάνει κρύο [kani krio] it's
cold

ΚΡΥΟ ΝΕΡΟ κρύο νερό
[krio nero] cold water

κρύος [krios] cold (adj)

κρύωμα (το) [krioma (to)] cold
(illness)

Κ.Τ.Ε.Λ. long-distance bus
station

κτηνίατρος (ο/η) [ktiniatros (o/
i)] vet

κτίριο (το) [ktirio (to)] building

κυβέρνηση (η) [kivernisi (i)]
government

κυκλοφορία (η) [kikloforia (i)]
traffic

κυκλοφοριακή συμφόρηση
(η) [kikloforiaki simforisi (i)]
traffic jam

ΚΥΛΙΚΕΙΟ κυλικείο (το)
[kilikio (to)] snackbar

ΚΥΛΟΤΕΣ κυλότες (οι)
[kilotes (i)] panties;
underpants

κύμα (το) [kima (to)] wave

κυνηγώ [kinigo] hunt (verb),
chase

ΚΥΠΡΟΣ Κύπρος (η) [Kipros
(i)] Cyprus

Κυρία (η) [Kiria (i)] Mrs; Ms

κυρία (η) [kiria (i)] lady;
madam

ΚΥΡΙΑΚΕΣ ΚΑΙ ΕΟΡΤΕΣ

Κυριακές και Εορτές
Sundays and holidays
ΚΥΡΙΑΚΗ Κυριακή (η)
[Kuriaki (i)] Sunday
ΚΥΡΙΑΚΗ ΤΟΥ ΠΑΣΧΑ
Κυριακή του Πάσχα (η)
[Kiriaki too Paskha (i)] Easter
Sunday
κύριε [kiri-eh] sir
ΚΥΡΙΕΣ κυρίες [kiries] Mrs
ΚΥΡΙΟΙ κύριοι Messrs
ΚΥΡΙΟΣ Κύριος [Kirios] Mr
κύριος (ο) [kirios (o)]
gentleman
κύριος [kirios] main
κύστη (η) [kisti (i)] bladder
κυττάζω [kitazo] look (verb)
ΚΩΔΙΚΟΣ κωδικός (ο)
[kothikos (o)] code
ΚΩΔΙΚΟΣ ΑΡΙΘΜΟΣ
κωδικός αριθμός [kothikos
ariTHmos] dialling code

Λ

ΛΑΔΙ λάδι (το) [lathi (to)] oil
ΛΑΔΙΑ λάδια (τα) [lathia (ta)]
engine oil
ΛΑΔΙ ΜΑΥΡΙΣΜΑΤΟΣ
λάδι μαυρίσματος [lathi
mavrismatos] suntan oil
λάθος (το) [laTHos (to)]
mistake
λάθος [laTHos] wrong
λάθος νούμερο [laTHos
noomero] wrong number
λαιμός (ο) [lemos (o)] neck;
throat
λακ (η) [lak (i)] hairspray

λάμπα (η) [lamba (i)] light
bulb; lamp
λαστιχάκι (το) [lastikhaki (to)]
rubber band
λάστιχο (το) [lastikho (to)]
rubber (material); tyre
λεβιές ταχυτήτων (ο) [levies
takhititon (o)] gear lever
λείπω [lipo] be missing; be
out; be away
λειτουργία (η) [litooryia (i)]
mass (church)
λεκές (ο) [lekes (o)] stain
ΛΕΜΒΟΣ λέμβος (η) [lemvos
(i)] lifeboat
λένε: λένε ότι [leneh oti]
they say that
με λένε ... [meh leneh ...] my
name is ...
πως σε λένε; [pos seh leneh?]
what's your name?
λέξη (η) [lexi (i)] word
λεξικό (το) [lexiko (to)]
dictionary
λεπτό (το) [lepto (to)] minute
λεπτός [leptos] slim
λέσχη (η) [leskhi (i)] club
λευκοπλάστ (το) [lefkoplast
(to)] (sticking) plaster,
Bandaid®
ΛΕΦΤΑ λεφτά (τα) [lefta (ta)]
money
λέω [leo] say
ΛΕΩΦΟΡΕΙΟ λεωφορείο
(το) [leoforio (to)] bus
ΛΕΩΦΟΡΕΙΟ ΥΠ' ΑΡΙΘΜ
... λεωφορείο υπ' αριθμ ...
bus number ...
ΛΕΩΦΟΡΟΣ λεωφόρος (η)

A
B
Γ
Δ
E
Z
H
Θ
I
K
Λ
M
N
Ξ
O
Π
P
Σ
T
Y
Φ
X
Ψ
Ω

[leoforos (i)] avenue

ΛΗΓΕΙ ΤΗΝ ... λήγει την ... expires on ...

λιακάδα (η) [liakatha (i)] sunshine

λίγα [liga] a few

λίγο [ligo] a little bit

ΣΕ ΛΙΓΟ σε λίγο [seh ligo] in a little while

λίγος [ligos] little, short

λιγότερος [ligoteros] fewer

λιγότερο [ligotero] less

ΛΙΜΑΝΙ λιμάνι (το) [limani (to)] harbour

λίμα νυχιών (η) [lima nikhion (i)] nailfile

ΛΙΜΕΝΑΡΧΕΙΟ λιμεναρχείο (το) port authorities

ΛΙΜΕΝΑΡΧΗΣ λιμενάρχης (ο) harbour master

ΛΙΜΕΝΙΚΗ ΑΣΤΥΝΟΜΙΑ Λιμενική Αστυνομία (η) [limeniki Astinomia (i)] harbour police

ΛΙΜΗΝ λιμήν (ο) [limin (o)] port

λίμνη (η) [limni (i)] lake

λιμνούλα (η) [limnoola (i)] pond

λίμπρα (η) [libra (i)] pound (weight)

λιπαρός [liparos] greasy

λιποθυμώ [lipoTHimo] faint (verb)

ΛΙΡΑ ΑΓΓΛΙΑΣ λίρα Αγγλίας (η) [lira Anglias (i)] pound sterling

ΛΙΤΑΝΕΙΑ λιτανεία (η) litany

ΛΙΤΡΟ λίτρο (το) [litro (to)] litre

ΛΟΓΑΡΙΑΣΜΟΣ λογαριασμός (ο) [logariasmos (o)] bill, (US) check

λογικός [loyikos] sensible

ΛΟΓΙΣΤΗΡΙΟ λογιστήριο (το) [loyistirio (to)] purser's office

ΛΟΝΔΙΝΟ Λονδίνο (το) [Lonthino (to)] London

λόξυγγας (ο) [loxingas (o)] hiccups

λουλούδι (το) [looloothi (to)] flower

λούσιμο (το) [loosimo (to)] wash

ΛΟΥΤΡΟ λουτρό (το) [lootro (to)] bathroom

λόφος (ο) [lofos (o)] hill

λυπάμαι [lipameh] I'm sorry

λυπημένος [lipimenos] sad

ΛΥΡΙΚΗ ΣΚΗΝΗ λυρική σκηνή (η) [liriki skini (i)] opera house

M

μαγαζί (το) [magazi (to)] shop

μαγειρεύω [mayirevo] cook (verb)

μαγειρικά σκεύη (τα) [mayirika skevi (ta)] cooking utensils

μαγείρισσα (η) [mayirisa (i)] cook

μάγειρος (ο) [mayiros (o)] cook

μάγκας (ο) [mangas (o)]
streetwise/smart person

μαγιό (το) [mayo (to)]
swimming trunks

μάγουλο (το) [magoolo (to)]
chin

μαζί [mazi] together

μαζί με [mazi meh] with,
together with

μαθαίνω [maTHeno] learn

μάθημα (το) [maTHima (to)]
lesson

κάνω μάθημα [kano maTHima]
teach; take a lesson

ΜΑΘΗΜΑΤΑ ΣΚΙ
μαθήματα σκι [maTHimata ski]
skiing lessons

ΜΑΙΟΣ Μάιος (ο) [Maios (o)]
May

μακριά [makria] far, at a
distance

μαλάκας (ο) [malakas (o)]
arsehole, wanker

μακρύς [makris] long

ΜΑΛΑΚΟΙ ΦΑΚΟΙ
μαλακοί φακοί (οι) [malaki
faki (i)] soft lenses

μάλιστα [malista] yes,
certainly

μάλιστα! [malista!] well!

ΜΑΛΛΙ μαλλί (το) [mali (to)]
wool

μαλλιά (τα) [malia (ta)] hair

ΜΑΛΛΙΝΟ μάλλινο [malino]
wool

μάλλον [malon] rather;
probably

μαλώνω [malono] fight (verb)

μαμά (η) [mama (i)] mum

ΜΑΝΑΒΗΣ μανάβης (ο)
[manavis (o)] greengrocer's

ΜΑΝΟ μανό (το) [mano (to)]
nail polish

μανταλάκι (το) [madalaki (to)]
clothes peg

μαντήλι (το) [madili (to)]
handkerchief; headscarf

μαξιλάρι (το) [maxilari (to)]
pillow

μαραγκός (ο) [marangos (o)]
carpenter

ΜΑΡΙΝΑ μαρίνα (η) [marina
(i)] marina

μαρκαδόρος (ο) [markathoros
(o)] felt-tip pen

ΜΑΡΤΙΟΣ Μάρτιος (ο)
[Martios (o)] March

μάρτυρας (ο) [martiras (o)]
witness

μασέλα (η) [masela (i)]
dentures

μας [mas] us; our

μάτι (το) [mati (to)] eye; ring
(on cooker)

ματς (το) [mats (to)] match
(sport)

μαυρίζω [mavrizo] tan (verb)

μαύρισμα (το) [mavrisma (to)]
tan (colour)

μαύρισμα από τον ήλιο
[mavrisma apo ton ilio] suntan

μαύρος [mavros] black

μαχαίρι (το) [makheri (to)]
knife

μαχαιροπήρουνα (τα)
[makheropiroona (ta)] cutlery

με [meh] with; by; me
με αυτοκίνητο [meh

A
B
Γ
Δ
E
Z
H
Θ
I
K
Λ
M
N
Ξ
O
Π
P
Σ
T
Y
Φ
X
Ψ
Ω

aftokinito] by car

ΜΕΓΑΛΗ ΒΡΕΤΑΝΝΙΑ
Μεγάλη Βρεταννία (η)
[Megali Vretania (i)] Great
Britain

Μεγάλη Παρασκευή (η)
[Megali Paraskevi (i)] Good
Friday

μεγάλος [megalos] big

μεγαλύτερος [megaliteros]
bigger

ΜΕΓΕΘΟΣ μέγεθος (το)
[meyeTHos (to)] size

μεγέθυνση (η) [meyeTHinsi (i)]
enlargement

ΜΕΓΙΣΤΟ ΒΑΡΟΣ μέγιστο
βάρος maximum permitted
weight

μέγιστος (ο) [meyistos (o)]
biggest

μεζ (η) [mez (i)] highlights (in
hair)

μεθαύριο [meTHavrio] the day
after tomorrow

μεθυσμένος [meTHismenos]
drunk

μέικ απ (το) [meik ap (to)]
make-up

μελανιά (η) [melania (i)]
bruise

μέλλον (το) [melon (to)] future

ΜΕ ΜΠΑΝΙΟ με μπάνιο
[meh banio] with bathroom

ΜΕ ΝΤΟΥΣ με ντους [meh
doos] with shower

μένω [meno] live (in town etc);
stay (in hotel etc)

μέρα (η) [mera (i)] day

μερίδα (η) [meritha (i)] portion

μερικά, μερικές, μερικοί
[merika, merikes, meriki] some

μέρος (το) [meros (to)] part,
place; WC

μέσα [mesa] in; inside

μεσάνυχτα (τα) [mesanikhta
(ta)] midnight

μέση (η) [mesi (i)] middle;
waist

μεσημέρι (το) [mesimeri (to)]
midday

Μεσόγειος (η) [Mesoyios (i)]
Mediterranean

μετά [meta] after; afterwards
μετά από σας [meta apo sas]
after you
μετά μεσημβρίας [meta
mesimvrias] p.m.

μετακινούμαι [metakinoomeh]
move (verb)

μέταλλο (το) [metalo (to)]
metal

ΜΕΤΑΞΙ μετάξι (το) [metaxi
(to)] silk

μεταξύ [metaxi] between

μεταφέρω [metafero] carry

μεταφράζω [metafrazo]
translate

μετεωρολογικό δελτίο (το)
[meteoroloyiko theltio (to)]
weather forecast

ΜΕΤΡΗΤΑ μετρητά [metrita]
cash
ΤΟΙΣ ΜΕΤΡΗΤΟΙΣ τοις
μετρητοίς [tis metritis] in
cash

μετρητής βενζίνης (ο)
[metritis venzinis (o)] fuel
gauge

μέτριο μέγεθος [metrio meyeTHos] medium-sized

ΜΕΤΡΙΟΣ μέτριος [metrios] medium; average

ΜΕΤΡΟ μέτρο (το) [metro (to)] metre

μέτωπο (το) [metopo (to)] forehead

μέχρι [mekhri] until

ΜΗ μη do not

ΜΗ ΒΓΑΖΕΤΕ ΤΗΝ ΚΑΡΤΑ μη βγάζετε την κάρτα do not remove the card yet

μηδέν [mithen] zero

ΜΗΝ ΚΑΠΝΙΖΕΤΕ μην καπνίζετε no smoking

ΜΗ ΚΑΠΝΙΖΟΝΤΕΣ μη καπνίζοντες [mi kapnizontes] non-smoking

ΜΗ ΚΑΠΝΙΣΤΕΣ μη καπνιστές [mi kapnistes] non-smokers

μήκος (το) [mikos (to)] length

μήνας (ο) [minas (o)] month

μήνας του μέλιτος [minas too melitos] honeymoon

ΜΗΝ ΕΝΟΧΛΕΙΤΕ μην ενοχλείτε do not disturb

ΜΗΝ ΟΜΙΛΕΙΤΕ ΣΤΟΝ ΟΔΗΓΟ μην ομιλείτε στον οδηγό do not speak to the driver

ΜΗΝ ΠΑΤΑΤΕ ΤΟ ΧΟΡΤΟ μην πατάτε το χόρτο keep off the grass

ΜΗ ΠΟΣΙΜΟ (ΝΕΡΟ) μη πόσιμο (νερό) not for drinking (water)

μητέρα (η) [mitera (i)] mother

ΜΗ ΤΟΞΙΚΟ μη τοξικό non-toxic

μητρόπολη (η) [mitropoli (i)] cathedral

μηχανάκι (το) [mikhanaki (to)] moped

μηχανή (η) [mikhani (i)] engine

μηχανικός (ο) [mikhanikos (o)] mechanic; engineer

μία [mia] a; one

μία φορά [mia fora] once

μιας [mias] of a

μίζα (η) [miza (i)] ignition

ΜΙΚΡΟ ΟΝΟΜΑ μικρό όνομα (το) [mikro onoma (to)] Christian name

ΜΙΚΡΟΣ μικρός [mikros] little, small

ΜΙΚΤΟ ΒΑΡΟΣ μικτό βάρος gross weight

μικρότερος [mikroteros] smaller

ΜΙΛΑΕΙ μιλάει [milai] engaged, occupied

μιλάω [milao] speak μιλάτε ...; [milateh ...?] do you speak ...?

μισός [misos] half

ΜΙΣΟΤΙΜΗΣ μισοτιμής half-price

μισώ [miso] hate (verb)

μ.μ. [m.m.] p.m.

μνημείο (το) [mnimio (to)] monument

μόδα (η) [motha (i)] fashion της μόδας [tis mothas] fashionable

ΜΟΔΕΣ μόδες fashions
μοιάζει [miazi] it looks/seems
μοιράζομαι [mirazomeh] share
~(verb)
μοκέτα (η) [moketa (i)] carpet
μολύβι (το) [molivi (to)] pencil
μόλυνση (η) [molinsi (i)]
  infection
ΜΟΛΥΣΜΕΝΑ ΥΔΑΤΑ
  μολυσμένα ύδατα polluted
  water
μολυσμένος [molismenos]
  polluted
ΜΟΝΑΔΕΣ μονάδες units
ΜΟΝΑΔΙΚΗ ΕΥΚΑΙΡΙΑ
  μοναδική ευκαιρία (η)
  special offer
μονή [moni] monastery
μόνο [mono] only
ΜΟΝΟΔΡΟΜΟΣ
  μονόδρομος one-way street
ΜΟΝΟ ΔΩΜΑΤΙΟ μονό
  δωμάτιο (το) [mono thomatio
  (to)] single room
ΜΟΝΟΚΛΙΝΟ ΔΩΜΑΤΙΟ
  μονόκλινο δωμάτιο (το)
  [monoklino thomatio (to)]
  single room
μονό κρεβάτι [mono krevati]
  single bed
μόνον δύο [monon thio] just
  two
μονοπάτι (το) [monopati (to)]
  path
μόνος [monos] alone
μοντέρνος [modernos] modern
μοτοσυκλέτα (η) [motosikleta
  (i)] motorbike
μου [moo] my

ΜΟΥΣΕΙΟ μουσείο (το)
  [moosio (to)] museum
ΜΟΥΣΙΚΑ ΟΡΓΑΝΑ
  μουσικά όργανα [moosika
  organa] musical instruments
μουσική (η) [moosiki (i)] music
μουσική ποπ (η) [moosiki pop
  (i)] pop music
μουστάκι (το) [moostaki (to)]
  moustache
μπαίνω [beno] go in, enter
ΜΠΑΚΑΛΙΚΟ μπακάλικο
  (το) [bakaliko (to)] grocer's
μπαλκόνι (το) [balkoni (to)]
  balcony
μπάλλα (η) [bala (i)] ball (large)
μπαλλάκι (το) [balaki (to)] ball
  (small)
μπαμπάς (ο) [babas (o)] dad
μπανιέρα (η) [baniera (i)]
  bathtub
ΜΠΑΝΙΟ μπάνιο (το) [banio
  (to)] bath
  κάνω μπάνιο [kano banio]
  swim (verb); have a bath
  πάω για μπάνιο [pao ya
  banio] go swimming
ΜΠΑΡ μπαρ (το) [bar (to)]
  bar
μπάρμαν (ο) [barman (o)]
  barman
μπάρ γούμαν (η) [bar woman
  (i)] barmaid
μπαταρία (η) [bataria (i)]
  battery
μπεζ [bez] beige
μπέιμπι-σίττερ (η) [baby-sitter
  (i)] babysitter
μπερδεμένος [berthemenos]

complicated

μπικίνι (το) [bikini (to)] bikini

μπλε [bleh] blue

μπλούζα (η) [blooza (i)] blouse

μπλουζάκι (το) [bloozaki (to)] T-shirt

μπόρα (η) [bora (i)] shower (rain)

μπορείς [boris] you can
μπορείς να ...; [boris na ...?] can you ...?

μπορείτε [boriteh] you can
μπορείτε να ...; [boritch na ...?] can you ...?

μπρος [bros] forwards; in front of
βάζω μπρος [vazo bros] switch on (engine)

μπορώ [boro] I can

μπότα (η) [bota (i)] boot (shoe)

μπουγάδα (η) [boogatha (i)] washing
βάζω μπουγάδα [vazo boogatha] do the washing

μπουζί (το) [boozi (to)] spark plug

ΜΠΟΥΖΟΥΚΙΑ
μπουζούκια (τα) [boozookia (ta)] club with bouzouki music

μπουκάλι (το) [bookali (to)] bottle

μπουκιά (η) [bookia (i)] bite

μπούτι (το) [booti (to)] thigh

ΜΠΟΥΤΙΚ μπουτίκ (η) [bootik (i)] boutique

μπροστινό μέρος (το) [brostino meros (to)] front

(part)

μπωλ (το) [bol (to)] bowl

μύγα (η) [miga (i)] fly

μυθιστόρημα (το) [miTHistorima (to)] novel

μυρίζω [mirizo] smell (verb)

μυρμήγκι (το) [mirmingi (to)] ant

μυρωδιά (η) [mirothia (i)] smell

μυστικός [mistikos] secret

μυς (ο) [mis (o)] muscle

μύτη (η) [miti (i)] nose

μύωπας [miopas] shortsighted

μωβ [mov] purple

μωρό (το) [moro (to)] baby

N

να [na] here is/are

ναι [neh] yes
ναι, ναι! [neh neh!] oh yes I do!

νάιτκλαμπ (το) [nightclub (to)] nightclub

ΝΑ ΛΑΜΒΑΝΕΤΑΙ ΜΟΝΟΝ ΑΠΟ ΤΟ ΣΤΟΜΑ να λαμβάνεται μόνον από το στόμα to be taken orally only

ΝΑ ΛΑΜΒΑΝΕΤΑΙ ... ΦΟΡΕΣ ΗΜΕΡΗΣΙΩΣ να λαμβάνεται ... φορές ημερησίως to be taken ... times daily

ναρκωτικά (τα) [narkotika (ta)] drugs (narcotics)

νάυλον κάλτσες (οι) [na-ilon kaltses (i)] stockings

Α
Β
Γ
Δ
Ε
Ζ
Η
Θ
Ι
Κ
Λ
Μ
Ν
Ξ
Ο
Π
Ρ
Σ
Τ
Υ
Φ
Χ
Ψ
Ω

ΝΑ ΦΥΛΑΣΣΕΤΑΙ
ΜΑΚΡΙΑ ΑΠΟ ΠΑΙΔΙΑ
να φυλάσσεται μακριά από
παιδιά keep out of reach of
children

νέα (η) [nea (i)] teenager

νέα (τα) [nea (ta)] news

ΝΕΑ ΖΗΛΑΝΔΙΑ Νέα
Ζηλανδία (η) [Nea Zilanthia
(i)] New Zealand

ΝΕΚΡΟΤΑΦΕΙΟ
νεκροταφείο (το) [nekrotafio
(to)] cemetery

Νέο Έτος (το) [Neo Etos (to)]
New Year

ΝΕΟΖΗΛΑΝΔΕΖΑ
Νεοζηλανδέζα (η)
[Neozilantheza (i)] New
Zealander

ΝΕΟΖΗΛΑΝΔΟΣ
Νεοζηλανδός (ο)
[Neozilanthos (o)] New
Zealander

νέοι (οι) [nei (i)] young
people

νέος (ο) [neos (o)] teenager

νέος [neos] new; young

ΝΕΡΟ νερό (το) [nero (to)]
water

νεροχύτης (ο) [nerokhitis (o)]
sink

νευρικός [nevrikos] nervous

νεφρά (τα) [nefra (ta)] kidneys

νησί (το) [nisi (to)] island

νιπτήρας (ο) [niptiras (o)]
washbasin

νιώθω [nioTHo] feel

ΝΟΕΜΒΡΙΟΣ Νοέμβριος (ο)
[Noemvrios (o)] November

νοικιάζω [nikiazo] rent (verb)

ΝΟΜΑΡΧΙΑ νομαρχία (η)
local government office

νομίζω [nomizo] think

ΝΟΜΟΣ νομός (ο) county

νόμος (ο) [nomos (o)] law

ΝΟΣΟΚΟΜΕΙΟ νοσοκομείο
(το) [nosokomio (to)] hospital

νόστιμο [nostimo] tasty

νοστιμώτατο [nostimotato]
delicious

ΝΟΥΜΕΡΟ νούμερο (το)
[noomero (to)] number

ΝΤΕΜΙ ΠΑΝΣΙΟΝ ντεμί
πανσιόν (η) [ndemi pansion
(i)] half board

ντεπόζιτο (το) [depozito (to)]
tank

ΝΤΗΖΕΛ ντήζελ (το) [dizel
(to)] diesel

ντισκοτέκ (η) [diskotek (i)]
disco

ντιστριμπυτέρ (το) [distribiter
(to)] distributor

ντουλάπι (το) [doolapi (to)]
cupboard

ΝΤΟΥΣ ντους (το) [doos (to)]
shower (in bathroom)

ΝΤΡΑΙΒ - ΙΝ ντραιβ - ιν
drive-in

ντροπαλός [dropalos] shy

ντύνομαι [dinomeh] dress
(oneself)

ντύνω [dino] dress (verb:
someone)

νύφη (η) [nifi (i)] daughter-in-
law; sister-in-law; bride

νύχι (το) [nikhi (to)] fingernail

νυχοκόπτης (ο) [nikhokoptis
(o)] nail clippers

νύχτα (η) [nikhta (i)] night
ΝΥΧΤΕΡΙΝΟ ΚΕΝΤΡΟ
νυχτερινό κέντρο [nikhterino kedro] nightclub
νυχτικό (το) [nikhtiko (to)] nightdress
νωρίς [noris] early

Ξ

ξαδέλφη (η) [xathelfi (i)] cousin
ξάδελφος (ο) [xathelfos (o)] cousin
ξανά [xana] again
ξανθός [xanthos] blond
ξαπλώνω [xaplono] lie down
ξαφνικά [xafnika] suddenly
ξεκουράζομαι [xekoorazomeh] relax
ξεναγός (ο/η) [xenagos (o/i)] guide
ΞΕΝΟΔΟΧΕΙΟ ξενοδοχείο (το) [xenothokhio (to)] hotel
ξένος [xenos] foreign
ΞΕΝΩΝΑΣ ξενώνας (ο) [xenonas (o)] guesthouse
ΞΕΝΩΝΑΣ ΝΕΟΤΗΤΑΣ ξενώνας νεότητας [xenonas neotitas] youth hostel
ΞΕΝΩΝΑΣ ΝΕΩΝ ξενώνας νέων [xenonas neon] youth hostel
ΞΕΠΟΥΛΗΜΑ ξεπούλημα closing-down sale
ξέρω [xero] know
δεν ξέρω [then xero] I don't know
ξεφωνίζω [xefonizo] scream

(verb)
ξεχνώ [xekhno] leave (verb); forget
ξεχωριστά [xekhorista] separately
ξηρός [xiros] dry
ξοδεύω [xothevo] spend
ξύλο (το) [xilo (to)] wood
ξινός [xinos] sour
ξυπνάω [xipnao] wake up
ξυπνητήρι (το) [xipnitiri (to)] alarm clock
ξύπνιος [xipnios] awake
ξυραφάκι (το) [xirafaki (to)] razor
ξυρίζομαι [xirizomeh] shave (verb)
ξύρισμα (το) [xirisma (to)] shave
ξυριστική μηχανή (η) [xiristiki mikhani (i)] electric shaver

Ο

ο [o] the
Ο.Α. Olympic Airways
Ο/Γ ferry
ογδόντα [ogthoda] eighty
όγδοος [ogthoos] eighth
οδηγάω [othigao] drive
οδηγός (ο/η) [othigos (o/i)] driver
ΟΔΙΚΑ ΕΡΓΑ οδικά έργα roadworks
ΟΔΟΝΤΙΑΤΡΟΣ
οδοντίατρος (ο/η) [othodiatros (o/i)] dentist
οδοντόβουρτσα (η) [othodovoortsa (i)] toothbrush

A
B
Γ
Δ
E
Z
H
Θ
I
K
Λ
M
N
Ξ
O
Π
P
Σ
T
Y
Φ
X
Ψ
Ω

ΟΔΟΝΤΟΓΙΑΤΡΟΣ
οδοντογιατρός (ο/η)
[othodoyatros (o/i)] dentist
ΟΔΟΝΤΙΑΤΡΕΙΟ
οδοντιατρείο (το)
[othodiatrio (to)] dentist's
ΟΔΟΝΤΟΚΡΕΜΑ
οδοντόκρεμα (η)
[othodokrema (i)] toothpaste
ΟΔΟΣ οδός (η) [othos (i)]
road, street
ΟΔΟΣ ΑΝΕΥ ΣΗΜΑΝΣΕΩΣ
ΣΕ ΜΗΚΟΣ ... ΧΙΛ. οδός
άνευ σημάνσεως σε μήκος
... χιλ no road markings for
... kms
οδυνηρός [othiniros] painful
όζα (η) [oza (i)] nail polish
Ο.Η.Ε. UN
ΟΧΙ ΕΠΙΤΑΓΕΣ όχι
επιταγές no cheques/checks
οι [i] the
οικογένεια (η) [ikoyenia (i)]
family
ΟΚΤΩΒΡΙΟΣ Οκτώβριος (ο)
[Oktovrios (o)] October
όλα [ola] all
όλα καλά [ola kala] that'll do
nicely, everything's fine
όλα πληρωμένα [ola
pliromena] all inclusive
όλες, όλη [oles, oli] all
ΟΛΙΣΘΗΡΟ ΟΔΟΣΤΡΩΜΑ
ολισθηρό οδόστρωμα
slippery road surface
όλο [olo] all
όλοι [oli] everyone; all
ολόκληρος [olokliros] whole
όλος [olos] all

Ο.Λ.Π. Piraeus Port
Authorities
ΟΛΥΜΠΙΑΚΗ
ΑΕΡΟΠΟΡΙΑ Ολυμπιακή
Αεροπορία Olympic
Airways
ομάδα (η) [omatha (i)] group;
team
ομάδα αίματος (η) [omatha
ematos (i)] blood group
ομίχλη (η) [omikhli (i)] fog
όμοιος [omios] similar
όμορφος [omorfos] fine,
beautiful
ομοφυλόφιλος (ο) [omofilofilos
(o)] gay
ομπρέλλα (η) [ombrella (i)]
umbrella
όνειρο (το) [oniro (to)] dream
ΟΝΟΜΑ όνομα (το) [onoma
(to)] name; first name
οπά! [opa!] watch it!
ΟΠΕΡΑ όπερα (η) [opera (i)]
opera
όπισθεν (η) [opisTHen (i)]
reverse (gear)
όπλο (το) [oplo (to)] gun; rifle
ΟΠΤΙΚΑ οπτικά (τα) [optika
(ta)] optician's
ΟΠΤΙΚΟΣ οπτικός (ο)
[optikos (o)] optician
ΟΠΩΡΟΠΩΛΕΙΟ
οπωροπωλείο (το)
[oporopolio (to)] grocer's
όπως [opos] like; as
όπως και νάναι [opos keh
naneh] anyway
ΟΡΓΑΝΙΣΜΟΣ
ΗΝΩΜΕΝΩΝ ΕΘΝΩΝ

Οργανισμός Ηνωμένων Εθνών United Nations Organization

οργανωμένη εκδρομή (η) [organomeni ekthromi (i)] package tour

οργανώνω [organono] organize

όρεξη (η) [orexi (i)] appetite καλή όρεξη! [kali orexi!] enjoy your meal!, bon appetit!

ΟΡΘΙΩΝ ορθίων standing

ΟΡΙΟ ΤΑΧΥΤΗΤΑΣ όριο ταχύτητας (το) speed limit

ορίστε; [oristeh?] can I help you?

όροφος (ο) [orofos (o)] floor, storey

ΟΡΥΚΤΕΛΑΙΟ ορυκτέλαιο (το) [orikteleo (to)] engine oil

ορχήστρα (η) [orkhistra (i)] orchestra

Ο.Σ.Ε. Greek Railways

όταν [otan] when

Ο.Τ.Ε. Greek Telecommunications Company

ότι [oti] that

οτιδήποτε [otithipoteh] anything

Ο.Υ. water authorities

Ουαλλή (η) [Ooali (i)] Welshwoman

ΟΥΑΛΛΙΑ Ουαλλία (η) [Ooalia (i)] Wales

Ουαλικός [Ooalikos] Welsh (adj)

Ουαλλός (ο) [Ooalos (o)] Welshman

ΟΥΖΕΡΙ ουζερί [oozeri] bar serving ouzo and beer with snacks or full meals

ούλο (το) [oolo (to)] gum (in mouth)

ΟΥΡΑ ουρά (η) [oora (i)] queue; tail; queue here κάνω ουρά [kano oora] queue (verb)

ουρανός (ο) [ooranos (o)] sky

ούτε ... ούτε ... [oote ... oote ...] neither ... nor ...

ΟΦΘΑΛΜΙΑΤΡΟΣ οφθαλμίατρος (ο/η) eye specialist

όχημα (το) [okhima (to)] vehicle

ΟΧΙ όχι [okhi] no; not όχι άλλο [okhi allo] no more

ΟΧΙ ΥΠΕΡΑΣΤΙΚΑ όχι υπεραστικά no long-distance calls

οχτώ [okhto] eight

Π

ΠΑΓΟΣ πάγος (ο) [pagos (o)] ice

παγωτό ξυλάκι [pagoto xilaki] ice lolly

πάει: πώς πάει; [pos pai?] how are things?

ΠΑΖΑΡΙ παζάρι (το) [pazari (to)] bazaar

ΠΑΘΟΛΟΓΟΣ παθολόγος (ο/η) [paTHologos (o/i)] doctor, general practitioner

ΠΑΙΔΙ παιδί (το) [pethi (to)] child

A
B
Γ
Δ
E
Z
H
Θ
I
K
Λ
M
N
Ξ
O
Π
P
Σ
T
Y
Φ
X
Ψ
Ω

ΠΑΙΔΙΑΤΡΟΣ παιδίατρος
(ο/η) paediatrician
ΠΑΙΔΙΚΑ παιδικά (τα)
[pethika (ta)] children's wear
ΠΑΙΔΙΚΑ ΕΙΔΗ παιδικά
είδη (τα) [pethika ithi (ta)]
children's department
ΠΑΙΔΙΚΑ ΕΣΩΡΟΥΧΑ
παιδικά εσώρουχα [pethika
esorookha] children's
underwear
ΠΑΙΔΙΚΑ ΦΟΡΜΑΚΙΑ
παιδικά φορμάκια [pethika
formakia] babywear,
toddlers' clothes
ΠΑΙΔΙΚΟ παιδικό [pethiko]
children's (adj)
παίζω [pezo] play (verb)
παίρνω [perno] get; take
παίρνω τηλέφωνο [perno
tilefono] phone (verb)
ΠΑΙΧΝΙΔΙ παιχνίδι (το)
[pekhnithi (to)] game; toy
ΠΑΚΕΤΟ πακέτο (το)
[paketo (to)] package; packet
ΠΑΛΑΙΟΠΩΛΕΙΟ
παλαιοπωλείο (το)
[paleopolio (to)] antique shop
παλαιός [paleos] old, ancient,
antique
παλάτι (το) [palati (to)] palace
παλίρροια (η) [paliria (i)] tide
παλτό (το) [palto (to)] coat
πάνα (η) [pana (i)] nappy,
diaper
ΠΑΝΕΠΙΣΤΗΜΙΟ
πανεπιστήμιο (το)
[panepistimio (to)] university
ΠΑΝΗΓΥΡΙ πανηγύρι (το)

[paniyiri (to)] fair, funfair
πανί (το) [pani (to)] sail
ΠΑΝ/ΜΙΟ παν/μιο
university
ΠΑΝΣΙΟΝ πανσιόν (η)
[pansion (i)] guesthouse
πάντα [pada] always; still
πανταλόνι (το) [padaloni (to)]
trousers, (US) pants
παντζούρια (τα) [padzooria
(ta)] shutters
ΠΑΝΤΟΠΩΛΕΙΟ
παντοπωλείο (το) [padopolio
(to)] grocery store
πάντοτε [padoteh] always
παντού [padoo] everywhere
παντόφλες (οι) [padofles (i)]
slippers
παντρεμένος [padremenos]
married
παντρεμένη [padremeni]
married
πάνω [pano] on; up; upstairs
πάνω από [pano apo] above
παξιμάδι (το) [paximathi (to)]
nut (for bolt)
παπάς (ο) [papas (o)] priest
πάπια (η) [papia (i)] duck
πάπλωμα (το) [paploma (to)]
quilt
παπούτσι (το) [papootsi (to)]
shoe
παππούς (ο) [pappoos (o)]
grandfather
παραγγελία (η) [parangelia (i)]
message
παραγγέλνω [paragelno] order
(verb: in restaurant)
παράδειγμα (το) [parathigma

(to)] example
παραδείγματος χάρι [parathigmatos khari] for example

παράδοση (η) [parathosi (i)] tradition

παραδοσιακός [parathosiakos] traditional

παράθυρο (το) [paraTHiro (to)] window

παρακαλώ [parakalo] please; excuse me; don't mention it
παρακαλώ; [parakalo?] can I help you?

ΠΑΡΑΚΑΜΠΤΗΡΙΟΣ παρακαμπτήριος (η) diversion

ΠΑΡΑΛΑΒΗ ΑΠΟΣΚΕΥΩΝ παραλαβή αποσκευών (η) [paralavi aposkevon (i)] baggage claim

ΠΑΡΑΛΙΑ παραλία (η) [paralia (i)] beach
κοντά στην παραλία [koda stin paralia] at the seaside

παραμάνα (η) [paramana (i)] safety pin

παραμένω [parameno] stay (verb), remain

παράξενος [paraxenos] strange

παραπονούμαι [paraponoomeh] complain

ΠΑΡΑΣΚΕΥΗ Παρασκευή (η) [Paraskevi (i)] Friday

παρατηρώ [paratiro] watch (verb)

παρατσούκλι (το) [paratsookli (to)] nickname

παρεξήγηση (η) [parexiyisi (i)] misunderstanding

παρκάρω [parkaro] park (verb)

ΠΑΡΚΙΝΓΚ πάρκινγκ (το) [parking (to)] car park, parking lot

πάρκο (το) [parko (to)] park

ΠΑΡΟΔΟΣ πάροδος (η) [parothos (i)] side street

παρπρίζ (το) [parpriz (to)] windscreen

πάρτυ (το) [parti (to)] party, celebration

παστίλιες λαιμού (οι) [pastilies lemoo (i)] throat pastilles

Πάσχα (το) [Paskha (to)] Easter

πατέρας (ο) [pateras (o)] father

πατερίτσες (οι) [pateritses (i)] crutches

πάτωμα (το) [patoma (to)] floor (of room)

ΠΑΥΣΙΠΟΝΟ παυσίπονο (το) [pafsipono (to)] painkiller

πάχος (το) [pakhos (to)] fat (on meat)

παχύς [pakhis] fat; thick

πάω [pao] go (verb)

πεζοδρόμιο (το) [pezothromio (to)] pavement, sidewalk

ΠΕΖΟΔΡΟΜΟΣ πεζόδρομος (ο) pedestrian precinct

ΠΕΖΟΙ πεζοί pedestrians

πεθαίνω [peTHeno] die

πεθαμένος [peTHamenos] dead

πεθερά (η) [peTHera (i)] mother-in-law

πεθερός (ο) [peTHeros (o)] father-in-law

πειράζει [pirazi] it matters

θα σε πείραζε αν ...; [THa seh pirazeh an ...?] do you mind if I ...?

δεν πειράζει [then pirazi] it doesn't matter

ΠΕΙΡΑΙΑΣ Πειραιάς [Pireas] Piraeus

ΠΕΜΠΤΗ Πέμπτη (η) [Pempti (i)] Thursday

πέμπτος [pemptos] fifth

πενήντα [penida] fifty

ΠΕΝΗΝΤΑΡΙΚΟ πενηντάρικο (το) [penidariko (to)] 50-drachma coin or note/bill

πενικιλλίνη (η) [penikilini (i)] penicillin

πέννα (η) [pena (i)] pen

πένσα (η) [pensa (i)] pliers

ΠΕΝΤΑΚΟΣΑΡΙΚΟ πεντακοσάρικο (το) [pedakosariko (to)] 500-drachma note/bill

πέντε [pedeh] five

πέος (το) [peos (to)] penis

περάστε [perasteh] come in; come back

ΠΕΡΙΕΧΟΜΕΝΟ περιεχόμενο contains

περίμενε [perimeneh] wait

περιμένω [perimeno] wait (for); expect

ΠΕΡΙΟΔΙΚΟ περιοδικό (το) [periothiko (to)] magazine

περίοδος (η) [periothos (i)] period

περιοχή (η) [periokhi (i)] area

περίπατος (ο) [peripatos (o)] walk

πάω περίπατο [pao peripato] go for a walk

περίπου [peripoo] about, approximately

ΠΕΡΙΠΤΕΡΟ περίπτερο [periptero] newspaper kiosk

ΣΕ ΠΕΡΙΠΤΩΣΗ ΑΝΑΓΚΗΣ ΣΠΑΣΤΕ ΤΟ ΤΖΑΜΙ σε περίπτωση ανάγκης σπάστε το τζάμι [seh periptosi anangis spasteh to tzami] in emergency break glass

περισσότερο [perisotero] more, most (of)

περισσότερος [perisoteros] more, most (of)

ΠΕΡΜΑΝΑΝΤ περμανάντ (η) [permanant (i)] perm

περνάω [pernao] cross, go through

περπατάω [perpatao] walk (verb)

πέρσυ [persi] last year

πετάλι (το) [petali (to)] pedal

πετάω [petao] throw away (verb)

πέτρα (η) [petra (i)] stone

πετσέτα (η) [petseta (i)] napkin; towel

πετσέτα κουζίνας [petseta koozinas] tea towel

πετώ [peto] fly (verb)

πέφτω [pefto] fall (verb)

πηγή (η) [piyi (i)] fountain

πηγούνι (το) [pigooni (to)] chin

πηδάω [pithao] jump (verb)

πηρούνι (το) [pirooni (to)] fork

πιάνω [piano] catch (verb)

πιατάκι (το) [piataki (to)] saucer

πιατικά (τα) [piatika (ta)] crockery

πιάτο (το) [piato (to)] dish; plate

ΠΙΕΣΗ ΑΙΜΑΤΟΣ πίεση αίματος (η) blood pressure

πιθανώς [piThanos] probably

πικάντικος [pikadikos] spicy

πικάπ (το) [pikap (to)] record player

πικνίκ (το) [piknik (to)] picnic

πικρός [pikros] bitter

πιλότος (ο) [pilotos (o)] pilot

πινακίδες (οι) [pinakithes (i)] number plates

ΠΙΝΑΚΟΘΗΚΗ πινακοθήκη (η) [pinakoTHiki (i)] art gallery

πινγκ-πονγκ (το) [ping-pong (to)] table tennis

πινέλο (το) [pinelo (to)] paintbrush

πινέλο γιά ξύρισμα [pinelo ya xirisma] shaving brush

πίνω [pino] drink (verb)

πίπα (η) [pipa (i)] pipe (for smoking)

ΠΙΣΙΝΑ πισίνα (η) [pisina (i)] swimming pool

πιστεύω [pistevo] believe

πιστολάκι (το) [pistolaki (to)] hairdryer

πιστόλι (το) [pistoli (to)] gun, pistol

πιστοποιητικό (το) [pistopiitiko (to)] certificate

ΠΙΣΤΩΤΙΚΗ ΚΑΡΤΑ πιστωτική κάρτα (η) [pistotiki karta (i)] credit card

πίσω [piso] back; behind

πίσω φώτα (τα) [piso fota (ta)] rear lights

ΠΙΤΣΑΡΙΑ πιτσαρία (η) [pitsaria (i)] pizzeria

πλαστική σακούλα (η) [plastiki sakoola (i)] plastic bag

πλαστικός [plastikos] plastic

ΠΛΑΤΕΙΑ πλατεία (η) [platia (i)] square (in town); stalls (in theatre)

πλάτη (η) [plati (i)] back (of person)

πλατύς [platis] wide

ΠΛΑΤΦΟΡΜΑ πλατφόρμα (η) [platforma (i)] platform, (US) track

πλέκω [pleko] knit

πλένομαι [plenomeh] wash (oneself)

πλένω [pleno] wash (verb: something)

πλευρά (η) [plevra (i)] side

πλευρό (το) [plevro (to)] rib

πληγή (η) [pliyi (i)] wound

πλήθος (το) [pliTHos (to)] crowd

ΠΛΗΡΕΣ πλήρες no vacancies, full

ΠΛΗΡΟΦΟΡΙΕΣ πληροφορίες (οι) [plirofories (i)] information; directory enquiries

ΠΛΗΡΩΜΑ πλήρωμα (το) crew

Α
Β
Γ
Δ
Ε
Ζ
Η
Θ
Ι
Κ
Λ
Μ
Ν
Ξ
Ο
Π
Ρ
Σ
Τ
Υ
Φ
Χ
Ψ
Ω

πληρώνω [pli**rono**] pay (verb)
πλοίο (το) [pl**io** (to)] boat, ship
πλούσιος [pl**oo**sios] rich
πλυντήριο (το) [pli**di**rio (to)]
    washing machine
ΠΛΥΝΤΗΡΙΟ
    ΑΥΤΟΚΙΝΗΤΩΝ
    πλυντήριο αυτοκινήτων car
    wash
ΠΛΥΝΤΗΡΙΟ ΡΟΥΧΩΝ
    πλυντήριο ρούχων [pli**di**rio
    r**oo**khon] launderette,
    laundromat
ΠΛΥΣΙΜΟ ΜΕ ΤΟ ΧΕΡΙ
    πλύσιμο με το χέρι
    handwash only
πλύσιμο των πιάτων (το)
    [pl**i**simo ton pi**a**ton (to)]
    washing up
πνεύμονες (οι) [pn**ev**mones (i)]
    lungs
ποδηλασία (η) [pothila**si**a (i)]
    cycling
ποδηλάτης (ο/η) [pothil**a**tis (o/
    i)] cyclist
ΠΟΔΗΛΑΤΟ ποδήλατο (το)
    [poth**i**lato (to)] bicycle
πόδι (το) [p**o**thi (to)] foot; leg
    με τα πόδια [meh ta p**o**thia]
    on foot
ποδόσφαιρο (το) [poth**o**sfero
    (to)] football
ποιά; [pi**a**?] who?
ποιανού; [pian**oo**?] whose?
ποιό; [pi**o**?] which?
ποιός; [pi**os**?] who?
    ποιός είναι; [pi**os** ineh?] who
    is it?
πόλεμος (ο) [p**o**lemos (o)] war

πόλη (η) [p**o**li (i)] city, town
πολιτεία (η) [poli**ti**a (i)] state
πολιτικά (τα) [politik**a** (ta)]
    politics
πολιτικός [politik**os**] political;
    politician
πολλά, πολλές, πολλή,
    πολλοί [pol**a**, pol**es**, pol**i**, pol**i**]
    many, a lot (of)
πολύ [pol**i**] a lot of; very; too
    much
    πάρα πολύ [p**a**ra pol**i**] too
    much; very much
πολυσύχναστος
    [polisi**khnastos**] busy (place)
πολύς [pol**is**] a lot (of)
ΠΟΛΥΤΕΛΕΙΑΣ
    πολυτελείας luxury class,
    four-star (hotel)
πονάει [pon**ai**] hurt
πονόδοντος (ο) [pono**thodos**
    (o)] toothache
πονοκέφαλος (ο) [ponok**efalos**
    (o)] headache
πόνος (ο) [p**o**nos (o)] ache,
    pain
ποντίκι (το) [pod**i**ki (to)]
    mouse
πόνυ (το) [p**o**ni (to)] pony
πορεία (η) [por**i**a (i)] route
πόρτα (η) [p**o**rta (i)] door
πορτ-μπαγκάζ (το) [port-bang**az**
    (to)] boot (car), (US) trunk
πορτ-μπε-μπέ (το) [port-be-b**e**
    (to)] carrycot
πορτοκαλί [portokal**i**] orange
    (colour)
πορτοφολάς (ο) [portofol**as** (o)]
    pickpocket

πορτοφόλι (το) [portofoli (to)] wallet

πόσα;, πόσες;, [posa?, poses?] how many?

ΠΟΣΙΜΟ ΝΕΡΟ πόσιμο νερό (το) [posimo nero (to)] drinking water

πόσο; [poso?] how much?

πόσοι; [posi?] how many?

πόστερ (το) [poster (to)] poster

ΠΟΣΤ ΡΕΣΤΑΝΤ ποστ ρεστάντ [post restant] poste restante

ποτάμι (το) [potami (to)] river

ποτέ [poteh] never

πότε; [poteh?] when?

έχετε ποτέ ...; [ekheteh poteh ...?] have you ever ...?

ποτήρι (το) [potiri (to)] glass

ΠΟΤΟΠΩΛΕΙΟ ποτοπωλείο (το) [potopolio (to)] off-licence, liquor store

που [poo] who, which, that

πού; [poo?] where?

πούδρα ταλκ (η) [poothra talk (i)] talcum powder

πουθενά [pooTHena] nowhere

πουκάμισο (το) [pookamiso (to)] shirt

πουλί (το) [pooli (to)] bird

ΠΟΥΛΜΑΝ πούλμαν (το) [poolman (to)] bus, coach

πουλόβερ (το) [poolover (to)] jumper

πουλώ [poolo] sell

πούρο (το) [pooro (to)] cigar

πράγμα (το) [pragma (to)] thing

πραγματικά [pragmatika] really

πρακτικός [praktikos] practical

πρακτορείο (το) [praktorio (to)] agency

ΠΡΑΚΤΟΡΕΙΟ ΕΦΗΜΕΡΙΔΩΝ πρακτορείο εφημερίδων newsagent, news vendor

ΠΡΑΚΤΟΡΕΙΟ ΛΕΩΦΟΡΕΙΩΝ πρακτορείο λεωφορείων [praktorio leoforion] bus station

πράσινος [prasinos] green

ΠΡΑΤΗΡΙΟ ΒΕΝΖΙΝΗΣ πρατήριο βενζίνης (το) [pratirio venzinis (to)] petrol station, gas station

πρέπει να ... [prepi na ...] I must ...

ΠΡΕΣΒΕΙΑ πρεσβεία (η) [presvia (i)] embassy

πρησμένος [prismenos] swollen

πρίγκηπας (ο) [pringipas (o)] prince

πριγκίπισσα (η) [pringipisa (i)] princess

πρίζα (η) [priza (i)] socket; plug

πρίζα ταυ (η) [priza taf (i)] adaptor

πριν [prin] before; ago

πριν τρεις μέρες [prin tris meres] three days ago

προάστια (τα) [proastia (ta)] suburbs

πρόβατο (το) [provato (to)] sheep

πρόβλημα (το) [provlima (to)]

problem

ΠΡΟΒΛΗΤΑ προβλήτα (η)
[provlita (i)] quay

προβολείς (οι) [provolis (i)]
headlights

ΠΡΟΓΕΥΜΑ πρόγευμα (το)
[proyevma (to)] breakfast

πρόγονος (ο/η) [progonos (o/i)]
ancestor

ΠΡΟΓΡΑΜΜΑ πρόγραμμα
(το) [programa (to)]
timetable, (US) schedule;
programme

προκαταβάλλω [prokatavalo]
advance (verb)

προκαταβολικά [prokatavolika]
in advance

ΠΡΟΞΕΝΕΙΟ προξενείο
(το) [proxenio (to)] consulate

ΠΡΟΟΡΙΣΜΟΣ προορισμός
[pro-orismos] destination

προσβάλλω [prosvalo] offend

ΠΡΟΣ ΓΚΑΡΑΖ προς
γκαράζ to car deck

ΠΡΟΣΔΕΘΗΤΕ προσδεθήτε
fasten your seat belt

προσεκτικός [prosektikos]
careful

πρόσεξε! [prosexeh!] look out!

ΠΡΟΣΕΧΕ! πρόσεχε!
[prosekheh!] look out!

προσέχω [prosekho] take care
of

ΠΡΟΣΕΧΩΣ προσεχώς
coming soon

πρόσθετο (το) [prosTHeto (to)]
supplementary

προσκαλώ [proskalo] invite

πρόσκληση (η) [prosklisi (i)]

invitation

ΠΡΟΣ ΟΡΟΦΟΥΣ προς
ορόφους to all floors

ΠΡΟΣΟΧΗ! προσοχή!
caution!

ΠΡΟΣΟΧΗ ΑΡΓΑ προσοχή
αργά caution: slow

ΠΡΟΣΟΧΗ ΕΞΟΔΟΣ
ΟΧΗΜΑΤΩΝ προσοχή
έξοδος οχημάτων caution:
vehicle exit

ΠΡΟΣΟΧΗ ΕΥΦΛΕΚΤΟΝ
προσοχή εύφλεκτον
caution: highly inflammable

ΠΡΟΣΟΧΗ ΚΙΝΔΥΝΟΣ
προσοχή κίνδυνος caution:
danger

προσοχή παρακαλώ [prosokhi
parakalo] attention please

ΠΡΟΣΟΧΗ ΣΚΥΛΟΣ
προσοχή σκύλος beware of
the dog

ΠΡΟΣ ΠΑΡΑΣΚΗΝΙΑ προς
παρασκήνια to dressing
rooms

προσπέκτους (το) [prospektoos
(to)] brochure

προσπερνώ [prosperno]
overtake

προστατεύω [prostatevo]
protect

ΠΡΟΣΤΙΜΟ πρόστιμο (το)
[prostimo (to)] fine

προσφέρω [prosfero] offer
(verb); give

ΠΡΟΣΦΟΡΑ προσφορά
special bargain

πρόσωπο (το) [prosopo (to)]
face

προς [pros] towards

προτείνω [protino] recommend

ΠΡΟΤΕΡΑΙΟΤΗΤΑ προτεραιότητα (η) right of way

προτιμώ [protimo] prefer

προφανής [profanis] obvious

προφέρω [profero] pronounce

προφορά (η) [profora (i)] accent

προφυλακτήρας (ο) [profilaktiras (o)] bumper, fender

ΠΡΟΦΥΛΑΚΤΙΚΑ προφυλακτικά contraceptives

ΠΡΟΦΥΛΑΚΤΙΚΟ προφυλακτικό (το) [profilaktiko (to)] condom

προχτές [prokhtes] the day before yesterday

πρωί (το) [proi (to)] morning το πρωί [to proi] in the morning

ΠΡΩΙΝΟ πρωινό (το) [pro-ino (to)] breakfast

πρώτα [prota] first, firstly

ΠΡΩΤΕΣ ΒΟΗΘΕΙΕΣ πρώτες βοήθειες (οι) [protes voiTHi-es (i)] first aid

ΠΡΩΤΗ ΘΕΣΗ πρώτη θέση first class

πρώτο! [proto!] great!

ΠΡΩΤΟ ΠΑΤΩΜΑ πρώτο πάτωμα (το) [proto patoma (to)] first floor, (US) second floor

πρώτος [protos] first

ΠΡΩΤΟΣ ΟΡΟΦΟΣ πρώτος όροφος [protos orofos] first floor, (US) second floor

Πρωτοχρονιά (η) [Protokhronia (i)] New Year's Day

ΠΤΗΣΕΙΣ ΕΞΩΤΕΡΙΚΟΥ πτήσεις εξωτερικού international flights

ΠΤΗΣΕΙΣ ΕΣΩΤΕΡΙΚΟΥ πτήσεις εσωτερικού domestic flights

ΠΤΗΣΗ πτήση (η) [ptisi (i)] flight

ΠΤΗΣΗ ΤΣΑΡΤΕΡ πτήση τσάρτερ charter flight

πυζάμες (οι) [pizames (i)] pyjamas

πυξίδα (η) [pixitha (i)] compass

πύργος (ο) [pirgos (o)] tower

πυρετός (ο) [piretos (o)] fever

πυρκαγιά (η) [pirkaya (i)] fire

ΠΥΡΟΣΒΕΣΤΗΡ πυροσβεστήρ (ο) fire extinguisher

ΠΥΡΟΣΒΕΣΤΗΡΑΣ πυροσβεστήρας (ο) fire extinguisher

ΠΥΡΟΣΒΕΣΤΙΚΗ ΣΩΛΗΝΑ πυροσβεστική σωλήνα (η) fire hose

ΠΥΡΟΣΒΕΣΤΙΚΗ (ΥΠΗΡΕΣΙΑ) πυροσβεστική (υπηρεσία) (η) [pirosvestiki ipiresia (i)] fire brigade

πυροτεχνήματα (τα) [pirotekhnimata (ta)] fireworks

πυτζάμες (οι) [pitzames (i)]

Α Β Γ Δ Ε Ζ Η Θ Ι Κ Λ Μ Ν Ξ Ο **Π** Ρ Σ Τ Υ Φ Χ Ψ Ω

pyjamas
ΠΩΛΕΙΤΑΙ πωλείται for sale
ΠΩΛΗΣΗ πώληση (η) sale
πώς; [pos?] how?; what?

Ρ

ράβω [ravo] sew
ραδιόφωνο (το) [rathiofono (to)] radio
ραντεβού (το) [randevoo (to)] appointment
ράντζο (το) [radzo (to)] campbed
ΡΑΦΕΙΟ ραφείο (το) [rafio (to)] tailor's
ρεζέρβα (η) [rezerva (i)] spare tyre
ΡΕΣΕΨΙΟΝ ρεσεψιόν (η) [resepsion (i)] reception
ρεσεψιονίστ (ο/η) [resepsionist (o/i)] receptionist
ρε συ! [reh si!] you there!, oy you!
ρεύμα (το) [revma (to)] current; draught
ρευματισμοί (οι) [revmatismi (i)] rheumatism
ρίχνω [rikhno] throw (verb)
ρόδα (η) [rotha (i)] wheel
ροζ [roz] pink
ρόκ (η) [rok (i)] rock music
ρολόι (το) [roloi (to)] clock; watch
ρόμπα (η) [roba (i)] dressing gown
ΡΟΥΦ - ΓΚΑΡΝΤΕΝ Ρουφ -

Γκάρντεν [Roof - Garden] roof garden
ρούχα (τα) [rookha (ta)] clothes
ροχαλίζω [rokhalizo] snore
ρυμούλκα (η) [rimoolka (i)] trailer (for car)
ρυμουλκό [rimoolko] trailer (for car etc)
ρωτώ [roto] ask

Σ

ΣΑΒΒΑΤΟ Σάββατο (το) [Savato (to)] Saturday
σαββατοκύριακο (το) [savatokiriako (to)] weekend
ΣΑΓΙΟΝΑΡΕΣ σαγιονάρες [sayonares] beach sandals, flip-flops
σαγόνι (το) [sagoni (to)] jaw
σακάκι (το) [sakaki (to)] jacket
σακβουαγιάζ (το) [sakvooayaz (to)] hand luggage, hand baggage
σακίδιο (το) [sakithio (to)] rucksack
σάκος (ο) [sakos (o)] backpack, rucksack
ΣΑΛΟΝΙ σαλόνι (το) [saloni (to)] lounge
ΣΑΜΠΟΥΑΝ σαμπουάν (το) [sampooan (to)] shampoo
σαμπρέλα (η) [sabrela (i)] inner tube
σαν [san] like, as
σανδάλια (τα) [santhalia (ta)] sandals
σάουνα (η) [saoona (i)] sauna

σάπιος [sapios] rotten

ΣΑΠΟΥΝΙ ΠΙΑΤΩΝ
σαπούνι πιάτων (το)
[sapooni piaton (to)] washing-up liquid

ΣΑΠΟΥΝΙ σαπούνι (το)
[sapooni (to)] soap

σαράντα [sarada] forty

σας [sas] you; your

σβήνω [svino] switch off
(engine); put out (fire)

ΣΒΗΣΤΕ ΤΗΝ ΜΗΧΑΝΗ
σβήστε την μηχανή switch off engine

σβήστρα (η) [svistra (i)]
rubber, eraser

σγουρά [sgoora] curly

σε [seh] you; to; at; in

σεζ λόνγκ (ή) [sez long (i)]
deckchair

ΣΕΙΡΑ σειρά (η) [sira (i)] row
(of seats)

σελίδα (η) [selitha (i)] page

ΣΕΛΛΟΤΕΗΠ σέλλοτέηπ
(το) [selloteip (to)]
Sellotape®, Scotch tape®

ΣΕΛΦ ΣΕΡΒΙΣ σελφ σέρβις
[self servis] self-service

σεντόνι (το) [sedoni (to)] sheet

σέξυ [sexi] sexy

ΣΕ ΠΕΡΙΠΤΩΣΗ
ΑΝΑΓΚΗΣ ΣΠΑΣΤΕ ΤΟ
ΤΖΑΜΙ σε περίπτωση
ανάγκης σπάστε το τζάμι in emergency break glass

ΣΕΠΤΕΜΒΡΙΟΣ
Σεπτέμβριος (ο) [Septemvrios
(o)] September

ΣΕΡΒΙΕΤΕΣ σερβιέτες (οι)
[servietes (i)] sanitary towels/napkins

σερβιτόρα (η) [servitora (i)]
barmaid; waitress

σερβιτόρος (ο) [servitoros (o)]
waiter

ΣΗΚΩΣΤΕ ΤΟ
ΑΚΟΥΣΤΙΚΟ σηκώστε το ακουστικό lift receiver

σημαδούρα (η) [simathoora (i)]
buoy

σημαία (η) [simea (i)] flag

σημειωματάριο (το)
[simiomatario (to)] notebook

ΣΗΜΕΡΑ σήμερα [simera]
today

ΣΗΜΕΡΟΝ σήμερον
showing today

σήραγγα (η) [siranga (i)]
tunnel

σιγά-σιγά [siga-siga] slowly;
slow down

σίγουρος [sigooros] sure

σίδερο (το) [sithero (to)] iron

σιδερώνω [sitherono] iron
(verb)

ΣΙΔΗΡΟΔΡΟΜΙΚΟΣ
ΣΤΑΘΜΟΣ
σιδηροδρομικός σταθμός
(ο) [sithirothromikos staTHmos
(o)] railway station

σιδηρόδρομος (ο)
[sithirothromos (o)] railway

ΣΙΔΗΡΟΥΡΓΕΙΟ
σιδηρουργείο (το)
[sithirooryio (to)] hardware store

ΣΙΝΕΜΑ σινεμά (το) [sinema
(to)] cinema, movie theater

A
B
Γ
Δ
E
Z
H
Θ
I
K
Λ
M
N
Ξ
O
Π
P
Σ
T
Y
Φ
X
Ψ
Ω

σιωπή (η) [siopi (i)] silence

σκάλα (η) [skala (i)] ladder

ΣΚΑΛΕΣ σκάλες (οι) [skales (i)] stairs

σκέπτομαι [skeptomeh] think

ΣΚΗΝΗ σκηνή (η) [skini (i)] tent

σκιά (η) [skia (i)] shade, shadow

στη σκιά [sti skia] in the shade

ΣΚΙΑ ΜΑΤΙΩΝ σκιά ματιών (η) [skia mation (i)] eye shadow

ΣΚΛΗΡΟΙ ΦΑΚΟΙ σκληροί φακοί (οι) [skliri faki (i)] hard lenses

σκληρός [skliros] hard

ΣΚΟΝΗ ΠΛΥΝΤΗΡΙΟΥ σκόνη πλυντηρίου (η) [skoni plidirioo (i)] washing powder

σκοτεινός [skotinos] dark

σκοτώνω [skotono] kill (verb)

σκουλαρίκια (τα) [skoolarikia (ta)] earrings

σκούπα [skoopa] broom

σκουπίδια (τα) [skoopithia (ta)] rubbish, (US) garbage

σκουπιδοντενεκές (ο) [skoopithodenekes (o)] dustbin, trashcan

σκύλος (ο) [skilos (o)] dog

σκωληκοειδίτις (η) [skoliko-ithitis (i)] appendicitis

ΣΚΩΤΙΑ Σκωτία (η) [Skotia (i)] Scotland

Σκωτσέζικος [Skotsezikos] Scottish

σλάιντ (το) [slaid (to)] slide

σλίπ (το) [slip (to)] underpants; panties

ΣΛΙΠΙΝΓΚ ΜΠΑΓΚ σλίπινγκ μπαγκ (το) [sliping bag (to)] sleeping bag

σοβαρός [sovaros] serious

σοκ (το) [sok (to)] shock

ΣΟΚΟΛΑΤΑ σοκολάτα (η) [sokolata (i)] chocolate

ΣΟΚΟΛΑΤΑ ΓΑΛΑΚΤΟΣ σοκολάτα γάλακτος (η) [sokolata galaktos (i)] milk chocolate

ΣΟΚΟΛΑΤΑΚΙΑ σοκολατάκια (τα) [sokolatakia (ta)] chocolates

σόλα (η) [sola (i)] sole (of shoe)

σόμπα (η) [soba (i)] oil heater

σορτς (το) [sorts (to)] shorts

σου [soo] you; your

σουγιάς (ο) [sooyas (o)] penknife

ΣΟΥΠΕΡ ΒΕΝΖΙΝΗ σούπερ βενζίνη (η) [sooper venzini (i)] four-star petrol, premium

ΣΟΥΠΕΡΜΑΡΚΕΤ σούπερμάρκετ (το) [soopermarket (to)] supermarket

σουτιέν (το) [sootien (to)] bra

ΣΠΑΓΓΟΣ σπάγγος (ο) [spangos (o)] string

σπασμένος [spasmenos] broken

σπάω [spao] break (verb)

σπηλιά (το) [spilia (to)] cave

σπιράλ (το) [spiral (to)] spiral; IUD; incense coil (mosquito repellent)

σπίρτα (τα) [spirta (ta)] matches

σπίτι (το) [spiti (to)] house

στο σπίτι [sto spiti] at home

σπορ (το) [spor (to)] sport

σπουδαίος [spootheos] important

σπρώχνω [sprokhno] push (verb)

σταγόνα (η) [stagona (i)] drop

ΣΤΑΓΟΝΕΣ σταγόνες drops

ΣΤΑΔΙΟ στάδιο (το) [stathio (to)] stadium

ΣΤΑΘΜΟΣ σταθμός (ο) [staTHmos (o)] station

ΣΤΑΘΜΟΣ ΑΝΕΦΟΔΙΑΣΜΟΥ ΘΑΛΑΜΗΓΩΝ σταθμός ανεφοδιασμού θαλαμηγών yacht refuelling station

ΣΤΑΘΜΟΣ ΛΕΩΦΟΡΕΙΩΝ σταθμός λεωφορείων [staTHmos leoforion] bus station

ΣΤΑΘΜΟΣ ΠΡΩΤΩΝ ΒΟΗΘΕΙΩΝ σταθμός πρώτων βοηθειών [staTHmos proton vo-iTHion] first aid post

ΣΤΑΘΜΟΣ ΤΑΞΙ σταθμός ταξί [staTHmos taxi] taxi stand

ΣΤΑΘΜΟΣ ΥΠΕΡΑΣΤΙΚΩΝ ΛΕΩΦΟΡΕΙΩΝ σταθμός υπεραστικών λεωφορείων [staTHmos iperastikon leoforion] bus station (long distance)

ΣΤΑΘΜΟΣ ΧΩΡΟΦΥΛΑΚΗΣ σταθμός χωροφυλακής [staTHmos khorofilakis] police station

σταματάω [stamatao] stop (verb)

ΣΤΑΣΗ στάση (η) [stasi (i)] stop (for bus, train)

ΣΤΑΣΗ ΑΣΤΙΚΩΝ ΣΥΓΚΟΙΝΩΝΙΩΝ στάση αστικών συγκοινωνιών city bus stop

ΣΤΑΣΗ ΛΕΩΦΟΡΕΙΟΥ στάση λεωφορείου bus stop

ΣΤΑΣΗ ΤΑΞΙ στάση ταξί [stasi taxi] taxi stand

ΣΤΑΣΙΣ στάσις (η) [stasis (i)] bus stop

στέγη (η) [steyi (i)] roof

ΣΤΕΓΝΟ ΚΑΘΑΡΙΣΜΑ ΜΟΝΟΝ στεγνό καθάρισμα μόνον dryclean only

ΣΤΕΓΝΟΚΑΘΑΡΙΣΤΗΡΙΟ στεγνοκαθαριστήριο (το) [stegnokaTHaristirio (to)] dry cleaner's

στεγνός [stegnos] dry

στεγνώνω [stegnono] dry (verb)

στέλνω [stelno] send

στενός [stenos] narrow; tight

στενοχώρια (η) [stenokhoria (i)] worry (verb)

στήθος (το) [stiTHos (to)] breast; chest

στην [stin] at; in; to; on

ΣΤΙΒΟΣ στίβος (ο) athletics stadium

στο [sto] at; in; to

στόμα (το) [stoma (to)] mouth

στομάχι (το) [stomakhi (to)]

A
B
Γ
Δ
E
Z
H
Θ
I
K
Λ
M
N
Ξ
O
Π
P
Σ
T
Y
Φ
X
Ψ
Ω

stomach

στον [ston] at; in; to;

ΣΤΟΠ! στοπ! stop!

στριφτό (το) [strifto (to)] hand-rolled cigarette

στρογγυλός [strongilos] round

στρόφαλος (ο) [strofalos (o)] crankshaft

στροφή (η) [strofi (i)] bend

στρώμα (το) [stroma (to)] mattress

στυλό (το) [stilo (to)] biro®

συγγενείς (οι) [singenis (i)] relatives

συγγνώμη [signomi] sorry; excuse me
συγγνώμη; [signomi?] pardon (me)?, sorry?

σύγκρουση (η) [singroosi (i)] crash

συγχαρητήρια! [sinkharitiria!] congratulations!

συγχωρείτε: με συγχωρείτε [meh sinkhoriteh] excuse me

σύζυγος (ο) [sizigos (o)] husband

συκότι (το) [sikoti (to)] liver

συλλαμβάνω [silamvano] arrest

συλλογή (η) [siloyi (i)] collection

συμβαίνω [simveno] happen

συμβουλεύω [simvoolevo] advise

ΣΥΜΠΕΡΙΛΑΜΒΑΝΕΤΑΙ συμπεριλαμβάνεται included

συμπλέκτης (ο) [siblektis (o)] clutch

συμφωνώ [simfono] agree

ΣΥΝΑΓΕΡΜΟΣ συναγερμός (ο) [sinayermos (o)] alarm

συναίσθημα (το) [sinesTHima (to)] feeling

ΣΥΝΑΛΛΑΓΜΑ συνάλλαγμα (το) [sinalagma (to)] foreign exchange

ΣΥΝΑΛΛΑΓΜΑΤΙΚΗ ΙΣΟΤΙΜΙΑ συναλλαγματική ισοτιμία (η) [sinalagmatiki isotimia (i)] exchange rate

συνάντηση (η) [sinadisi (i)] meeting

συναντώ [sinado] meet

συναρπαστικός [sinarpastikos] exciting

συναυλία (η) [sinavlia (i)] concert

ΣΥΝ/ΓΕΙΟ συν/γειο auto repairs

σύνδεση (η) [sinthesi (i)] connection (electrical)

ΣΥΝΕΡΓΕΙΟ (ΑΥΤΟΚΙΝΗΤΩΝ) συνεργείο (αυτοκινήτων) (το) auto repairs

συνήθεια (η) [siniTHia (i)] habit

συνηθισμένος [siniTHismenos] usual

συνήθως [siniTHos] usually

ΣΥΝΘΕΤΙΚΟ συνθετικό synthetic

συννεφιασμένος [sinefiasmenos] cloudy

σύννεφο (το) [sinefo (to)] cloud

συνοδεύω [sinothevo]
accompany
ΣΥΝΟΙΚΙΑ συνοικία (η)
[sinikia (i)] district
συνολικά [sinolika] altogether
σύνορα (τα) [sinora (ta)]
border
συνταγή (η) [sidayi (i)]
prescription; recipe
συνταξιούχος (ο/η)
[sidaxiookhos (o/i)] old-age
pensioner
ΣΥΝΤΗΡΗΤΙΚΟ ΔΙΑΛΥΜΑ
συντηρητικό διάλυμα (το)
[sidiritiko thialima (to)]
soaking solution
σύντομα [sidoma] soon
ΣΥΡΑΤΕ σύρατε pull
σύρμα (το) [sirma (to)] wire
ΣΥΣΤΑΤΙΚΑ συστατικά
ingredients
ΣΥΣΤΗΜΕΝΑ συστημένα
[sistimena] registered mail
συστήνω [sistino] introduce;
recommend
συχνά [sikhna] often
σφήγγα (η) [sfinga (i)] wasp
σφράγισμα (το) [sfrayisma (to)]
filling (in tooth)
σφυρί (το) [sfiri (to)] hammer
σχάρα αυτοκινήτου (η)
[skhara aftokinitoo (i)] roof
rack
σχέδιο (το) [skhethio (to)] plan
σχεδόν [skhethon] almost
σχοινί (το) [skhini (to)] rope
ΣΧΟΛΕΙΟ σχολείο (το)
[skholio (to)] school
σωλήνας (ο) [solinas (o)] pipe

(water)
σώμα (το) [soma (to)] body
ΣΩΣΙΒΙΑ σωσίβια lifejackets
σωστός [sostos] correct

Τ

τα [ta] the; them
ταβάνι (το) [tavani (to)] ceiling
ΤΑΒΕΡΝΑ ταβέρνα (η)
[taverna (i)] restaurant
τακούνι (το) [takooni (to)] heel
(of shoe)
ΤΑΛΗΡΟ τάληρο (το) [taliro
(to)] 5-drachma coin
ΤΑΜΕΙΟ ταμείο (το) [tamio
(to)] box office; cash desk,
till, cashier
ΤΑΜΙΕΥΤΗΡΙΟ
ταμιευτήριο (το) [tami-eftirio
(to)] savings bank
ΤΑΜΠΛΕΤΑ ταμπλέτα (η)
[tableta (i)] tablet
ΤΑΜΠΟΝ ταμπόν (τα)
[tampon (ta)] tampons
τάξη (η) [taxi (i)] class
ΤΑΞΙ ταξί (το) [taxi (to)] taxi
ταξιδεύω [taxithevo] travel
(verb)
ταξίδι (το) [taxithi (to)]
journey, trip
καλό ταξίδι! [kalo taxithi!]
have a good journey!, bon
voyage!
ταξίδι για δουλειές [taxithi ya
thoolies] business trip
ΤΑΞΙΔΙΩΤΙΚΗ ΕΠΙΤΑΓΗ
ταξιδιωτική επιταγή (η)
[taxithiotiki epitayi (i)]

travellers' cheque/check

ΤΑΞΙΔΙΩΤΙΚΟ ΓΡΑΦΕΙΟ
ταξιδιωτικό γραφείο (το)
[taxithiotiko grafio (to)] travel
agent's

τάπα (η) [tapa (i)] plug (in sink)

ΤΑ ΡΕΣΤΑ ΣΑΣ τα ρέστα
σας your change

ΤΑΡΙΦΑ ταρίφα [tarifa] taxi
tariff

τασάκι (το) [tasaki (to)]
ashtray

ταύρος (ο) [tavros (o)] bull

ΤΑΥΤΟΤΗΤΑ ταυτότητα (η)
[taftotita (i)] pass, identity
card

ΤΑΧΥΔΡΟΜΕΙΟ
ταχυδρομείο (το)
[takhithromio (to)] post office

ΤΑΧΥΔΡΟΜΙΚΟΣ
ΤΟΜΕΥΣ ταχυδρομικός
τομεύς (ο) [takhithromikos
tomefs (o)] postcode,
zipcode

ταχυδρόμος (ο) [takhithromos
(o)] postman

ταχυδρομώ [takhithromo] post,
mail (verb)

ταχύτητα (η) [takhititita (i)] gear
(in car)

ταχύτητα (η) [takhititita (i)]
speed

τέλειος [telios] perfect

τελειώνω [teliono] finish (verb)

ΤΕΛΕΥΤΑΙΑ ΠΑΡΑΣΤΑΣΗ
τελευταία παράσταση last
performance

τελευταίος [telefteos] last

τελεφερίκ (το) [teleferik (to)]

cable car

ΤΕΛΟΣ τέλος (το) [telos (to)]
end

ΤΕΛΩΝΕΙΟ Τελωνείο (το)
[Telonio (to)] Customs

τεμπέλης [tebelis] lazy

τέννις (το) [tenis (to)] tennis

τέντα (η) [tenta (i)] tent,
marquee

τέσσερα [tesera] four

ΤΕΤΑΡΤΗ Τετάρτη (η)
[Tetarti (i)] Wednesday

τέταρτο (το) [tetarto (to)]
quarter

τέταρτος [tetartos] fourth

τέχνη (η) [tekhni (i)] art

τεχνητός [tekhnitos] artificial

ΤΕΧΝΗΤΟ ΧΡΩΜΑ
τεχνητό χρώμα artificial
colouring

τζαζ (η) [tzaz (i)] jazz

τζηνς (τα) [tzins (ta)] jeans

τζόγγιγκ (το) [tzoging (to)]
jogging

τη [ti] the

τηγάνι (το) [tigani (to)] frying
pan

τηγανίζω [tiganizo] fry

ΤΗΛΕΓΡΑΦΗΜΑ
τηλεγράφημα (το)
[tilegrafima (to)] telegram

ΤΗΛΕΓΡΑΦΗΜΑΤΑ
τηλεγραφήματα telegrams

ΤΗΛΕΓΡΑΦΙΚΗ ΕΝΤΟΛΗ
τηλεγραφική εντολή
[tilegrafiki entoli] telegram

ΤΗΛΕΚΑΡΤΑ τηλεκάρτα
(η) [tilekarta (i)] phonecard

ΤΗΛΕΟΡΑΣΗ τηλεόραση

(η) [tileorasi (i)] television

ΤΗΛΕΦΩΝΗΜΑ
τηλεφώνημα [tilefonima] call

ΤΗΛΕΦΩΝΗΜΑ
ΚΟΛΛΕΚΤ τηλεφώνημα
κολλέκτ (το) [tilefonima
kollekt (to)] reverse charge
call

ΤΗΛΕΦΩΝΙΚΗ ΕΝΤΟΛΗ
τηλεφωνική εντολή
operator-controlled phone
call

ΤΗΛΕΦΩΝΙΚΟΣ
ΘΑΛΑΜΟΣ τηλεφωνικός
θάλαμος (ο) [tilefonikos
THalamos (o)] phone box

ΤΗΛΕΦΩΝΙΚΟΣ
ΚΑΤΑΛΟΓΟΣ
τηλεφωνικός κατάλογος (ο)
[tilefonikos katalogos (o)]
phone book

ΤΗΛΕΦΩΝΟ τηλέφωνο (το)
[tilefono (to)] phone

ΤΗΛΕΦΩΝΩ τηλεφωνώ
[tilefono] ring, phone (verb)

την [tin] her; on; per; the
την εβδομάδα [tin
evthomatha] per week

της [tis] her; to her; of her

τι; [ti?] what?

ΤΙΜΗ τιμή (η) [timi (i)] price

ΤΙΜΗ ΑΓΟΡΑΣ τιμή αγοράς
buying rate

ΤΙΜΗ ΑΝΕΥ ΠΟΣΟΣΤΩΝ
τιμή άνευ ποσοστών price
exclusive of extras

ΤΙΜΗ ΔΩΜΑΤΙΟΥ τιμή
δωματίου room price

ΤΙΜΗ ΚΑΤ' ΑΤΟΜΟ τιμή

κατ' άτομο price per person

ΤΙΜΗ ΚΛΙΝΗΣ τιμή κλίνης
price per bed

ΤΙΜΗ ΜΕΤΑ ΠΟΣΟΣΤΩΝ
τιμή μετά ποσοστών price
inclusive of extras

ΤΙΜΗ ΠΩΛΗΣΗΣ τιμή
πώλησης selling rate

τίμιος [timios] honest

τιμόνι (το) [timoni (to)]
steering wheel

τίνος; [tinos?] whose

τίποτε [tipoteh] nothing

ΤΙΠΟΤΕ ΠΡΟΣ ΔΗΛΩΣΗ
τίποτε προς δήλωση
nothing to declare

τις [tis] them

ΤΜΗΜΑ τμήμα (το) [tmima
(to)] department

το [to] in; it; the; per

τοις εκατό [tis ekato] per cent

ΤΟΙΣ ΜΕΤΡΗΤΟΙΣ τοις
μετρητοίς cash only, no
credit cards

τοίχος (ο) [tikhos (o)] wall

ΤΟ ΚΑΤΑΣΤΗΜΑ
ΜΕΤΑΦΕΡΘΗΚΕ ΕΙΣ ...
το κατάστημα μεταφέρθηκε
εις ... we have moved to ...

ΤΟ ΚΟΜΜΑΤΙ το κομμάτι
per item

ΤΟΚΟΣ τόκος (ο) [tokos (o)]
interest

τολμάω [tolmao] dare (verb)

τον [ton] him; the

ΤΟΞΙΚΟ τοξικό toxic

ΤΟΠΙΚΗ ΩΡΑ τοπική ώρα
local time

ΤΟΠΙΚΟ (ΤΗΛΕΦΩΝΗΜΑ)

A
B
Γ
Δ
E
Z
H
Θ
I
K
Λ
M
N
Ξ
O
Π
P
Σ
T
Y
Φ
X
Ψ
Ω

τοπικό (τηλεφώνημα) (το)
[topiko tilefonima (to)] local
call

τοπίο (το) [topio (to)]
landscape

τόσο [toso] so (much); that
much

τότε [toteh] then

του [too] his; its; to him

ΤΟΥΑΛΕΤΑ τουαλέτα (η)
[tooaleta (i)] toilet, rest room

ΤΟΥΑΛΕΤΑ ΤΩΝ
ΓΥΝΑΙΚΩΝ τουαλέτα των
γυναικών (η) [tooaleta ton
yinekon (i)] ladies' toilet,
ladies' room

ΤΟΥΑΛΕΤΕΣ τουαλέτες
[tooaletes] toilets, rest room

τουλάχιστον [toolakhiston] at
least

του οποίου [too opioo] whose

τουρίστας (ο) [tooristas (o)]
tourist

ΤΟΥΡΙΣΤΙΚΗ
ΑΣΤΥΝΟΜΙΑ Τουριστική
Αστυνομία (η) [Tooristiki
Astinomia (i)] Tourist Police

τουριστικός οδηγός (ο)
[tooristikos othigos (o)]
guidebook

τουρίστρια (η) [tooristria (i)]
tourist

ΤΟΥΡΚΑΛΑ τουρκάλα (η)
[toorkala (i)] Turk

ΤΟΥΡΚΙΑ Τουρκία (η)
[Toorkia (i)] Turkey

Τούρκος (ο) [Toorkos (o)]
Turk

ΤΟΥΡΚΙΚΟΣ Τουρκικός

[Toorkikos] Turkish (adj)

τους [toos] them; to them

τραβάω [travao] pull (verb)

τραγούδι (το) [tragoothi (to)]
song

τραγουδώ [tragootho] sing

ΤΡΑΠΕΖΑΡΙΑ τραπεζαρία
(η) [trapezaria (i)] dining
room

ΤΡΑΠΕΖΑ τράπεζα (η)
[trapeza (i)] bank

τραπέζι (το) [trapezi (to)] table

τραπεζομάντηλο (το)
[trapezomadilo (to)] tablecloth

τραυματίζομαι [travmatizomeh]
hurt, injure

τραυματισμένος
[travmatismenos] injured

τρελλός [trelos] mad

ΤΡΕΝΟ τρένο (το) [treno
(to)] train

τρέχω [trekho] run (verb)

τρία [tria] three

τριακόσια [triakosia] three
hundred

τριάντα [triada] thirty

τριαντάφυλλο (το) [triadafilo
(to)] rose

ΤΡΙΚΛΙΝΟ ΔΩΜΑΤΙΟ
τρίκλινο δωμάτιο (το)
[triklino thomatio (to)] triple
room

ΤΡΙΤΗ Τρίτη (η) [Triti (i)]
Tuesday

ΤΡΙΤΗ ΘΕΣΗ τρίτη θέση
third class

τρίτος [tritos] third

τρόλλεϋ (το) [troleh-i (to)]
trolley, trolleybus

τρομερός [tromeros]
tremendous
ΤΡΟΦΗ ΓΙΑ
ΔΙΑΒΗΤΙΚΟΥΣ τροφή γιά
διαβητικούς [trofi ya
thiavitikoos] diabetic foods
τροφική δηλητηρίαση (η)
[trofiki thilitiriasi (i)] food
poisoning
ΤΡΟΧΑΙΑ τροχαία (η)
traffic police
τροχονόμος (ο) [trokhonomos
(o)] traffic warden
τροχόσπιτο (το) [trokhospito
(to)] caravan, (US) trailer
ΤΡΟΧΟΣΠΙΤΑ τροχόσπιτα
(το) caravans, (US) trailers
τρύπα (η) [tripa (i)] hole
τρώω [troo] eat
τρώω [troo] have dinner
τσαγιέρα (η) [tsayera (i)]
teapot
ΤΣΑΓΚΑΡΗΣ τσαγκάρης (ο)
[tsangaris (o)] shoe repairer's
τσάντα (η) [tsada (i)] bag;
handbag, (US) purse
ΤΣΑΝΤΕΣ ΜΠΑΝΙΟΥ
τσάντες μπάνιου beach bags
τσέπη (η) [tsepi (i)] pocket
ΤΣΙΓΑΡΟ τσιγάρο (το)
[tsigaro (to)] cigarette
τσίμπημα (το) [tsibima (to)]
bite (insect)
τσιμπιδάκι (το) [tsibithaki (to)]
tweezers
τσιμπώ [tsibo] sting (verb)
ΤΣΙΠΣ τσιπς (τα) [tsips (ta)]
crisps, (US) potato chips
ΤΣΙΧΛΑ τσίχλα (η) [tsikhla

(i)] chewing gum
τσόκ (το) [tsok (to)] choke (on
car)
τσούχτρα (η) [tsookhtra (i)]
jellyfish
τυλίγω [tiligo] wrap (verb)
τυφλός [tiflos] blind
τύχη (η) [tikhi (i)] luck
καλή τύχη! [kali tikhi!] good
luck!
των [ton] of them
τώρα [tora] now

Υ

υαλοκαθαριστήρας (ο)
[ialokaτHaristiras (o)]
windscreen wiper
υγεία: στην υγειά σας/σου!
[stin iya sas/soo!] your health!,
cheers!
υγιής [iyi-is] healthy
ΥΓΡΑΕΡΙΟ υγραέριο (το)
[igraerio (to)] camping gas
υγρός [igros] damp, wet
ΥΔΡΑΥΛΙΚΑ υδραυλικά
(τα) [ithravlika (ta)] plumber
ΥΔΡΑΥΛΙΚΟΣ υδραυλικός
(ο) [ithravlikos (o)] plumber
υπάρχει [iparkhi] there is
υπάρχουν [iparkhoon] there
are
ΥΠΕΡΑΣΤΙΚΟ
(ΤΗΛΕΦΩΝΗΜΑ)
υπεραστικό (τηλεφώνημα)
(το) [iperastiko tilefonima (to)]
long-distance call,
international call
υπερβάλλω [ipervallo]

A
B
Γ
Δ
E
Z
H
Θ
I
K
Λ
M
N
Ξ
O
Π
P
Σ
T
Y
Φ
X
Ψ
Ω

exaggerate

υπέρβαρο (το) [ipervaro (to)] excess baggage

υπερβολικά [ipervolika] too (too much)

υπερήφανος [iperifanos] proud

ΥΠΕΡΠΟΛΥΤΕΛΕΙΑΣ υπερπολυτελειας five-star (hotel)

υπεύθυνος [ipefтнinos] responsible

ΥΠΗΡΕΣΙΑ υπηρεσία (η) [ipiresia (i)] service

ύπνο: πάω για ύπνο [pao ya ipno] go to bed

υπνοδωμάτιο (το) [ipnothomatio (to)] bedroom

ύπνος (ο) [ipnòs (o)] sleep

ΥΠΝΩΤΙΚΟ ΧΑΠΙ υπνωτικό χάπι (το) [ipnotiko khapi (to)] sleeping pill

ΥΠΟΓΕΙΑ ΔΙΑΒΑΣΗ ΠΕΖΩΝ υπόγεια διάβαση πεζών (η) pedestrian subway

ΥΠΟΓΕΙΟ υπόγειο (το) [ipoyio (to)] basement

ΥΠΟΓΕΙΟΣ υπόγειος (ο) [ipoyios (o)] underground, (US) subway

υπογράφω [ipografo] sign (verb)

ΥΠΟΔΗΜΑΤΑ υποδήματα (τα) [ipothimata (ta)] shoes

ΥΠΟΔΗΜΑΤΑ ΓΥΝΑΙΚΕΙΑ υποδήματα γυναικεία [ipothimata yinekia] ladies' shoes

ΥΠΟΔΗΜΑΤΟΠΟΙΕΙΟ υποδηματοποιείο (το)

[ipothimatopi-io (to)] shoe shop

υπολογιστής (ο) [ipoloyistis (o)] computer

υπόλοιπο (το) [ipolipo (to)] rest, remainder

υπόσχομαι [iposkhomeh] promise (verb)

ΥΠΟΥΡΓΕΙΟ υπουργείο (το) ministry

ύφασμα (το) [ifasma (to)] material

ΥΦΑΣΜΑΤΑ υφάσματα [ifasmata] clothing; cloth, material

Φ

ΦΑΓΗΤΟ φαγητό (το) [fayito (to)] food; meal; lunch

φαγούρα (η) [fagoora (i)] itch

φάκελος (ο) [fakelos (o)] envelope

ΦΑΚΟΙ ΕΠΑΦΗΣ φακοί επαφής (οι) [faki epafis (i)] contact lenses

φακός (ο) [fakos (o)] lens; torch

φαλακρός [falakros] bald

φαλλοκράτης (ο) [falokratis (o)] male chauvinist

φανάρια τροχαίας (τα) [fanaria trokheas (ta)] traffic lights

φανταστικός [fantastikos] fantastic

ΦΑΡΜΑΚΕΙΟ φαρμακείο (το) [farmakio (to)] chemist's, pharmacy

φάρμακο (το) [farmako (to)]

medicine

φαρμακοποιός (ο) [farmakopios (o)] chemist, pharmacist

φασαρία (η) [fasaria (i)] noise

ΦΕΒΡΟΥΑΡΙΟΣ
Φεβρουάριος (ο) [Fevrooarios (o)] February

φεγγάρι (το) [fengari (to)] moon

φεμινίστρια (η) [feministria (i)] feminist

φερμουάρ (το) [fermooar (to)] zip

φέρνω [ferno] bring

ΦΕΡΡΥ ΜΠΩΤ φέρρυ μπωτ (το) [feri bot (to)] ferry

φέτα (η) [feta (i)] slice

φεύγω [fevgo] go away

φθινόπωρο (το) [fthinoporo (to)] autumn, (US) fall

φίδι (το) [fithi (to)] snake

φιλενάδα (η) [filenatha (i)] girlfriend; friend

φιλί (το) [fili (to)] kiss

ΦΙΛΜ φιλμ (το) [film (to)] film, movie

ΦΙΛΟΔΩΡΗΜΑ
φιλοδώρημα (το) [filothorima (to)] service charge; tip

φιλοξενία (η) [filoxenia (i)] hospitality

φιλοξενούμενη (η) [filoxenoomeni (i)] guest

φιλοξενούμενος (ο) [filoxenoomenos (o)] guest

φίλος (ο) [filos (o)] boyfriend; friend

φιλοφρόνηση (η) [filofronisi (i)] compliment

φίλτρο (το) [filtro (to)] filter

φιλώ [filo] kiss (verb)

φλας (το) [flas (to)] flash; indicator

φλέβα (η) [fleva (i)] vein

φλυτζάνι (το) [flitzani (to)] cup

φοβάμαι [fovameh] be afraid

φοβερός [foveros] terrible

φόβος (ο) [fovos (o)] fear

φοιτητής (ο) [fititis (o)] student

ΦΟΙΤΗΤΙΚΑ ΕΙΣΙΤΗΡΙΑ
φοιτητικά εισιτήρια [fititika isitiria] student tickets

φοιτήτρια (η) [fititria (i)] student

φορά (η) [fora (i)] time, occasion

φόρεμα (το) [forema (to)] dress

φορτηγό (το) [fortigo (to)] lorry

ΦΟΥΑΓΙΕ φουαγιέ (το) [fooaye (to)] foyer

ΦΟΥΛ ΠΑΝΣΙΟΝ φουλ πανσιόν (η) [fool pansion (i)] full board

ΦΟΥΛ-ΣΑΙΖΟΝ φουλ-σαιζόν high season

ΦΟΥΡΝΟΣ φούρνος (ο) [foornos (o)] baker's; oven

φουσκάλα (η) [fooskala (i)] blister

φούστα (η) [foosta (i)] skirt

φρακαρισμένος [frakarismenos] blocked; stuck

φράκτης (ο) [fraktis (o)] fence

φρενάρω [frenaro] brake (verb)

φρένο (το) [freno (to)] brake

ΦΡΕΣΚΟΣ φρέσκος [freskos]

178

fresh

φρικτός [friktos] horrible

φρύδι (το) [frithi (to)] eyebrow

φτάνει [ftani] that's enough

φτάνω [ftano] arrive

φτέρνα (η) [fterna (i)] heel (of foot)

φτερνίζομαι [fternizomeh] sneeze (verb)

φτερό (το) [ftero (to)] wing

ΦΤΗΝΟΣ φτηνός [ftinos] cheap, inexpensive

φτιάχνω τις βαλίτσες [ftiakhno tis valitses] pack (verb)

φτυάρι (το) [ftiari (to)] spade

φτωχός [ftokhos] poor

φύγε! [fiyeh!] go away!

φύκια (τα) [fikia (ta)] seaweed

ΦΥΛΑΚΗ φυλακή (η) [filaki (i)] prison

ΦΥΛΑΞΗ ΑΠΟΣΚΕΥΩΝ φύλαξη αποσκευών [filaxi aposkevon] left luggage, baggage check

φύλλο (το) [filo (to)] leaf

φύλο (το) [filo (to)] gender

φύση (η) [fisi (i)] nature

ΦΥΣΙΚΟ ΠΡΟΪΟΝ φυσικό προϊόν natural product

ΦΥΣΙΚΟΣ φυσικός [fisikos] natural

ΦΥΣΙΚΟ ΧΡΩΜΑ φυσικό χρώμα natural colouring

φυσιολογικός [fisioloyikos] normal

ΦΥΤΟ φυτό (το) [fito (to)] plant

φωνάζω [fonazo] call; shout (verb)

φωνή (η) [foni (i)] voice

ΦΩΣ φως (το) [fos (to)] light

φώτα (τα) [fota (ta)] lights (on car)

ΦΩΤΙΑ φωτιά (η) [fotia (i)] fire

έχεις φωτιά; [ekhis fotia?] have you got a light?

φωτογραφία (η) [fotografia (i)] photograph

ΦΩΤΟΓΡΑΦΙΚΑ φωτογραφικά cameras

φωτογραφική μηχανή (η) [fotografiki mikhani (i)] camera

φωτόμετρο (το) [fotometro (to)] light meter

X

χαίρετε [khereteh] hello

χαλάκι (το) [khalaki (to)] rug

χαλί (το) [khali (to)] carpet

χάλια [khalia] awful

χαμηλά φώτα (τα) [khamila fota (ta)] sidelights

χαμηλός [khamilos] low

χαμόγελο (το) [khamoyelo (to)] smile

χαμογελώ [khamoyelo] smile (verb)

χάνω [khano] lose; miss

ΧΑΠΙ χάπι (το) [khapi (to)] pill

χάρηκα! [kharika!] pleased to meet you!

ΧΑΡΠΙΚ χάρπικ (το) [kharpik (to)] bleach (for toilet)

ΧΑΡΤΗΣ χάρτης (ο) [khartis

(ο)] map

ΧΑΡΤΙ χαρτί (το) [kharti (to)]
paper

χαρτιά (τα) [khartia (ta)]
playing cards

ΧΑΡΤΙ ΑΛΛΗΛΟΓΡΑΦΙΑΣ
χαρτί αλληλογραφίας (το)
[kharti alilografias (to)] writing
paper

ΧΑΡΤΙΚΑ χαρτικά (τα)
[khartika (ta)] stationery

ΧΑΡΤΙ ΠΕΡΙΤΥΛΙΓΜΑΤΟΣ
χαρτί περιτυλίγματος [kharti
peritiligmatos] wrapping
paper

ΧΑΡΤΙ ΥΓΕΙΑΣ χαρτί
υγείας [kharti iyias] toilet
paper

ΧΑΡΤΟΜΑΝΤΗΛΑ
χαρτομάντηλα (τα)
[khartomantila (ta)] tissues,
Kleenex®

χαρτόνι (το) [khartoni (to)]
cardboard

χαρτονόμισμα [khartonomisma]
banknote, (US) bill

ΧΑΡΤΟΠΩΛΕΙΟ
χαρτοπωλείο (το)
[khartopolio (to)] stationer's

χαρτοφύλακας (ο)
[khartofilakas (o)] briefcase

ΧΑΣΑΠΗΣ χασάπης (ο)
[khasapis (o)] butcher's

χείλι (το) [khili (to)] lip

ΧΕΙΜΕΡΙΝΟΣ χειμερινός
[khimerinos] (winter) cinema/
movie theater

χειμώνας (ο) [khimonas (o)]
winter

ΧΕΙΡΟΠΟΙΗΤΟ
χειροποίητο [khiropi-ito]
handmade

χειρότερος [khiroteros] worse

χειρότερος (ο) [khiroteros (o)]
worst

ΧΕΙΡΟΤΕΧΝΙΑ
χειροτεχνία (η) crafts

χειρόφρενο (το) [khirofreno
(to)] handbrake

χέρι (το) [kheri (to)] arm; hand

χερούλι (το) [kherooli (to)]
handle

χήρα (η) [khira (i)] widow

χήρος (ο) [khiros (o)] widower

χθες [khтHes] yesterday

ΧΙΛ. χιλ. thousand,
thousands

ΧΙΛΙΑ χίλια [khilia]
thousand, thousands

ΧΙΛΙΑΔΕΣ χιλιάδες
[khiliathes] thousand,
thousands

ΧΙΛΙΑΡΙΚΟ χιλιάρικο (το)
[khiliariko (to)] 1,000-
drachma note/bill

χιλιόμετρο (το) [khiliometro
(to)] kilometre

χιούμορ (το) [khioomor (to)]
humour

χλιαρός [khliaros] lukewarm;
cool

ΧΛΩΡΙΝΗ χλωρίνη (η)
[khlorini (i)] bleach

χόμπυ (το) [khobi (to)] hobby

ΧΟΝΔΡΙΚΗΣ χονδρικής
wholesale

χορεύω [khorevo] dance (verb)

χορός (ο) [khoros (o)] dance

χορτάρι (το) [khortari (to)]
grass

χορτοφαγικός [khortofayikos]
vegetarian

χορτοφάγος (ο/η) [khortofagos
(o/i)] vegetarian

χρειάζομαι [khriazomeh] need
(verb)

ΧΡΗΜΑΤΙΣΤΗΡΙΟ
χρηματιστήριο (το)
[khrimatistirio (to)] currency
exchange; stock exchange

χρήση (η) [khrisi (i)] use

χρησιμοποιώ [khrisimopio] use
(verb)

χρήσιμος [khrisimos] useful

Χριστούγεννα (τα)
[KHristooyena (ta)] Christmas
Καλά Χριστούγεννα! [Kala
KHristooyena!] happy
Christmas!

χρονιά (η) [khronia (i)] year
χρόνια πολλά! [khronia pola!]
happy birthday!

του χρόνου [too khronoo]
next year

πόσο χρονών είσαι; [poso
khronon iseh?] how old are
you?

χρόνος (ο) [khronos (o)] time;
year

ΧΡΥΣΟΣ χρυσός (ο) [khrisos
(o)] gold

ΧΡΥΣΟΣ ΟΔΗΓΟΣ χρυσός
οδηγός (ο) [khrisos othigos
(o)] yellow pages

ΧΡΥΣΟΧΟΕΙΟ χρυσοχοείο
(το) [khrisokhoio (to)]
jeweller's

χρώμα (το) [khroma (to)]
colour

ΧΡΩΜΑΤΑ - ΣΙΔΕΡΙΚΑ
χρώματα - σιδερικά paint
and hardware store

χτένα (η) [khtena (i)] comb

χτυπώ [khtipo] hit (verb)

χώμα (το) [khoma (to)] earth

χώρα (η) [khora (i)] country

χωράφι (το) [khorafi (to)] field

ΧΩΡΗΤΙΚΟΤΗΤΟΣ ...
ΑΤΟΜΩΝ χωρητικότητος
... ατόμων max load ...
persons

χωριό (το) [khorio (to)] village

χωρίς [khoris] without

ΧΩΡΙΣ ΕΙΣΠΡΑΚΤΟΡΑ
χωρίς εισπράκτορα no
ticket collector

χωρισμένος [khorismenos]
divorced

ΧΩΡΙΣ ΜΠΑΝΙΟ χωρίς
μπάνιο [khoris banio] without
bathroom

ΧΩΡΙΣ ΝΤΟΥΣ χωρίς ντους
[khoris doos] without shower

ΧΩΡΙΣ ΣΥΝΤΗΡΗΤΙΚΑ
χωρίς συντηρητικά no
preservatives

χωριστός [khoristos] separate

ΧΩΡΟΣ ΔΙΑ ΠΟΔΗΛΑΤΕΣ
χώρος διά ποδηλάτες cycle
path

χώρος φύλαξης αποσκευών
(ο) [khoros filaxis aposkevon
(o)] left luggage, baggage
check

Ψ

ψαλίδι (το) [psalithi (to)] scissors

ΨΑΡΑΔΙΚΟ ψαράδικο (το) [psarathiko (to)] fishmonger's

ψάρεμα (το) [psarema (to)] fishing

ΨΑΡΟΤΑΒΕΡΝΑ ψαροταβέρνα (η) [psarotaverna (i)] restaurant specializing in seafood

ψάχνω [psakhno] look for

ψέματα: λέω ψέματα [leo psemata] lie (say untruth)

ψεύτικος [pseftikos] false

ψήνω [psino] bake

ΨΗΣΤΑΡΙΑ ψησταριά (η) [psistaria (i)] restaurant specialising in charcoal-grilled food

ψιλά (τα) [psila (ta)] small change

ΨΙΛΙΚΑ ψιλικά (τα) [psilika (ta)] small shop

ψυγείο (το) [psiyio (to)] fridge

ψυγείο αυτοκινήτου (το) [psiyio aftokinitoo (to)] radiator (car)

ΨΩΜΑΔΙΚΟ ψωμάδικο [psomathiko] baker's

ψωμάς (ο) [psomas (o)] baker

ψηλός [psilos] high; tall

ψώνια (τα) [psonia (ta)] shopping

πάω για ψώνια [pao ya psonia] go shopping

Ω

ΩΘΗΣΑΤΕ ωθήσατε push

ώμος (ο) [omos (o)] shoulder

ώρα (η) [ora (i)] hour

τι ώρα είναι; [ti ora ineh?] what time is it?

σε λίγη ώρα [seh liyi ora] soon

στην ώρα του [stin ora too] on time

ωραίος [oreos] beautiful; handsome; lovely

ΩΡΕΣ ΕΠΙΣΚΕΨΕΩΣ ώρες επισκέψεως visiting hours

ΩΡΕΣ ΛΕΙΤΟΥΡΓΕΙΑΣ ώρες λειτουργείας opening hours

ως [os] as, since

ΩΤΟΡΙΝΟΛΑΡΥΓΓΟΛΟΓΟΣ ωτορινολαρυγγολόγος (ο/η) ear, nose and throat specialist

ωτοστόπ (το) [otostop (to)] hitchhiking

ωτοστόπ: κάνω ωτοστόπ [kano otostop] hitchhike

A
B
Γ
Δ
E
Z
H
Θ
I
K
Λ
M
N
Ξ
O
Π
P
Σ
T
Y
Φ
X
Ψ
Ω

Menu Reader:

Food

ΑΓΓΙΝΑΡΕΣ
ΑΥΓΟΛΕΜΟΝΟ
αγγινάρες αυγολέμονο
[aginares avgolemono]
artichokes in egg and lemon
sauce

ΑΓΓΟΥΡΑΚΙΑ αγγουράκια
[agoorakia] cucumbers

ΑΓΓΟΥΡΙ αγγούρι [agoori]
cucumber

ΑΓΓΟΥΡΙΑ ΚΑΙ
ΝΤΟΜΑΤΕΣ ΣΑΛΑΤΑ
αγγούρια και ντομάτες
σαλάτα [agooria keh domates
salata] cucumber and
tomato salad

ΑΚΤΙΝΙΔΙΟ ακτινίδιο
[aktinithio] kiwi fruit

ΑΛΑΤΙ αλάτι [alati] salt

ΑΛΕΥΡΙ αλεύρι [alevri] flour
ΑΛΕΥΡΙ
ΚΑΛΑΜΠΟΚΙΟΥ αλεύρι
καλαμποκιού [alevri
kalabokioo] cornflour

ΑΛΕΥΡΙ ΣΤΑΡΙΟΥ αλεύρι
σταριού [alevri starioo]
wheat flour

ΑΛΛΑΝΤΙΚΑ αλλαντικά
[aladika] sausages, salami,
ham etc

ΑΜΥΓΔΑΛΑ αμύγδαλα
[amigthala] almonds

ΑΜΥΓΔΑΛΩΤΑ
αμυγδαλωτά [amigthalota]
macaroons; almond pastries

ΑΝΑΝΑΣ ανανάς [ananas]
pineapple

ΑΝΘΟΤΥΡΟ ανθότυρο
[anTHotiro] type of cottage
cheese

ΑΝΤΖΟΥΓΙΑ ΣΤΟ ΛΑΔΙ
αντζούγια στο λάδι [antsoo-
yia sto lathi] anchovies in oil

ΑΡΑΚΑΣ αρακάς [arakas]
peas

ΑΡΑΚΑΣ ΛΑΔΕΡΟΣ
αρακάς λαδερός [arakas
latheros] peas cooked with
tomato and oil

ΑΡΑΚΑΣ ΣΩΤΕ αρακάς
σωτέ [arakas soteh] peas
fried in butter

ΑΡΝΑΚΙ αρνάκι [arnaki]
lamb

ΑΡΝΑΚΙ ΕΞΟΧΙΚΟ
αρνάκι εξοχικό [arnaki
exokhiko] leg of lamb baked
in greaseproof paper

ΑΡΝΑΚΙ ΜΕ ΜΠΑΜΙΕΣ
αρνάκι με μπάμιες [arnaki
meh bami-es] lamb and okra
stew

ΑΡΝΑΚΙ ΜΕ ΠΑΤΑΤΕΣ
ΣΤΟ ΦΟΥΡΝΟ αρνάκι με
πατάτες στο φούρνο [arnaki
meh patates sto foorno] roast
lamb and potatoes

ΑΡΝΑΚΙ ΤΑΣ ΚΕΜΠΑΠ
αρνάκι τας κεμπάπ [arnaki
tas kebap] lamb in tomato
sauce

ΑΡΝΑΚΙ ΤΗΣ ΣΟΥΒΛΑΣ
αρνάκι της σούβλας [arnaki
tis soovlas] spit-roast lamb

ΑΡΝΑΚΙ ΦΡΙΚΑΣΕ
αρνάκι φρικασέ με
μαρούλια [arnaki frikaseh meh
maroolia] lamb and lettuce

in egg and lemon sauce

ΑΡΝΙ αρνί [arni] mutton, lamb

ΑΡΝΙ ΓΕΜΙΣΤΟ ΣΤΟ ΦΟΥΡΝΟ αρνί γεμιστό στο φούρνο [arni yemisto sto foorno] oven-cooked stuffed lamb

ΑΡΝΙ ΕΞΟΧΙΚΟ αρνί εξοχικό [arni exohiko] lamb cooked in greased foil with cheese and spices

ΑΡΝΙ ΚΟΚΚΙΝΙΣΤΟ αρνί κοκκινιστό [arni kokinisto] lamb in tomato sauce

ΑΡΝΙ ΛΑΔΟΡΙΓΑΝΗ ΣΤΟ ΦΟΥΡΝΟ αρνί λαδορίγανη στο φούρνο [arni lathorigani sto foorno] oven-cooked lamb with oil and oregano

ΑΡΝΙ ΜΕ ΑΡΑΚΑ αρνί με αρακά [arni meh araka] lamb with peas

ΑΡΝΙ ΜΕ ΚΟΛΟΚΥΘΑΚΙΑ ΑΥΓΟΛΕΜΟΝΟ αρνί με κολοκυθάκια αυγολέμονο [arni meh kolokiTHakia avgolemono] lamb with courgettes/zucchini in egg and lemon sauce

ΑΡΝΙ ΜΕ ΚΡΙΘΑΡΑΚΙ αρνί με κριθαράκι [arni meh kriTHaraki] lamb with pasta

ΑΡΝΙ ΜΕ ΜΑΚΑΡΟΝΙΑ αρνί με μακαρόνια [arni meh makaronia] lamb with spaghetti

ΑΡΝΙ ΜΕ ΜΕΛΙΤΖΑΝΕΣ

αρνί με μελιτζάνες [arni meh melitzanes] lamb with aubergines/eggplants

ΑΡΝΙ ΜΕ ΜΠΑΜΙΕΣ αρνί με μπάμιες [arni meh bami-es] lamb with okra

ΑΡΝΙ ΜΕ ΠΑΤΑΤΕΣ ΡΑΓΟΥ αρνί με πατάτες ραγού [arni meh patates ragoo] lamb with potatoes cooked in tomato sauce

ΑΡΝΙ ΜΕ ΦΑΣΟΛΑΚΙΑ ΦΡΕΣΚΑ αρνί με φασολάκια φρέσκα [arni meh fasolakia freska] lamb with runner beans

ΑΡΝΙ ΜΕ ΧΥΛΟΠΙΤΕΣ αρνί με χυλοπίτες [arni meh khilopites] lamb with a type of lasagne

ΑΡΝΙ ΜΠΟΥΤΙ ΣΤΟ ΦΟΥΡΝΟ αρνί μπούτι στο φούρνο [arni booti sto foorno] oven-cooked leg of lamb

ΑΡΝΙ ΜΠΡΙΖΟΛΕΣ αρνί μπριζόλες [arni brizoles] lamb chops

ΑΡΝΙ ΠΑΪΔΑΚΙΑ αρνί παϊδάκια [arni paithakia] grilled lamb chops

ΑΡΝΙ ΤΑΣ ΚΕΜΠΑΠ αρνί τας κεμπάπ [arni tas kebab] chopped lamb kebab with tomato sauce

ΑΡΝΙ ΤΗΣ ΚΑΤΣΑΡΟΛΑΣ ΜΕ ΠΑΤΑΤΕΣ αρνί της κατσαρόλας με πατάτες [arni tis katsarolas meh patates] casseroled lamb cooked with potatoes

ΑΡΝΙ ΤΗΣ ΣΟΥΒΛΑΣ
αρνί της σούβλας [arni tis
soovlas] spit-roast lamb

ΑΡΝΙ ΦΡΙΚΑΣΕ αρνί
φρικασέ [arni frikaseh] lamb
fricassee

ΑΣΤΑΚΟΣ αστακός [astakos]
lobster

ΑΣΤΑΚΟΣ ΜΕ
ΛΑΔΟΛΕΜΟΝΟ αστακός
με λαδολέμονο [astakos meh
latholemono] lobster cooked
in lemon and oil sauce

ΑΣΤΑΚΟΣ ΜΕ
ΜΑΓΙΟΝΕΖΑ αστακός με
μαγιονέζα [astakos meh
mayoneza] lobster with
mayonnaise

ΑΤΖΕΜ ΠΙΛΑΦΙ ατζέμ
πιλάφι [atzem pilafi] rice
pilaf

ΑΥΓΑ αυγά [avga] eggs

ΑΥΓΑ ΒΡΑΣΤΑ αυγά
βραστά [avga vrasta] boiled
eggs

ΑΥΓΑ ΒΡΑΣΤΑ ΣΦΙΧΤΑ
αυγά βραστά σφιχτά [avga
vrasta sfikhta] hard-boiled
eggs

ΑΥΓΑ ΓΕΜΙΣΤΑ αυγά
γεμιστά [avga yemista]
stuffed eggs

ΑΥΓΑ ΓΕΜΙΣΤΑ ΜΕ
ΜΑΓΙΟΝΕΖΑ αυγά
γεμιστά με μαγιονέζα [avga
yemista meh mayoneza]
stuffed eggs with
mayonnaise

ΑΥΓΑ ΜΑΤΙΑ αυγά μάτια
[avga matia] fried eggs

ΑΥΓΑ ΜΕΛΑΤΑ αυγά
μελάτα [avga melata] soft-
boiled eggs

ΑΥΓΑ ΜΕ ΜΑΝΙΤΑΡΙΑ
αυγά με μανιτάρια [avga meh
manitaria] mushroom
omelette

ΑΥΓΑ ΜΕ ΜΠΕΙΚΟΝ
αυγά με μπέικον [avga meh
bacon] bacon and eggs

ΑΥΓΑ ΜΕ ΝΤΟΜΑΤΕΣ
αυγά με ντομάτες [avga meh
domates] eggs cooked in
tomato sauce

ΑΥΓΑ ΜΕ ΤΥΡΙ αυγά με
τυρί [avga meh tiri] cheese
omelette

ΑΥΓΑ ΟΜΕΛΕΤΑ αυγά
ομελέτα [avga omeleta] plain
omelette

ΑΥΓΑ ΟΜΕΛΕΤΑ ΜΕ
ΠΑΤΑΤΕΣ αυγά ομελέτα
με πατάτες [avga omeleta meh
patates] omelette with chips/
fries

ΑΥΓΑ ΠΟΣΕ αυγά ποσέ
[avga poseh] poached eggs

ΑΥΓΑ ΣΦΙΧΤΑ αυγά
σφιχτά [avga sfikhta] hard-
boiled eggs

ΑΥΓΑ ΤΗΓΑΝΗΤΑ αυγά
τηγανητά [avga tiganita] fried
eggs

ΑΥΓΑ Ω ΓΚΡΑΤΕΝ αυγά
ω γκρατέν [avga o graten]
eggs au gratin

ΑΥΓΟ αυγό [avgo] egg

Α Β Γ Δ Ε Ζ Η Θ Ι Κ Λ Μ Ν Ξ Ο Π Ρ Σ Τ Υ Φ Χ Ψ Ω

ΑΥΓΟΛΕΜΟΝΟ
αυγολέμονο [avGolemono]
egg and lemon sauce
ΑΥΓΟΛΕΜΟΝΟ ΣΟΥΠΑ
αυγολέμονο σούπα
[avGolemono soopa] chicken
broth with egg and lemon
ΑΥΓΟΤΑΡΑΧΟ αυγοτάραχο
[avgotarakho] roe
ΑΧΛΑΔΙ αχλάδι [akhlathi]
pear

ΒΑΝΙΛΙΑ βανίλια [vanilia]
vanilla
ΒΑΤΟΜΟΥΡΟ βατόμουρο
[vatomooro] blackberry
ΒΕΡΙΚΟΚΟ βερίκοκο
[verikoko] apricot
ΒΟΔΙΝΟ βοδινό [vothino]
beef
ΒΟΔΙΝΟ ΒΡΑΣΤΟ βοδινό
βραστό [vothino vrasto]
boiled beef
ΒΟΔΙΝΟ ΡΟΣΜΠΙΦ
βοδινό ροσμπίφ [vothino
rosbif] roast beef
ΒΟΤΑΝΑ βότανα [votana]
herbs
ΒΟΥΤΥΡΟ βούτυρο [vootiro]
butter
ΒΡΑΣΤΟ βραστό [vrasto]
boiled
ΒΥΣΣΙΝΟ βύσσινο [visino]
sour cherries

ΓΑΛΑΚΤΟΜΠΟΥΡΕΚΟ
γαλακτομπούρεκο
[Galaktobooreko] cream-filled
sweet filo pastry with honey
ΓΑΛΟΠΟΥΛΑ γαλοπούλα

[Galopoola] turkey
ΓΑΛΟΠΟΥΛΑ ΓΕΜΙΣΤΗ
γαλοπούλα γεμιστή
[galopoola yemisti] stuffed
turkey
ΓΑΛΟΠΟΥΛΑ
ΚΟΚΚΙΝΙΣΤΗ γαλοπούλα
κοκκινιστή [galopoola
kokinisti] turkey cooked with
tomatoes
ΓΑΛΟΠΟΥΛΑ ΨΗΤΗ
ΣΤΟ ΦΟΥΡΝΟ γαλοπούλα
ψητή στο φούρνο [galopoola
psiti sto foorno] roast turkey
ΓΑΡΔΟΥΜΠΑ γαρδούμπα
[Garthoomba] spit-roast
rolled lamb offal
ΓΑΡΙΔΕΣ γαρίδες [Garithes]
prawns
ΓΑΡΙΔΕΣ ΒΡΑΣΤΕΣ
γαρίδες βραστές [garithes
vrastes] boiled shrimps
ΓΑΡΙΔΕΣ ΚΟΚΤΑΙΗΛ
γαρίδες κοκταίηλ [garithes
cocktail] shrimp cocktail
ΓΑΡΙΔΕΣ ΠΙΛΑΦΙ γαρίδες
πιλάφι [garithes pilafi] shrimp
pilaf
ΓΑΡΙΔΟΠΙΛΑΦΟ
γαριδοπίλαφο [garithopilafo]
prawns with rice cooked in
butter
ΓΑΡΝΙΤΟΥΡΑ γαρνιτούρα
[garnitoora] vegetables
ΓΑΡΝΙΤΟΥΡΑ ΚΑΡΟΤΑ
ΣΩΤΕ γαρνιτούρα καρότα
σωτέ [garnitoora karota soteh]
sautéed carrots
ΓΑΡΝΙΤΟΥΡΑ

ΚΟΥΝΟΥΠΙΔΙ ΣΩΤΕ
γαρνιτούρα κουνουπίδι
σωτέ [garnit**oo**ra koonoopithi
sot**eh**] sautéed cauliflower
ΓΑΡΝΙΤΟΥΡΑ ΠΑΤΑΤΕΣ
γαρνιτούρα πατάτες
[garnit**oo**ra patates] potatoes
ΓΑΡΝΙΤΟΥΡΑ ΣΠΑΝΑΚΙ
ΣΩΤΕ γαρνιτούρα σπανάκι
σωτέ [garnit**oo**ra spanaki
sot**eh**] sautéed spinach
ΓΑΡΝΙΤΟΥΡΑ ΦΑΣΟΛΙΑ
ΠΡΑΣΙΝΑ ΣΩΤΕ
γαρνιτούρα φασόλια
πράσινα σωτέ [garnit**oo**ra
fas**o**lia pra**s**ina sot**eh**] sautéed
runner beans
ΓΕΜΙΣΤΑ γεμιστά [yemist**a**]
stuffed, usually with rice
and/or minced meat
ΓΕΜΙΣΤΕΣ γεμιστές
[yemist**es**] stuffed vegetables
ΓΙΑΛΑΝΤΖΗ
ΝΤΟΛΜΑΔΕΣ γιαλαντζή
ντολμάδες [yalantz**i**
dolm**a**thes] vine leaves
stuffed with rice
ΓΙΑΟΥΡΤΙ γιαούρτι [ya-
oorti] yoghurt
ΓΙΓΑΝΤΕΣ γίγαντες
[yi**G**andes] white haricot
beans; butter beans
ΓΙΟΥΒΑΡΛΑΚΙΑ
γιουβαρλάκια [yoovarl**a**kia]
meatballs, rice and
seasoning in a sauce
ΓΙΟΥΒΑΡΛΑΚΙΑ
ΑΥΓΟΛΕΜΟΝΟ
γιουβαρλάκια αυγολέμονο

[yoovarl**a**kia avgol**e**mono]
meatballs with egg and
lemon sauce
ΓΙΟΥΒΑΡΛΑΚΙΑ ΜΕ
ΣΑΛΤΣΑ ΝΤΟΜΑΤΑΣ
γιουβαρλάκια με σάλτσα
ντομάτας [yoovarl**a**kia meh
s**a**ltsa dom**a**tas] meatballs
with rice cooked with
tomatoes
ΓΙΟΥΒΕΤΣΙ γιουβέτσι
[yoov**e**tsi] oven-roasted lamb
with pasta
ΓΚΡΕΙΠΦΡΟΥΤ
γκρέιπφρουτ [grapefruit]
grapefruit
ΓΛΥΚΑ γλυκά [**G**lik**a**] cakes,
desserts
ΓΛΥΚΙΣΜΑ γλύκισμα
[**G**likisma] dessert
ΓΛΥΚΟ γλυκό [**G**lik**o**] sweet,
dessert
ΓΛΥΚΟ ΒΥΣΣΙΝΟ γλυκό
βύσσινο [**G**lik**o** visino]
candied cherries in syrup
ΓΛΥΚΟ ΚΑΡΥΔΑΚΙ
ΦΡΕΣΚΟ γλυκό καρυδάκι
φρέσκο [**G**liko karith**a**ki fr**e**sko]
dried fresh green walnuts in
syrup
ΓΛΥΚΟ ΜΑΣΤΙΧΑ γλυκό
μαστίχα [**G**lik**o** mastikha]
vanilla-flavoured fudge
ΓΛΥΚΟ ΜΕΛΙΤΖΑΝΑΚΙ
γλυκό μελιτζανάκι [**G**liko
melitzan**a**ki] dried small
aubergine/eggplant in syrup
ΓΛΥΚΟ ΝΕΡΑΝΤΖΑΚΙ
γλυκό νεραντζάκι [**G**lik**o**

nerantz**a**ki] dried bitter orange in syrup

ΓΛΥΚΟ ΣΥΚΟ γλυκό σύκο [Glik**o** s**i**ko] candied figs in syrup

ΓΛΥΚΟ ΣΥΚΟ ΦΡΕΣΚΟ γλυκό σύκο φρέσκο [Glik**o** s**i**ko fr**e**sko] dried fig in syrup

ΓΛΥΚΟ ΤΡΙΑΝΤΑΦΥΛΛΟ γλυκό τριαντάφυλλο [Glik**o** triad**a**filo] dried rose petals in syrup

ΓΛΩΣΣΑ γλώσσα [gl**o**sa] sole; tongue

ΓΛΩΣΣΕΣ ΤΗΓΑΝΗΤΕΣ γλώσσες τηγανητές [gl**o**ses tigan**i**tes] fried sole

ΓΟΥΡΟΥΝΟΠΟΥΛΟ ΣΤΟ ΦΟΥΡΝΟ ΜΕ ΠΑΤΑΤΕΣ γουρουνόπουλο στο φούρνο με πατάτες [gooroon**o**poolo sto f**oo**rno meh pat**a**tes] oven-cooked pork with potatoes

ΓΡΑΒΙΕΡΑ γραβιέρα [grav**i**era] hard cheese like gruyère

ΓΡΑΝΙΤΑ γρανίτα [gran**i**ta] sorbet

ΓΡΑΝΙΤΑ ΛΕΜΟΝΙ γρανίτα λεμόνι [gran**i**ta lem**o**ni] lemon sorbet

ΓΡΑΝΙΤΑ ΜΠΑΝΑΝΑ γρανίτα μπανάνα [gran**i**ta ban**a**na] banana sorbet

ΓΡΑΝΙΤΑ ΠΟΡΤΟΚΑΛΙ γρανίτα πορτοκάλι [gran**i**ta portok**a**li] orange sorbet

ΓΡΑΝΙΤΑ ΦΡΑΟΥΛΕΣ γρανίτα φράουλες [gran**i**ta

fra**oo**les] strawberry sorbet

ΔΑΜΑΣΚΗΝΑ δαμάσκηνα [tham**a**skina] prunes

ΔΑΜΑΣΚΗΝΟ δαμάσκηνο [tham**a**skino] plum

ΔΙΠΛΕΣ δίπλες [th**i**ples] pancakes

ΕΛΑΙΟΛΑΔΟ ελαιόλαδο [ele**o**latho] olive oil

ΕΛΙΕΣ ελιές [eli-**e**s] olives

ΕΝΤΟΣΘΙΑ ΑΡΝΙΟΥ ΛΑΔΟΡΙΓΑΝΗ εντόσθια αρνιού λαδορίγανη [ent**o**sthia arn**ioo** lathor**i**gani] lambs' intestines cooked in lemon and oil

ΕΠΙΔΟΡΠΙΟ επιδόρπιο [epith**o**rpio] dessert

ΕΣΚΑΛΟΠ ΜΕ ΖΑΜΠΟΝ ΚΑΙ ΣΑΛΤΣΑ ΝΤΟΜΑΤΑΣ εσκαλόπ με ζαμπόν και σάλτσα ντομάτας [eskal**o**p meh zab**o**n keh s**a**ltsa dom**a**tas] escalope of veal with ham and tomato sauce

ΖΑΜΠΟΝ ζαμπόν [zab**o**n] ham

ΖΑΧΑΡΗ ζάχαρη [z**a**khari] sugar

ΖΕΛΕ ζελέ [zel**eh**] jelly

ΖΥΜΑΡΙΚΑ ζυμαρικά [zimarik**a**] pasta and rice

ΘΑΛΑΣΣΙΝΑ θαλασσινά [THalasin**a**] seafood

ΚΑΒΟΥΡΙΑ καβούρια [kav**oo**ria] crab

KAKABIA κακαβιά [kakavia]
mixed fish soup

KAKABIA ΨΑΡΟΣΟΥΠΑ
κακαβιά ψαρόσουπα
[kakavia psarosoopa] fish soup

ΚΑΛΑΜΑΡΑΚΙΑ
καλαμαράκια [kalamarakia]
baby squid

ΚΑΛΑΜΑΡΑΚΙΑ
ΓΕΜΙΣΤΑ καλαμαράκια
γεμιστά [kalamarakia yemista]
stuffed baby squid

ΚΑΛΑΜΑΡΑΚΙΑ
ΤΗΓΑΝΗΤΑ καλαμαράκια
τηγανητά [kalamarakia
tiganita] fried baby squid

ΚΑΛΑΜΑΡΙΑ καλαμάρια
[kalamaria] squid

ΚΑΝΑΠΕ καναπέ [kanapeh]
canapés

ΚΑΝΑΠΕ ΜΕ ΖΑΜΠΟΝ
καναπέ με ζαμπόν [kanapeh
meh zabon] ham canapés

ΚΑΝΑΠΕ ΜΕ ΚΡΕΑΣ
ΨΗΤΟ καναπέ με κρέας
ψητό [kanapeh meh kreas
psito] meat canapés

ΚΑΝΑΠΕ ΜΕ ΜΑΥΡΟ
ΧΑΒΙΑΡΙ καναπέ με μαύρο
χαβιάρι [kanapeh meh mavro
haviari] black caviar canapés

ΚΑΝΑΠΕ ΜΕ
ΤΑΡΑΜΟΣΑΛΑΤΑ
καναπέ με ταραμοσαλάτα
[kanapeh meh taramosalata]
taramosalata canapés

ΚΑΝΕΛΛΑ κανέλλα
[kanela] cinnamon

ΚΑΝΕΛΛΟΝΙΑ ΓΕΜΙΣΤΑ

κανελλόνια γεμιστά
[kanelonia yemista] stuffed
canelloni

ΚΑΝΤΑΪΦΙ κανταΐφι [kada-
ifi] shredded and rolled filo
pastry in syrup

ΚΑΠΑΜΑΣ ΑΡΝΙ καπαμάς
αρνί [kapamas arni] lamb
cooked in spices and tomato
sauce

ΚΑΠΝΙΣΤΟ καπνιστό
[kapnisto] smoked

ΚΑΠΠΑΡΗ κάππαρη
[kapari] caper

ΚΑΡΑΒΙΔΕΣ καραβίδες
[karavithes] king prawns;
crayfish

ΚΑΡΟΤΑ καρότα [karota]
carrots

ΚΑΡΠΟΥΖΙ καρπούζι
[karpoozi] watermelon

ΚΑΡΥΔΙ καρύδι [karithi] nut

ΚΑΡΥΔΟΠΙΤΤΑ
καρυδόπιττα [karithopita]
walnut cake; cake with nuts
and syrup

ΚΑΡΧΑΡΙΑΣ καρχαρίας
[karkharias] shark

ΚΑΣΕΡΙ κασέρι [kaseri]
Cheddar-type cheese

ΚΑΣΤΑΝΑ κάστανα
[kastana] chestnuts

ΚΑΣΤΑΝΑ ΓΛΑΣΕ
κάστανα γλασέ [kastana
glaseh] glazed chestnuts,
marrons glacés

ΚΑΤΑΪΦΙ καταΐφι [kata-ifi]
shredded filo pastry with
honey and nuts

A
B
Γ
Δ
E
Z
H
Θ
I
K
Λ
M
N
Ξ
O
Π
P
Σ
T
Y
Φ
X
Ψ
Ω

ΚΑΤΑΛΟΓΟΣ κατάλογος [katalogos] menu

ΚΕΙΚ κέικ [cake] cake

ΚΕΙΚ ΚΑΝΕΛΛΑΣ κέικ κανέλλας [cake kanelas] cinammon cake

ΚΕΙΚ ΜΕ ΑΜΥΓΔΑΛΑ κέικ με αμύγδαλα [cake meh amigthala] almond cake

ΚΕΙΚ ΜΕ ΚΑΡΥΔΙΑ ΚΑΙ ΣΤΑΦΙΔΕΣ κέικ με καρύδια και σταφίδες [cake meh karithia keh stafithes] nut and sultana cake

ΚΕΙΚ ΣΟΚΟΛΑΤΑΣ κέικ σοκολάτας [cake sokolatas] chocolate cake

ΚΕΙΚ ΦΡΟΥΤΩΝ κέικ φρούτων [cake frooton] fruit cake

ΚΕΡΑΣΙΑ κεράσια [kerasia] cherries

ΚΕΦΑΛΟΤΥΡΙ κεφαλοτύρι [kefalotiri] very salty, hard cheese

ΚΕΦΤΕΔΕΣ κεφτέδες [keftethes] meatballs

ΚΕΦΤΕΔΕΣ ΜΕ ΣΑΛΤΣΑ κεφτέδες με σάλτσα [keftethes meh saltsa] meatballs in tomato sauce

ΚΕΦΤΕΔΕΣ ΣΤΟ ΦΟΥΡΝΟ κεφτέδες στο φούρνο [keftethes sto foorno] oven-cooked meatballs

ΚΕΦΤΕΔΕΣ ΤΗΓΑΝΗΤΟΙ κεφτέδες τηγανητοί [keftethes tiganiti] fried meatballs

ΚΙΜΑΣ κιμάς [kimas] minced meat

ΚΛΕΦΤΙΚΟ κλέφτικο [kleftiko] meat, potatoes and vegetables cooked together in a pot or foil

ΚΟΚΚΙΝΙΣΤΟ κοκκινιστό [kokinisto] in tomato sauce

ΚΟΚΟΡΕΤΣΙ κοκορέτσι [kokoretsi] spit-roast rolled lamb offal

ΚΟΛΙΟΙ κολιοί [koli-i] mackerel

ΚΟΛΙΟΙ ΨΗΤΟΙ κολιοί ψητοί [koli-i psiti] fried mackerel

ΚΟΛΟΚΥΘΑΚΙΑ κολοκυθάκια [kolokiThakia] courgettes/zucchini

ΚΟΛΟΚΥΘΑΚΙΑ ΓΕΜΙΣΤΑ ΜΕ ΚΙΜΑ κολοκυθάκια γεμιστά με κιμά [kolokiThakia yemista meh kima] courgettes/zucchini stuffed with minced meat

ΚΟΛΟΚΥΘΑΚΙΑ ΓΕΜΙΣΤΑ ΜΕ ΡΥΖΙ κολοκυθάκια γεμιστά με ρύζι [kolokiThakia yemista meh rizi] courgettes/zucchini stuffed with rice

ΚΟΛΟΚΥΘΑΚΙΑ ΓΙΑΧΝΙ κολοκυθάκια γιαχνί [kolokiThakia yakhni] courgettes/zucchini and onions in a tomato sauce

ΚΟΛΟΚΥΘΑΚΙΑ ΛΑΔΕΡΑ κολοκυθάκια λαδερά [kolokiThakia lathera]

courgettes/zucchini cooked in oil

ΚΟΛΟΚΥΘΑΚΙΑ ΜΕ ΚΡΕΑΣ κολοκυθάκια με κρέας [kolokiTHakia meh kreas] courgette/zucchini and beef stew

ΚΟΛΟΚΥΘΑΚΙΑ ΜΕ ΠΑΤΑΤΕΣ κολοκυθάκια με πατάτες [kolokiTHakia meh patates] courgettes/zucchini with potatoes

ΚΟΛΟΚΥΘΑΚΙΑ ΜΟΥΣΑΚΑΣ κολοκυθάκια μουσακάς [kolokiTHakia moosakas] courgettes/zucchini with minced meat and béchamel

ΚΟΛΟΚΥΘΑΚΙΑ ΠΑΠΟΥΤΣΑΚΙΑ κολοκυθάκια παπουτσάκια [kolokiTHakia papootsakia] courgettes/zucchini with minced meat and onions

ΚΟΛΟΚΥΘΑΚΙΑ ΤΗΓΑΝΗΤΑ κολοκυθάκια τηγανητά [kolokiTHakia tiganita] fried courgettes/zucchini

ΚΟΛΟΚΥΘΟΚΕΦΤΕΔΕΣ κολοκυθοκεφτέδες [kolokiTHokeftethes] fried courgette/zucchini balls

ΚΟΛΟΚΥΘΟΤΥΡΟΠΙΤΤΑ κολοκυθοτυρόπιττα [kolokiTHotiropita] courgette/zucchini and cheese pie

ΚΟΜΠΟΣΤΑ κομπόστα [kobosta] fruit compote

ΚΟΤΑ κότα [kota] chicken

ΚΟΤΑ ΒΡΑΣΤΗ κότα βραστή [kota vrasti] boiled chicken

ΚΟΤΑ ΨΗΤΗ ΣΤΟ ΦΟΥΡΝΟ κότα ψητή στο φούρνο [kota psiti sto foorno] roast chicken

ΚΟΤΑ ΨΗΤΗ ΤΗΣ ΚΑΤΣΑΡΟΛΑΣ κότα ψητή της κατσαρόλας [kota psiti tis katsarolas] chicken casserole

ΚΟΤΑ ΨΗΤΗ ΤΗΣ ΣΟΥΒΛΑΣ κότα ψητή της σούβλας [kota psiti tis soovlas] spit-roast chicken

ΚΟΤΟΛΕΤΕΣ ΑΡΝΙΣΙΕΣ ΠΑΝΕ κοτολέτες αρνίσιες πανέ [kotoletes arnisi-es paneh] lamb cutlets

ΚΟΤΟΛΕΤΕΣ ΜΟΣΧΑΡΙΣΙΕΣ ΠΑΝΕ κοτολέτες μοσχαρίσιες πανέ [kotoletes moskharisi-es paneh] veal cutlets

ΚΟΤΟΠΙΤΤΑ κοτόπιττα [kotopita] chicken pie

ΚΟΤΟΠΟΥΛΟ κοτόπουλο [kotopoolo] chicken

ΚΟΤΟΠΟΥΛΟ ΓΙΟΥΒΕΤΣΙ ΜΕ ΧΥΛΟΠΙΤΤΕΣ κοτόπουλο γιουβέτσι με χυλοπίττες [kotopoolo yioovetsi meh hilopites] chicken with pasta

ΚΟΤΟΠΟΥΛΟ ΚΟΚΚΙΝΙΣΤΟ κοτόπουλο κοκκινιστό [kotopoolo

kokinisto] chicken in tomato sauce

ΚΟΤΟΠΟΥΛΟ ΜΕ ΜΠΑΜΙΕΣ κοτόπουλο με μπάμιες [kotopoolo meh bamies] chicken with okra

ΚΟΤΟΠΟΥΛΟ ΜΕ ΜΠΙΖΕΛΙΑ κοτόπουλο με μπιζέλια [kotopoolo meh bizelia] chicken with peas

ΚΟΤΟΠΟΥΛΟ ΠΑΝΕ κοτόπουλο πανέ [kotopoolo paneh] breaded chicken

ΚΟΤΟΠΟΥΛΟ ΠΙΛΑΦΙ κοτόπουλο πιλάφι [kotopoolo pilafi] chicken pilaf

ΚΟΤΟΠΟΥΛΟ ΤΗΣ ΣΟΥΒΛΑΣ κοτόπουλο της σούβλας [kotopoolo tis soovlas] spit-roast chicken

ΚΟΤΟΣΟΥΠΑ κοτόσουπα [kotosoopa] chicken soup

ΚΟΥΚΙΑ ΛΑΔΕΡΑ κουκιά λαδερά [kookia lathera] broad beans in tomato sauce

ΚΟΥΝΕΛΙ κουνέλι [kooneli] rabbit

ΚΟΥΝΕΛΙ ΜΕ ΣΑΛΤΣΑ κουνέλι με σάλτσα [kooneli meh saltsa] rabbit with tomato sauce

ΚΟΥΝΕΛΙ ΣΤΙΦΑΔΟ κουνέλι στιφάδο [kooneli stifatho] rabbit with onions

ΚΟΥΝΟΥΠΙΔΙ κουνουπίδι [koonoopithi] cauliflower

ΚΟΥΝΟΥΠΙΔΙ ΒΡΑΣΤΟ ΣΑΛΑΤΑ κουνουπίδι βραστό σαλάτα [koonopithi vrasto salata] boiled cauliflower salad

ΚΟΥΡΑΜΠΙΕΔΕΣ κουραμπιέδες [koorabi-ethes] Greek shortbread

ΚΟΥΡΑΜΠΙΕΔΕΣ ΜΕ ΑΜΥΓΔΑΛΟ κουραμπιέδες με αμύγδαλο [koorabi-ethes meh amigthalo] shortbread-type biscuits with sesame seeds and icing sugar

ΚΡΑΚΕΡΣ ΑΛΜΥΡΑ κράκερς αλμυρά [krakers almira] salted crackers

ΚΡΑΣΑΤΟ κρασάτο [krasato] cooked in wine sauce

ΚΡΕΑΣ κρέας [kreas] meat, usually beef

ΚΡΕΑΣ ΜΕ ΑΝΤΙΔΙΑ ΑΥΓΟΛΕΜΟΝΟ κρέας με αντίδια αυγολέμονο [kreas meh antithia avgolemono] beef with endives in egg and lemon sauce

ΚΡΕΑΣ ΜΕ ΦΑΣΟΛΙΑ ΞΕΡΑ κρέας με φασόλια ξερά [kreas meh fasolia xera] beef with butter beans

ΚΡΕΑΤΙΚΑ κρεατικά [krehatika] meat dishes

ΚΡΕΑΤΟΠΙΤΤΑ κρεατόπιττα [kreh-atopita] minced meat in filo pastry

ΚΡΕΜΑ κρέμα [krema] cream

ΚΡΕΜΑ ΚΑΡΑΜΕΛΕ κρέμα καραμελέ [krema karameleh] crème caramel

ΚΡΕΜΑ ΜΕ ΜΗΛΑ
κρέμα με μήλα [krema meh
mila] apples with cream
ΚΡΕΜΑ ΜΕ ΜΠΑΝΑΝΕΣ
κρέμα με μπανάνες [krema
meh bananes] bananas with
cream
ΚΡΕΜΜΥΔΑΚΙΑ ΦΡΕΣΚΑ
κρεμμυδάκια φρέσκα
[kremithakia freska] spring
onions
ΚΡΕΜΜΥ⌐ΙΑ κρεμμύδια
[kremithia] onions
ΚΡΕΜΜΥΔΟΣΟΥΠΑ
κρεμμυδόσουπα
[kremithosoopa] onion soup
ΚΡΕΠΑ κρέπα [krepa]
pancake
ΚΡΟΚΕΤΕΣ κροκέτες
[kroketes] croquettes
ΚΡΟΚΕΤΕΣ ΑΠΟ ΚΡΕΑΣ
κροκέτες από κρέας
[kroketes apo kreas] meat
croquettes
**ΚΡΟΚΕΤΕΣ ΜΕ ΑΥΓΑ
ΚΑΙ ΤΥΡΙ** κροκέτες με
αυγά και τυρί [kroketes meh
avga keh tiri] egg and cheese
croquettes
**ΚΡΟΚΕΤΕΣ
ΜΠΑΚΑΛΙΑΡΟΥ**
κροκέτες μπακαλιάρου
[kroketes bakaliaroo] cod
croquettes
ΚΡΟΚΕΤΕΣ ΠΑΤΑΤΕΣ
κροκέτες πατάτες [kroketes
patates] potato croquettes
ΚΡΟΥΑΣΑΝ κρουασάν
[croissants] croissants

ΚΥΔΩΝΙΑ κυδώνια
[kithonia] quinces
ΚΥΔΩΝΟΠΑΣΤΟ
κυδωνόπαστο [kithonopasto]
thick jelly made from quince
ΚΥΝΗΓΙ κυνήγι [kiniyi]
game
ΚΥΡΙΟ ΠΙΑΤΟ κύριο πιάτο
[kirio piato] main course
ΚΩΚ κωκ [kok] cake with
cream and chocolate
topping

ΛΑΓΟΣ λαγός [lagos] hare
ΛΑΓΟΣ ΜΕ ΣΑΛΤΣΑ
λαγός με σάλτσα [lagos meh
saltsa] hare in tomato sauce
ΛΑΓΟΣ ΣΤΙΦΑΔΟ λαγός
στιφάδο [lagos stifatho] hare
and shallot stew
ΛΑΔΕΡΑ λαδερά [lathera] in
olive oil and tomato sauce
ΛΑΔΙ λάδι [lathi] oil
ΛΑΔΟΛΕΜΟΝΟ
λαδολέμονο [latholemono]
olive oil and lemon dressing
ΛΑΔΟΞΥΔΟ λαδόξυδο
[lathoxitho] oil and vinegar
salad dressing
ΛΑΖΑΝΙΑ λαζάνια [lazania]
lasagne
ΛΑΧΑΝΙΚΑ λαχανικά
[lakhanika] vegetables
ΛΑΧΑΝΙΚΑ ΜΙΚΤΑ
λαχανικά μικτά [lakhanika
mikta] vegetables
**ΛΑΧΑΝΑΚΙΑ
ΒΡΥΞΕΛΛΩΝ** λαχανάκια
Βρυξελλών [lakhanakia

vrixel**on**] Brussels sprouts

ΛΑΧΑΝΟ λάχανο [l**a**khano]
cabbage

ΛΑΧΑΝΟ ΚΟΚΚΙΝΟ
λάχανο κόκκινο [l**a**khano
k**o**kino] red cabbage

ΛΑΧΑΝΟ ΝΤΟΛΜΑΔΕΣ
ΑΥΓΟΛΕΜΟΝΟ λάχανο
ντολμάδες αυγολέμονο
[l**a**khano dolm**a**thes
avgol**e**mono] cabbage leaves
stuffed with rice in egg and
lemon sauce

ΛΑΧΑΝΟ ΝΤΟΛΜΑΔΕΣ
λάχανο ντολμάδες [l**a**khano
dolm**a**thes] cabbage leaves
stuffed with minced meat
and rice

ΛΑΧΑΝΟ ΝΤΟΛΜΑΔΕΣ
ΜΕ ΣΑΛΤΣΑ ΝΤΟΜΑΤΑΣ
λάχανο ντολμάδες με
σάλτσα ντομάτας [l**a**khano
dolm**a**thes meh s**a**ltsa dom**a**tas]
vine leaves stuffed with rice
in tomato sauce

ΛΑΧΑΝΟΣΑΛΑΤΑ
λαχανοσαλάτα
[lakhanosal**a**ta] cabbage salad

ΛΕΜΟΝΙ λεμόνι [lem**o**ni]
lemon

ΛΙΘΡΙΝΙ λιθρίνι [li**TH**rini] red
snapper

ΛΙΘΡΙΝΙ ΨΗΤΟ λιθρίνι
ψητό [li**TH**rini psit**o**] grilled
red snapper

ΛΟΥΚΑΝΙΚΑ λουκάνικα
[look**a**nika] sausages

ΛΟΥΚΑΝΙΚΑ ΒΡΑΣΤΑ
λουκάνικα βραστά [look**a**nika

vrast**a**] boiled sausages

ΛΟΥΚΑΝΙΚΑ
ΚΑΠΝΙΣΤΑ ΣΤΗ ΣΧΑΡΑ
λουκάνικα καπνιστά στη
σχάρα [look**a**nika kapnist**a** sti
skh**a**ra] grilled smoked
sausages

ΛΟΥΚΑΝΙΚΑ
ΤΗΓΑΝΗΤΑ λουκάνικα
τηγανητά [look**a**nika tiganit**a**]
fried sausages

ΛΟΥΚΟΥΜΑΔΕΣ
λουκουμάδες [lookoom**a**thes]
doughnuts

ΛΟΥΚΟΥΜΙΑ λουκούμια
[look**oo**mia] Turkish delight

ΜΑΓΕΙΡΙΤΣΑ μαγειρίτσα
[mayir**i**tsa] traditional Easter
soup made from lambs'
intestines

ΜΑΓΙΑ μαγιά [may**a**] yeast

ΜΑΓΙΟΝΕΖΑ μαγιονέζα
[mayon**e**za] mayonnaise

ΜΑΪΝΤΑΝΟΣ μαϊντανός
[maidan**o**s] parsley

ΜΑΚΑΡΟΝΑΚΙ ΚΟΦΤΟ
μακαρονάκι κοφτό
[makaron**a**ki koft**o**] macaroni

ΜΑΚΑΡΟΝΙΑ μακαρόνια
[makar**o**nia] pasta

ΜΑΚΑΡΟΝΙΑ ΜΕ ΚΙΜΑ
μακαρόνια με κιμά
[makar**o**nia meh kim**a**]
spaghetti bolognaise

ΜΑΚΑΡΟΝΙΑ ΜΕ
ΦΡΕΣΚΟ ΒΟΥΤΥΡΟ ΚΑΙ
ΠΑΡΜΕΖΑΝΑ μακαρόνια
με φρέσκο βούτυρο και

παρμεζάνα [makaronia meh fresko vootiro keh parmezana] spaghetti with butter and parmesan cheese

ΜΑΚΑΡΟΝΙΑ ΠΑΣΤΙΤΣΙΟ ΜΕ ΚΙΜΑ μακαρόνια παστίτσιο με κιμά [makaronia pastitsio meh kima] baked pasta dish with minced meat and béchamel

ΜΑΝΙΤΑΡΙΑ μανιτάρια [manitaria] mushrooms

ΜΑΝΙΤΑΡΙΑ ΤΗΓΑΝΗΤΑ μανιτάρια τηγανητά [manitaria tiganita] fried mushrooms

ΜΑΝΟΥΡΙ μανούρι [manoori] hard cheese

ΜΑΝΤΑΡΙΝΙ μανταρίνι [madarini] satsuma, tangerine

ΜΑΡΓΑΡΙΝΗ μαργαρίνη [margarini] margarine

ΜΑΡΙΔΕΣ ΤΗΓΑΝΗΤΕΣ μαρίδες τηγανητές [marithes tiganites] small fried fish

ΜΑΡΜΕΛΑΔΑ μαρμελάδα [marmelatha] jam, marmalade

ΜΑΡΜΕΛΑΔΑ ΒΕΡΥΚΟΚΚΑ μαρμελάδα βερύκοκκα [marmelatha verikoka] apricot jam

ΜΑΡΜΕΛΑΔΑ ΠΟΡΤΟΚΑΛΙ μαρμελάδα πορτοκάλι [marmelatha portokali] orange jam

ΜΑΡΜΕΛΑΔΑ ΡΟΔΑΚΙΝΑ μαρμελάδα ροδάκινα [marmelatha

pothakina] peach jam

ΜΑΡΜΕΛΑΔΑ ΦΡΑΟΥΛΕΣ μαρμελάδα φράουλες [marmelatha fraooles] strawberry jam

ΜΑΡΟΥΛΙ μαρούλι [marooli] lettuce

ΜΑΡΟΥΛΙΑ ΣΑΛΑΤΑ μαρούλια σαλάτα [maroolia salata] green salad

ΜΕ ΛΑΔΟΛΕΜΟΝΟ με λαδολέμονο [meh latholemono] with olive oil and lemon dressing

ΜΕΛΙ μέλι [meli] honey

ΜΕΛΙΤΖΑΝΕΣ μελιτζάνες [melidzanes] aubergines/ eggplants

ΜΕΛΙΤΖΑΝΕΣ ΓΕΜΙΣΤΕΣ ΜΕ ΚΙΜΑ μελιτζάνες γεμιστές με κιμά [melitzanes yemistes meh kima] aubergines/eggplants stuffed with minced meat

ΜΕΛΙΤΖΑΝΕΣ ΓΙΑΧΝΙ μελιτζάνες γιαχνί [melitzanes yakhni] aubergines/eggplants with tomato and onions

ΜΕΛΙΤΖΑΝΕΣ ΙΜΑΜ ΜΠΑΪΛΝΤΙ μελιτζάνες ιμάμ μπαϊλντί [melitzanes imam baildi] aubergines/ eggplants with garlic and tomato

ΜΕΛΙΤΖΑΝΕΣ ΜΟΥΣΑΚΑ μελιτζάνες μουσακά [melidzanes moosaka] layers of aubergine/eggplant and minced meat topped with béchamel

ΜΕΛΙΤΖΑΝΕΣ ΠΑΠΟΥΤΣΑΚΙΑ μελιτζάνες παπουτσάκια [melidzaness papootsakia] stuffed aubergines/ eggplants

ΜΕΛΙΤΖΑΝΕΣ ΤΗΓΑΝΗΤΕΣ μελιτζάνες τηγανητές [melitzanes tiganites] fried aubergines/ eggplants

ΜΕΛΙΤΖΑΝΟΣΑΛΑΤΑ μελιτζανοσαλάτα [melidzanosalata] puréed aubergine/eggplant dip

ΜΕΛΟΜΑΚΑΡΟΝΑ μελομακάρονα [melomakarona] sweet cakes with cinammon, nuts and syrup

ΜΕΝΟΥ μενού [menoo] menu

ΜΕ ΣΑΛΤΣΑ με σάλτσα [meh saltsa] with sauce, usually tomato sauce

ΜΗΛΑ ΓΕΜΙΣΤΑ μήλα γεμιστά [mila yemista] stuffed apples with cinammon

ΜΗΛΟ μήλο [milo] apple

ΜΗΛΟΠΙΤΤΑ μηλόπιττα [milopita] apple pie

μισοψημένο [misopsimeno] medium (steak)

ΜΟΣΧΑΡΙ μοσχάρι [moskhari] veal; tender beef

ΜΟΣΧΑΡΙ ΒΡΑΣΤΟ μοσχάρι βραστό [moskhari vrasto] veal stew

ΜΟΣΧΑΡΙ ΚΟΚΚΙΝΙΣΤΟ μοσχάρι κοκκινιστό [moskhari kokinisto] veal in tomato sauce

ΜΟΣΧΑΡΙ ΜΕ ΑΡΑΚΑ μοσχάρι με αρακά [moskhari meh araka] veal with peas

ΜΟΣΧΑΡΙ ΜΕ ΚΡΙΘΑΡΑΚΙ μοσχάρι με κριθαράκι [moskhari meh kriTHaraki] veal with pasta

ΜΟΣΧΑΡΙ ΜΕ ΜΕΛΙΤΖΑΝΕΣ μοσχάρι με μελιτζάνες [moskhari meh melitzanes] veal with aubergines/eggplants

ΜΟΣΧΑΡΙ ΜΕ ΜΠΑΜΙΕΣ μοσχάρι με μπάμιες [moskhari meh bami-es] veal with okra

ΜΟΣΧΑΡΙ ΜΕ ΠΑΤΑΤΕΣ μοσχάρι με πατάτες [moskhari meh patates] veal with potatoes

ΜΟΣΧΑΡΙ ΜΕ ΠΑΤΑΤΕΣ ΣΤΟ ΦΟΥΡΝΟ μοσχάρι με πατάτες στο φούρνο [moskhari meh patates sto foorno] veal with potatoes cooked in the oven

ΜΟΣΧΑΡΙ ΜΕ ΠΟΥΡΕ μοσχάρι με πουρέ [moskhari meh pooreh] veal with mashed potatoes

ΜΟΣΧΑΡΙ ΜΕ ΦΑΣΟΛΑΚΙΑ μοσχάρι με

φασολάκια [moskhari meh fasolakia] veal and green beans

ΜΟΣΧΑΡΙ ΡΟΣΜΠΙΦ
μοσχάρι ροσμπίφ [moskhari rosbif] roast beef

ΜΟΣΧΑΡΙΣΙΟΣ ΚΙΜΑΣ
μοσχαρίσιος κιμάς [moskharisios kimas] minced meat

ΜΟΣΧΑΡΙ ΣΝΙΤΖΕΛ ΜΕ ΠΑΤΑΤΕΣ ΤΗΓΑΝΗΤΕΣ
μοσχάρι σνίτζελ με πατάτες τηγανητές [moskhari schnitzel meh patates tiganites] steak and chips/fries

ΜΟΣΧΑΡΙ ΣΝΙΤΖΕΛ ΜΕ ΠΟΥΡΕ μοσχάρι σνίτζελ με πουρέ [moskhari schnitzel meh patates pooreh] steak with mashed potatoes

ΜΟΣΧΑΡΙ ΨΗΤΟ μοσχάρι ψητό [moskhari psito] veal pot roast

ΜΟΥΣΑΚΑΣ μουσακάς [moosakas] moussaka – layers of vegetables and minced meat topped with béchamel sauce

ΜΟΥΣΑΚΑΣ ΠΑΤΑΤΕΣ μουσακάς πατάτες [moosakas patates] potatoes with minced meat and béchamel

ΜΟΥΣΤΑΡΔΑ μουστάρδα [moostartha] mustard

ΜΟΥΣΤΟΚΟΥΛΟΥΡΑ μουστοκούλουρα [moostokooloora] Greek biscuits

ΜΠΑΚΑΛΙΑΡΟΣ

μπακαλιάρος [bakaliaros] cod; salt cod; haddock

ΜΠΑΚΑΛΙΑΡΟΣ ΚΡΟΚΕΤΕΣ μπακαλιάρος κροκέτες [bakaliaros kroketes] haddock croquettes

ΜΠΑΚΑΛΙΑΡΟΣ ΠΛΑΚΙ μπακαλιάρος πλακί [bakaliaros plaki] salted cod cooked in tomato sauce

ΜΠΑΚΑΛΙΑΡΟΣ ΤΗΓΑΝΗΤΟΣ μπακαλιάρος τηγανητός [bakaliaros tiganitos] fried salted cod

ΜΠΑΚΛΑΒΑΔΕΣ μπακλαβάδες [baklavathes] baklava – layers of thin pastry with nuts and syrup

ΜΠΑΚΛΑΒΑΔΕΣ ΜΕ ΚΑΡΥΔΙΑ μπακλαβάδες με καρύδια [baklavathes meh karithia] baklava – layers of thin pastry with walnuts and syrup

ΜΠΑΚΛΑΒΑΣ μπακλαβάς [baklavas] baklava – filo pastry with nuts and syrup

ΜΠΑΜΙΕΣ μπάμιες [bami-es] okra

ΜΠΑΜΙΕΣ ΛΑΔΕΡΕΣ μπάμιες λαδερές [bami-es latheres] okra in olive oil and tomato sauce

ΜΠΑΝΑΝΑ μπανάνα [banana] banana

ΜΠΑΡΜΠΟΥΝΙΑ μπαρμπούνια [barboonia] red mullet

Α Β Γ Δ Ε Ζ Η Θ Ι Κ Λ **Μ** Ν Ξ Ο Π Ρ Σ Τ Υ Φ Χ Ψ Ω

ΜΠΑΡΜΠΟΥΝΙΑ ΠΑΝΕ
μπαρμπούνια πανέ
[barboonia paneh] breaded
red mullet

ΜΠΑΧΑΡΙΚΟ μπαχαρικό
[bakhariko] spice

ΜΠΕΖΕΔΕΣ μπεζέδες
[bezethes] meringues with
cream

ΜΠΕΙΚΟΝ μπέικον [bacon]
bacon

ΜΠΕΙΚΟΝ ΚΑΠΝΙΣΤΟ
μπέικον καπνιστό [bacon
kapnisto] smoked bacon

ΜΠΕΣΑΜΕΛ ΣΑΛΤΣΑ
μπεσαμέλ σάλτσα [besamel
saltsa] béchamel sauce

ΜΠΙΖΕΛΙΑ μπιζέλια
[bizelia] peas

ΜΠΙΣΚΟΤΑ μπισκότα
[biskota] biscuits

ΜΠΙΣΚΟΤΑΚΙΑ ΑΛΜΥΡΑ
μπισκοτάκια αλμυρά
[biskotakia almira] savoury
crackers

ΜΠΙΣΚΟΤΑ ΣΟΚΟΛΑΤΑΣ
μπισκότα σοκολάτας
[biskota sokolatas] chocolate
biscuits

ΜΠΙΦΤΕΚΙ μπιφτέκι
[bifteki] hamburger; grilled
meatballs

ΜΠΟΝ ΦΙΛΕ μπον φιλέ [bon
fileh] fillet steak

ΜΠΟΥΓΑΤΣΑ μπουγάτσα
[boogatsa] puff pastry with
various fillings

ΜΠΟΥΓΑΤΣΑ ΓΛΥΚΙΑ
μπουγάτσα γλυκιά [boogatsa

glikia] puff pastry with
cream and icing sugar

ΜΠΟΥΡΕΚΑΚΙΑ
μπουρεκάκια [boorekakia]
cheese or minced meat pies

ΜΠΟΥΡΕΚΙ μπουρέκι
[booreki] courgette, potato
and cheese pie

ΜΠΡΙΑΜΙ μπριάμι [briami]
ratatouille

ΜΠΡΙΑΜΙ ΜΕ
ΚΟΛΟΚΥΘΑΚΙΑ μπριάμι
με κολοκυθάκια [briami meh
kolokiτΗakia] courgettes/
zucchini cooked with
potatoes in the oven

ΜΠΡΙΖΟΛΑ μπριζόλα
[brizola] chop; steak

ΜΠΡΙΖΟΛΑ
ΜΟΣΧΑΡΙΣΙΑ μπριζόλα
μοσχαρίσια [brizola
moskharisia] beef steak

ΜΠΡΙΖΟΛΕΣ μπριζόλες
[brizoles] chops; steaks

ΜΠΡΙΖΟΛΕΣ ΒΟΔΙΝΕΣ
ΣΤΗ ΣΧΑΡΑ μπριζόλες
βοδινές στη σχάρα [brizoles
vothines sti skhara] grilled T-
bone steak

ΜΠΡΙΖΟΛΕΣ ΣΤΟ
ΤΗΓΑΝΙ μπριζόλες στο
τηγάνι [brizoles sto tigani]
fried T-bone steak

ΜΠΡΙΖΟΛΕΣ ΧΟΙΡΙΝΕΣ
μπριζόλες χοιρινές [brizoles
khirines] pork chops

ΜΠΡΙΖΟΛΕΣ ΧΟΙΡΙΝΕΣ
ΣΤΗ ΣΧΑΡΑ μπριζόλες
χοιρινές στη σχάρα [brizoles

khirines sti skhara] charcoal-grilled pork chops

ΜΠΡΟΚΟΛΟ μπρόκολο [brokolo] broccoli

ΜΥΑΛΑ μυαλά [miala] brains
ΜΥΑΛΑ ΠΑΝΕ μυαλά πανέ [miala paneh] breaded cows' brains

ΜΥΔΙΑ μύδια [mithia] mussels
ΜΥΔΙΑ ΤΗΓΑΝΗΤΑ μύδια τηγανητά [mithia tiganita] fried mussels

ΝΕΦΡΑ νεφρά [nefra] kidneys
ΝΕΦΡΑ ΨΗΤΑ/ ΤΗΓΑΝΗΤΑ νεφρά ψητά/ τηγανητά [nefra psita/ tiganita] grilled/fried kidneys

ΝΤΟΛΜΑΔΑΚΙΑ ντολμαδάκια [dolmathakia] vine leaves stuffed with minced meat, rice and herbs

ΝΤΟΛΜΑΔΕΣ ντολμάδες [dolmathes] vine or cabbage leaves stuffed with minced meat and/or rice
ΝΤΟΛΜΑΔΕΣ ΑΥΓΟΛΕΜΟΝΟ ΜΕ ΚΙΜΑ ντολμάδες αυγολέμονο με κιμά [dolmathes avgolemono meh kima] vine leaves with rice and minced meat in egg and lemon sauce
ΝΤΟΛΜΑΔΕΣ ΓΙΑΛΑΝΤΖΙ ντολμάδες

γιαλαντζί [dolmathes yialantzi] vine leaves stuffed with rice

ΝΤΟΜΑΤΕΣ ντομάτες [domates] tomatoes
ΝΤΟΜΑΤΕΣ ΓΕΜΙΣΤΕΣ ΜΕ ΚΙΜΑ ντομάτες γεμιστές με κιμά [domates yemistes meh kima] stuffed tomatoes with minced meat
ΝΤΟΜΑΤΕΣ ΓΕΜΙΣΤΕΣ ΜΕ ΡΥΖΙ ντομάτες γεμιστές με ρύζι [domates yemistes meh rizi] tomatoes stuffed with rice
ΝΤΟΜΑΤΕΣ ΓΕΜΙΣΤΕΣ ντομάτες γεμιστές [domates yemistes] stuffed tomatoes

ΝΤΟΜΑΤΟΣΑΛΑΤΑ ντοματοσαλάτα [domatosalata] tomato salad

ΝΤΟΜΑΤΟΣΟΥΠΑ ντοματόσουπα [domatosoopa] tomato soup

ΝΤΟΝΑΤΣ ντόνατς [doughnuts] doughnuts

ΞΗΡΟΙ ΚΑΡΠΟΙ ξηροί καρποί [xiri karpi] nuts, dried fruit

ΞΙΦΙΑΣ ξιφίας [xifias] swordfish

ΞΥΔΙ ξύδι [xithi] vinegar

ΟΜΕΛΕΤΑ ομελέτα [omeleta] omelette
ΟΜΕΛΕΤΑ ΛΟΥΚΑΝΙΚΑ ομελέτα λουκάνικα [omeleta lookanika] omelette with sausages

Α Β Γ Δ Ε Ζ Η Θ Ι Κ Λ Μ Ν Ξ Ο Π Ρ Σ Τ Υ Φ Χ Ψ Ω

ΟΡΕΚΤΙΚΑ ορεκτικά [orektika] hors d'œuvres, starters

ΟΣΤΡΑΚΟΕΙΔΗ οστρακοειδή [ostrako-ithi] shellfish

ΠΑΓΩΤΟ παγωτό [pagoto] ice cream
ΠΑΓΩΤΟ ΒΕΡΥΚΟΚΚΟ παγωτό βερύκοκκο [pagoto verikoko] apricot ice cream
ΠΑΓΩΤΟ ΚΟΚΤΑΙΗΛ παγωτό κοκταίηλ [pagoto cocktail] ice cream cocktail
ΠΑΓΩΤΟ ΚΡΕΜΑ παγωτό κρέμα [pagoto krema] vanilla ice cream
ΠΑΓΩΤΟ ΜΕ ΣΑΝΤΙΓΥ παγωτό με σαντιγύ [pagoto meh sadiyi] ice cream with whipped cream
ΠΑΓΩΤΟ ΜΟΚΚΑ παγωτό μόκκα [pagoto moka] coffee-flavoured ice cream
ΠΑΓΩΤΟ ΜΠΑΝΑΝΑ παγωτό μπανάνα [pagoto banana] banana ice cream
ΠΑΓΩΤΟ ΠΑΡΦΑΙ παγωτό παρφαί [pagoto parfeh] ice cream parfait
ΠΑΓΩΤΟ ΠΡΑΛΙΝΑ παγωτό πραλίνα [pagoto pralina] praline ice cream
ΠΑΓΩΤΟ ΣΟΚΟΛΑΤΑ παγωτό σοκολάτα [pagoto sokolata] chocolate ice cream
ΠΑΓΩΤΟ ΦΡΑΟΥΛΑ

παγωτό φράουλα [pagoto fraoola] strawberry ice cream
ΠΑΓΩΤΟ ΦΥΣΤΙΚΙ παγωτό φυστίκι [pagoto fistiki] pistachio ice cream
ΠΑΞΙΜΑΔΙ παξιμάδι [paximathi] dried, hard bread
ΠΑΝΤΖΑΡΙ παντζάρι [pandzari] beetroot
ΠΑΠΙΑ πάπια [papia] duck
ΠΑΠΡΙΚΑ πάπρικα [paprika] paprika
ΠΑΡΜΕΖΑΝΑ παρμεζάνα [parmezana] parmesan
ΠΑΣΤΑ πάστα [pasta] cake
ΠΑΣΤΑ ΑΜΥΓΔΑΛΟΥ πάστα αμυγδάλου [pasta amigthaloo] almond gâteau
ΠΑΣΤΑ ΚΟΡΜΟΣ πάστα κορμός [pasta kormos] chocolate log
ΠΑΣΤΑ ΝΟΥΓΚΑΤΙΝΑ πάστα νουγκατίνα [pasta noogatin] cream gâteau
ΠΑΣΤΑ ΣΟΚΟΛΑΤΙΝΑ πάστα σοκολατίνα [pasta sokolatina] chocolate gâteau
ΠΑΣΤΑ ΦΡΑΟΥΛΑ πάστα φράουλα [pasta fraoola] strawberry gâteau
ΠΑΣΤΙΤΣΙΟ παστίτσιο [pastitsio] macaroni cheese or lasagne-type dish, with minced meat and white sauce
ΠΑΣΤΙΤΣΙΟ ΛΑΖΑΝΙΑ παστίτσιο λαζάνια [pastitsio lazania] lasagne

ΠΑΣΤΙΤΣΙΟ
ΜΑΚΑΡΟΝΙΑ ΜΕ ΚΙΜΑ
παστίτσιο μακαρόνια με
κιμά [pastitsio makaronia meh
kima] baked pasta dish with
minced meat and béchamel

ΠΑΣΤΟ παστό [pasto] salted

ΠΑΤΑΤΕΣ πατάτες [patates]
potatoes

ΠΑΤΑΤΕΣ ΓΑΡΝΙΤΟΥΡΑ
πατάτες γαρνιτούρα [patates
garnitoora] potatoes

ΠΑΤΑΤΕΣ ΓΙΑΧΝΙ
πατάτες γιαχνί [patates
yakhni] potatoes cooked with
onion and tomato

ΠΑΤΑΤΕΣ ΚΑΙ
ΚΟΛΟΚΥΘΑΚΙΑ ΣΤΟ
ΦΟΥΡΝΟ πατάτες και
κολοκυθάκια στο φούρνο
[patates keh kolokiTHakia sto
foorno] potatoes,
courgettes/zucchini and
tomatoes baked in the oven

ΠΑΤΑΤΕΣ ΚΟΛΟΚΥΘΙΑ
ΜΟΥΣΑΚΑΣ πατάτες
κολοκύθια μουσακάς
[patates kolokiTHia moosakas]
potatoes with courgettes/
zucchini, minced meat and
cheese sauce

ΠΑΤΑΤΕΣ ΠΟΥΡΕ
πατάτες πουρέ [patates
pooreh] mashed potatoes

ΠΑΤΑΤΕΣ ΡΙΓΑΝΑΤΕΣ
πατάτες ριγανάτες στο
φούρνο [patates riganates sto
foorno] oven-cooked
potatoes with oregano

ΠΑΤΑΤΕΣ ΣΟΥΦΛΕ
πατάτες σουφλέ [patates
soofleh] potato soufflé

ΠΑΤΑΤΕΣ ΣΤΟ ΦΟΥΡΝΟ
ΡΙΓΑΝΑΤΕΣ πατάτες στο
φούρνο ριγανάτες [patates
sto foorno riganates] potatoes
baked in the oven with
oregano, lemon and olive oil

ΠΑΤΑΤΕΣ ΤΗΓΑΝΙΤΕΣ
πατάτες τηγανιτές [patates
tiganites] chips, French fries

ΠΑΤΑΤΕΣ ΤΣΙΠΣ πατάτες
τσιπς [patates tsips] chips,
French fries

ΠΑΤΑΤΟΣΑΛΑΤΑ
πατατοσαλάτα [patatosalata]
potato salad

ΠΑΤΖΑΡΙΑ πατζάρια
[patzaria] beetroot

ΠΑΤΣΑΣ πατσάς [patsas]
tripe; soup made from
lambs' intestines

ΠΑΤΣΑΣ ΣΟΥΠΑ πατσάς
σούπα [patsas soopa] tripe
soup

ΠΕΠΟΝΙ πεπόνι [peponi]
melon

ΠΕΣΤΡΟΦΑ πέστροφα
[pestrofa] trout

ΠΕΣΤΡΟΦΑ ΨΗΤΗ
πέστροφα ψητή [pestrofa
psiti] grilled trout

ΠΗΧΤΗ πηχτή [pikhti]
potted meat

ΠΙΛΑΦΙ πιλάφι [pilafi] rice

ΠΙΛΑΦΙ ΜΕ ΓΑΡΙΔΕΣ
πιλάφι με γαρίδες [pilafi meh
garithes] shrimp pilaf

Β
Γ
Δ
Ε
Ζ
Η
Θ
Ι
Κ
Λ
Μ
Ν
Ξ
Ο
Π
Ρ
Σ
Τ
Υ
Φ
Χ
Ψ
Ω

ΠΙΛΑΦΙ ΜΕ ΜΥΔΙΑ
πιλάφι με μύδια [pilafi meh
mithia] pilaf with mussels
ΠΙΛΑΦΙ ΜΕ ΣΑΛΤΣΑ
ΝΤΟΜΑΤΑ πιλάφι με
σάλτσα ντομάτα [pilafi meh
saltsa domata] pilaf with
tomato sauce
ΠΙΛΑΦΙ ΤΑΣ-ΚΕΜΠΑΠ
πιλάφι τας-κεμπάπ [pilafi tas
kebab] rice with cubes of
beef in tomato sauce
ΠΙΠΕΡΙ πιπέρι [piperi]
pepper (spice)
ΠΙΠΕΡΙΕΣ πιπεριές [piperi-
es] peppers
ΠΙΠΕΡΙΕΣ ΓΕΜΙΣΤΕΣ ΜΕ
ΚΙΜΑ πιπεριές γεμιστές
με κιμά [piperi-es yemistes
meh kima] peppers stuffed
with minced meat
ΠΙΠΕΡΙΕΣ ΓΕΜΙΣΤΕΣ ΜΕ
ΡΥΖΙ πιπεριές γεμιστές με
ρύζι [piperi-es yemistes meh
rizi] peppers stuffed with
rice
ΠΙΠΕΡΙΕΣ ΓΕΜΙΣΤΕΣ
πιπεριές γεμιστές [piperi-es
yemistes] stuffed peppers
ΠΙΠΕΡΙΕΣ ΚΟΚΚΙΝΕΣ
πιπεριές κόκκινες [piperi-es
kokines] red peppers
ΠΙΠΕΡΙΕΣ ΠΡΑΣΙΝΕΣ
πιπεριές πράσινες [piperi-es
prasines] green peppers
ΠΙΡΟΣΚΙ πιροσκί [piroski]
minced meat or sausage
rolls
ΠΙΤΣΑ πίτσα [pizza] pizza

ΠΙΤΣΑ ΜΕ ΖΑΜΠΟΝ
πίτσα με ζαμπόν [pizza meh
zabon] ham pizza
ΠΙΤΣΑ ΜΕ ΜΑΝΙΤΑΡΙΑ
πίτσα με μανιτάρια [pizza
meh manitaria] mushroom
pizza
ΠΙΤΣΑ ΜΕ ΝΤΟΜΑΤΑ
ΤΥΡΙ πίτσα με ντομάτα
τυρί [pizza meh domata tiri]
cheese and tomato pizza
ΠΙΤΣΑ ΣΠΕΣΙΑΛ πίτσα
σπέσιαλ [pizza special]
special pizza
ΠΙΤΤΑ πίττα [pita] pie
ΠΙΤΤΑ ΜΕ ΚΙΜΑ πίττα
με κιμά [pita meh kima]
minced meat pie
ΠΛΑΚΙ πλακί [plaki] baked
in the oven in a tomato
sauce
πολύ ψημένο [poli psimeno]
overdone
ΠΟΡΤΟΚΑΛΙ πορτοκάλι
[portokali] orange
ΠΟΥΛΕΡΙΚΑ πουλερικά
[poulerika] poultry
ΠΟΥΤΙΓΚΑ πουτίγκα
[pootiga] pudding
ΠΟΥΤΙΓΚΑ ΜΕ ΑΝΑΝΑ
πουτίγκα με ανανά [pootiga
meh anana] pineapple
pudding
ΠΟΥΤΙΓΚΑ ΜΕ
ΚΑΡΥΔΙΑ πουτίγκα με
καρύδια [pootiga meh karithia]
walnut pudding
ΠΟΥΤΙΓΚΑ ΜΕ
ΣΤΑΦΙΔΕΣ πουτίγκα με

σταφίδες [pootiga meh stafithes] sultana pudding

ΠΡΑΣΑ πράσα [prasa] leeks

ΠΡΑΣΟΠΙΤΤΑ πρασόπιττα [prasopita] leek pie

ΠΡΩΤΟ ΠΙΑΤΟ πρώτο πιάτο [proto piato] starter

ΡΑΒΑΝΙ ραβανί [ravani] very sweet sponge cake

ΡΑΒΙΟΛΙΑ ραβιόλια [raviolia] ravioli

ΡΙΓΑΝΗ ρίγανη [riGani] oregano

ΡΟΔΑΚΙΝΟ ροδάκινο [rothakino] peaches

ΡΟΣΜΠΙΦ ΑΡΝΙ ΜΟΣΧΑΡΙ ροσμπίφ αρνί μοσχάρι [rozbif arni moskhari] roast beef, veal or lamb

ΡΥΖΙ ρύζι [rizi] rice

ΡΥΖΟΓΑΛΟ ρυζόγαλο [rizoGalo] rice pudding

ΡΩΣΙΚΗ ΣΑΛΑΤΑ ρώσικη σαλάτα [rosiki salata] Russian salad

ΣΑΛΑΜΙ σαλάμι [salami] salami

ΣΑΛΑΤΑ σαλάτα [salata] salad

ΣΑΛΑΤΑ ΑΜΠΕΛΟΦΑΣΟΥΛΑ σαλάτα αμπελοφάσουλα [salata abelofasoola] runner bean salad

ΣΑΛΑΤΑ ΚΟΥΝΟΥΠΙΔΙ ΒΡΑΣΤΟ σαλάτα κουνουπίδι βραστό [salata koonoopithi vrasto] boiled

cauliflower salad

ΣΑΛΑΤΑ ΜΑΡΟΥΛΙΑ σαλάτα μαρούλια [salata maroolia] lettuce salad

ΣΑΛΑΤΑ ΝΤΟΜΑΤΕΣ ΚΑΙ ΑΓΓΟΥΡΙΑ σαλάτα ντομάτες και αγγούρια [salata domates keh agooria] tomato and cucumber salad

ΣΑΛΑΤΑ ΝΤΟΜΑΤΕΣ-ΠΙΠΕΡΙΕΣ σαλάτα ντομάτες-πιπεριές [salata domates piperi-es] tomato and green pepper salad

ΣΑΛΑΤΑ ΣΠΑΡΑΓΓΙΑ σαλάτα σπαράγγια [salata sparagia] asparagus salad

ΣΑΛΑΤΑ ΦΑΣΟΛΙΑ ΞΗΡΑ σαλάτα φασόλια ξηρά [salata fasolia xira] butter bean salad

ΣΑΛΑΤΑ ΧΟΡΤΑ ΒΡΑΣΜΕΝΑ σαλάτα χόρτα βρασμένα [salata khorta vrasmena] chicory salad

ΣΑΛΑΤΑ ΧΩΡΙΑΤΙΚΗ σαλάτα χωριάτικη [salata khoriatiki] Greek salad – tomatoes, cucumber, feta cheese and olives

ΣΑΛΙΓΚΑΡΙΑ σαλιγκάρια [saligaria] snails

ΣΑΛΤΣΑ σάλτσα [saltsa] sauce

ΣΑΛΤΣΑ ΜΠΕΣΑΜΕΛ σάλτσα μπεσαμέλ [saltsa besamel] béchamel sauce

ΣΑΛΤΣΑ ΝΤΟΜΑΤΑ
σάλτσα ντομάτα [saltsa
domata] tomato sauce
ΣΑΜΑΛΙ σάμαλι [samali]
semolina cake with honey
ΣΑΝΤΙΓΥ σαντιγύ [sadiyi]
whipped cream
ΣΑΝΤΟΥΙΤΣ σάντουιτς
[sandwich] sandwich
ΣΑΡΔΕΛΛΕΣ σαρδέλλες
[sartheles] sardines
ΣΑΡΔΕΛΛΕΣ ΛΑΔΙΟΥ
σαρδέλλες λαδιού [sartheles
lathioo] sardines in oil
ΣΕΛΙΝΟ σέλινο [selino]
celery
ΣΙΜΙΓΔΑΛΙ σιμιγδάλι
[simigthali] semolina
ΣΙΡΟΠΙ σιρόπι [siropi] syrup
ΣΚΟΡΔΑΛΙΑ σκορδαλιά
[skorthalia] thick garlic sauce
ΣΚΟΡΔΑΛΙΑ ΜΕ ΨΩΜΙ
σκορδαλιά με ψωμί
[skorthalia meh psomi] thick
garlic sauce made with
bread or potatoes
ΣΚΟΡΔΟ σκόρδο [skortho]
garlic
ΣΟΚΟΛΑΤΑΚΙΑ
σοκολατάκια [sokolatakia]
little chocolate cakes; milk
chocolates
ΣΟΛΟΜΟΣ σολομός
[solomos] salmon
ΣΟΛΟΜΟΣ ΚΑΠΝΙΣΤΟΣ
σολομός καπνιστός [solomos
kapnistos] smoked salmon
ΣΟΥΒΛΑΚΙΑ σουβλάκια
[soovlakia] meat grilled on a

skewer, served in pitta
bread
ΣΟΥΒΛΑΚΙΑ ΑΠΟ
ΚΡΕΑΣ ΑΡΝΙΣΙΟ
σουβλάκια από κρέας
αρνίσιο [soovlakia apo kreas
arnisio] lamb kebab
ΣΟΥΒΛΑΚΙΑ ΑΠΟ
ΚΡΕΑΣ ΜΟΣΧΑΡΙΣΙΟ
σουβλάκια από κρέας
μοσχαρίσιο [soovlakia apo
kreas moskharisio] veal kebab
ΣΟΥΒΛΑΚΙΑ ΑΠΟ
ΚΡΕΑΣ ΧΟΙΡΙΝΟ
σουβλάκια από κρέας
χοιρινό [soovlakia apo kreas
khirino] pork kebab
ΣΟΥΒΛΑΚΙΑ ΝΤΟΝΕΡ
ΜΕ ΠΙΤΤΑ σουβλάκια
ντονέρ με πίττα [soovlaki
doner meh pita] donner kebab
with pitta bread
ΣΟΥΒΛΑΚΙ ΚΑΛΑΜΑΚΙ
σουβλάκι καλαμάκι [soovlaki
kalamaki] shish kebab
ΣΟΥΠΑ σούπα [soopa] soup
ΣΟΥΠΑ ΠΑΤΣΑΣ σούπα
πατσάς [soopa patsas] tripe
soup
ΣΟΥΠΑ ΡΕΒΥΘΙΑ σούπα
ρεβύθια [soopa reviThia]
chickpea soup
ΣΟΥΠΑ ΤΡΑΧΑΝΑΣ
σούπα τραχανάς [soopa
trakhanas] milk broth with
flour
ΣΟΥΠΑ ΦΑΚΕΣ σούπα
φακές [soopa fakes] lentil
soup

ΣΟΥΠΑ ΦΑΣΟΛΙΑ σούπα φασόλια [soopa fasolia] bean soup

ΣΟΥΠΑ ΨΑΡΙ σούπα ψάρι [soopa psari] fish soup

ΣΟΥΠΑ ΨΑΡΙ ΑΥΓΟΛΕΜΟΝΟ σούπα ψάρι αυγολέμονο [soopa psari avgolemono] fish soup with egg and lemon

ΣΟΥΠΕΣ σούπες [soopes] soups

ΣΟΥΠΙΕΣ σουπιές [soopi-es] cuttlefish

ΣΟΥΠΙΕΣ ΜΕ ΣΠΑΝΑΚΙ σουπιές με σπανάκι [soopi-es meh spanaki] cuttlefish and spinach stew

ΣΟΥΠΙΕΣ ΤΗΓΑΝΗΤΕΣ σουπιές τηγανητές [soopi-es tiganites] fried cuttlefish

ΣΟΥΣΑΜΙ σουσάμι [soosami] sesame

ΣΟΥΤΖΟΥΚΑΚΙΑ σουτζουκάκια [sootzookakia] spicy meatballs in red sauce

ΣΟΥΦΛΕ σουφλέ [soofleh] soufflé

ΣΠΑΓΓΕΤΟ ΜΕ ΦΡΕΣΚΟ ΒΟΥΤΥΡΟ ΚΑΙ ΠΑΡΜΕΖΑΝΑ σπαγγέτο με φρέσκο βούτυρο και παρμεζάνα [spageto meh fresko vootiro keh parmezana] spaghetti with butter and parmesan cheese

ΣΠΑΝΑΚΙ σπανάκι [spanaki] spinach

ΣΠΑΝΑΚΟΠΙΤΤΑ

σπανακόπιττα [spanakopita] spinach (and sometimes feta) in filo pastry

σπάνιος [spanios] rare (steak)

ΣΠΑΡΑΓΓΙΑ ΣΑΛΑΤΑ σπαράγγια σαλάτα [sparagia salata] asparagus salad

ΣΠΕΣΙΑΛΙΤΕ σπεσιαλιτέ [spesialiteh] speciality

ΣΠΛΗΝΑΝΤΕΡΟ σπληνάντερο [splinadero] intestines stuffed with spleen

ΣΤΑΦΙΔΕΣ σταφίδες [stafithes] dried fruit

ΣΤΑΦΙΔΟΨΩΜΟ σταφιδόψωμο [stafithopsomo] bread with raisins

ΣΤΑΦΥΛΙΑ σταφύλια [stafilia] grapes

ΣΤΙΦΑΔΟ στιφάδο [stifatho] chopped meat with onions; hare or rabbit stew with onions

ΣΤΟ ΦΟΥΡΝΟ στο φούρνο [sto foorno] baked in the oven

ΣΤΡΕΙΔΙΑ στρείδια [strithia] oysters

ΣΥΚΑ σύκα [sika] figs

ΣΥΚΩΤΑΚΙΑ συκωτάκια [sikotakia] liver

ΣΥΚΩΤΑΚΙΑ ΜΑΡΙΝΑΤΑ συκωτάκια μαρινάτα [sikotakia marinata] liver cooked in rosemary

ΣΥΚΩΤΑΚΙΑ ΠΙΛΑΦΙ συκωτάκια πιλάφι [sikotakia pilafi] liver pilaf

Α
Β
Γ
Δ
Ε
Ζ
Η
Θ
Ι
Κ
Λ
Μ
Ν
Ξ
Ο
Π
Ρ
Σ
Τ
Υ
Φ
Χ
Ψ
Ω

ΣΥΚΩΤΑΚΙΑ ΣΤΗ
ΣΧΑΡΑ συκωτάκια στη
σχάρα [sikotakia sti skhara]
grilled liver
ΣΥΚΩΤΑΚΙΑ
ΤΗΓΑΝΗΤΑ συκωτάκια
τηγανητά [sikotakia tiganita]
fried liver
ΣΥΚΩΤΙ ΨΗΤΟ συκώτι
ψητό [sikoti psito] charcoal-
grilled liver
ΣΥΝΑΓΡΙΔΑ ΨΗΤΗ
συναγρίδα ψητή [sinagritha
psiti] grilled sea bream
ΣΦΥΡΙΔΑ ΒΡΑΣΤΗ σφυρίδα
βραστή [sriritha vrasti] boiled
pike
ΣΩΤΕ σωτέ [soteh] lightly
fried, sautéed

ΤΑΡΑΜΑΣ ταραμάς
[taramas] cod roe
ΤΑΡΑΜΟΚΕΦΤΕΔΕΣ
ταραμοκεφτέδες
[taramokeftethes] roe pâté
balls with spices
ΤΑΡΑΜΟΣΑΛΑΤΑ
ταραμοσαλάτα [taramosalata]
cod roe dip
ΤΑΡΤΑ τάρτα [tarta] tart
ΤΑΡΤΑ ΜΕ ΚΕΡΑΣΙΑ
τάρτα με κεράσια [tarta meh
kerasia] cherry tart
ΤΑΡΤΑ ΜΕ ΚΡΕΜΑ ΚΑΙ
ΑΜΥΓΔΑΛΑ τάρτα με
κρέμα και αμύγδαλα [tarta
meh krema keh amigthala]
cream and almond tart
ΤΑΡΤΑ ΜΕ ΚΡΕΜΑ ΚΑΙ

ΚΑΡΥΔΙΑ τάρτα με κρέμα
και καρύδια [tarta meh krema
keh karithia] walnut and
cream tart
ΤΑΡΤΑ ΜΕ ΦΡΑΟΥΛΕΣ
τάρτα με φράουλες [tarta
meh fraooles] strawberry tart
ΤΑΡΤΑ ΜΗΛΟΥ τάρτα
μήλου [tarta miloo] apple tart
ΤΑΣ-ΚΕΜΠΑΠ τας-κεμπάπ
[tas kebab] spicy lamb cutlets
ΤΑΣ-ΚΕΜΠΑΠ ΠΙΛΑΦΙ
τας-κεμπάπ πιλάφι [tas kebab
pilafi] spicy lamb cutlets
pilaf
ΤΖΑΤΖΙΚΙ τζατζίκι [dzadziki]
yoghurt, cucumber and
garlic dip
ΤΗΓΑΝΗΤΟΣ τηγανητός
[tiganitos] fried
ΤΗΓΑΝΙΤΕΣ τηγανίτες
[tiganites] pancakes
ΤΗΣ ΚΑΤΣΑΡΟΛΑΣ της
κατσαρόλας [tis katsarolas]
casseroled
ΤΗΣ ΣΟΥΒΛΑΣ της
σούβλας [tis soovlas] roast
on a spit
ΤΗΣ ΣΧΑΡΑΣ της σχάρας
[tis skharas] grilled over
charcoal
ΤΟΝΝΟΣ τόννος [tonos]
tuna
ΤΟΝΝΟΣΑΛΑΤΑ
τοννοσαλάτα [tonosalata]
tuna salad
ΤΟΣΤ τοστ [tost] toasted
sandwich
ΤΟΣΤ ΚΛΑΜΠ τοστ

κλαμπ [tost club] toasted club sandwich

ΤΟΣΤ ΜΕ ΑΥΓΟ τοστ με αυγό [tost meh avgo] toasted egg sandwich

ΤΟΣΤ ΜΕ ΖΑΜΠΟΝ τοστ με ζαμπόν [tost meh zabon] toasted ham sandwich

ΤΟΣΤ ΜΕ ΚΟΤΟΠΟΥΛΟ τοστ με κοτόπουλο [tost meh kotopoolo] toasted chicken sandwich

ΤΟΣΤ ΜΕ ΚΡΕΑΣ τοστ με κρέας [tost meh kreas] toasted meat sandwich

ΤΟΣΤ ΜΕ ΜΠΙΦΤΕΚΙ τοστ με μπιφτέκι [tost meh bifteki] toasted hamburger

ΤΟΣΤ ΜΕ ΤΥΡΙ τοστ με τυρί [tost meh tiri] toasted cheese sandwich

ΤΟΥ ΑΤΜΟΥ του ατμού [too atmoo] steamed

ΤΟΥΡΣΙ τουρσί [toorsi] pickled

ΤΟΥΡΤΑ τούρτα [toorta] gâteau

ΤΟΥΡΤΑ ΑΜΥΓΔΑΛΟΥ τούρτα αμυγδάλου [toorta amigthaloo] almond gâteau

ΤΟΥΡΤΑ ΚΡΕΜΑ ΜΕ ΦΡΑΟΥΛΕΣ τούρτα κρέμα με φράουλες [toorta krema meh fraooles] strawberry cream gâteau

ΤΟΥΡΤΑ ΜΟΚΚΑ τούρτα μόκκα [toorta moka] coffee gâteau

ΤΟΥΡΤΑ ΝΟΥΓΚΑΤΙΝΑ

τούρτα νουγκατίνα [toorta noogatina] nougat gâteau

ΤΟΥΡΤΑ ΣΑΝΤΙΓΥ τούρτα σαντιγύ [toorta sadiyi] whipped cream gâteau

ΤΟΥΡΤΑ ΣΟΚΟΛΑΤΑΣ τούρτα σοκολάτας [toorta sokolatas] chocolate gâteau

ΤΡΟΥΦΑΚΙΑ τρουφάκια [troofakia] small chocolate fudge cake

ΤΣΙΠΟΥΡΕΣ τσιπούρες [tsipoores] sea bream

ΤΣΙΠΟΥΡΕΣ ΨΗΤΕΣ τσιπούρες ψητές [tsipoores psites] roast sea bream

ΤΣΙΠΣ τσιπς [tsips] crisps, (US) potato chips

ΤΣΟΥΡΕΚΙ τσουρέκι [tsooreki] light sponge

ΤΣΟΥΡΕΚΙΑ τσουρέκια [tsoorekia] sweet bread with fresh butter (Christmas/Easter dish)

ΤΥΡΙ τυρί [tiri] cheese

ΤΥΡΙΑ τυριά [tiria] cheese

ΤΥΡΟΠΙΤΤΑ τυρόπιττα [tiropita] cheese and egg in filo pastry

ΤΥΡΟΠΙΤΤΑΚΙΑ τυροπιττάκια [tiropitakia] small cheese pies

ΦΑΒΑ φάβα [fava] chick pea soup

ΦΑΚΕΣ φακές [fakes] lentil soup

ΦΑΣΟΛΑΔΑ φασολάδα

[fasolatha] bean soup with celery, carrots and tomatoes

ΦΑΣΟΛΑΚΙΑ φασολάκια [fasolakia] green beans

ΦΑΣΟΛΑΚΙΑ ΛΑΔΕΡΑ φασολάκια λαδερά [fasolakia lathera] green beans in olive oil and tomato sauce

ΦΑΣΟΛΑΚΙΑ ΦΡΕΣΚΑ ΓΙΑΧΝΙ φασολάκια φρέσκα γιαχνι [fasolakia freska yakhni] runner beans with onion and tomato

ΦΑΣΟΛΑΚΙΑ ΦΡΕΣΚΑ ΣΑΛΑΤΑ φασολάκια φρέσκα σαλάτα [fasolakia freska salata] runner bean salad

ΦΑΣΟΛΙΑ φασόλια [fasolia] beans

ΦΑΣΟΛΙΑ ΓΙΓΑΝΤΕΣ ΓΙΑΧΝΙ φασόλια γίγαντες γιαχνι [fasolia yiGandes yakhni] butter beans with onion and tomato

ΦΑΣΟΛΙΑ ΓΙΓΑΝΤΕΣ ΣΤΟ ΦΟΥΡΝΟ φασόλια γίγαντες στο φούρνο [fasolia yiGandes sto foorno] oven-cooked butter beans

ΦΑΣΟΛΙΑ ΓΙΓΑΝΤΕΣ φασόλια γίγαντες [fasolia yiGandes] large dried beans in tomato sauce

ΦΑΣΟΛΙΑ ΣΟΥΠΑ φασόλια σούπα [fasolia soopa] bean soup

ΦΕΤΑ φέτα [feta] feta cheese

ΦΙΛΕ ΜΙΝΙΟΝ φιλέ μινιόν [fileh minion] thin fillet steak

ΦΙΛΕΤΟ φιλέτο [fileto] fillet steak

ΦΛΟΓΕΡΕΣ ΜΕ ΚΡΕΜΑ φλογέρες με κρέμα [floyeres meh krema] round sweets filled with cream

ΦΟΝΤΑΝ φοντάν [fodan] sweets

ΦΟΝΤΑΝ ΑΜΥΓΔΑΛΟΥ φοντάν αμυγδάλου [fodan amigthaloo] almond sweets

ΦΟΝΤΑΝ ΑΠΟ ΚΑΡΥΔΑ φοντάν από καρύδα [fodan apo karitha] coconut sweets

ΦΟΝΤΑΝ ΑΠΟ ΚΑΡΥΔΙΑ φοντάν από καρύδια [fodan apo karithia] walnut sweets

ΦΟΝΤΑΝ ΙΝΔΙΚΗΣ ΚΑΡΥΔΑΣ φοντάν ινδικής καρύδας [fodan inthikis karithas] coconut sweets

ΦΟΝΤΑΝ ΠΟΡΤΟΚΑΛΙΟΥ φοντάν πορτοκαλιού [fodan portokali-oo] orange sweets

ΦΟΥΝΤΟΥΚΙΑ φουντούκια [foodookia] hazelnuts

ΦΡΑΟΥΛΕΣ φράουλες [fra-ooles] strawberries

ΦΡΑΟΥΛΕΣ ΜΕ ΣΑΝΤΙΓΥ φράουλες με σαντιγύ [fra-ooles meh sadiyi] strawberries with whipped cream

ΦΡΙΚΑΣΕ ΑΡΝΙ φρικασέ αρνί [frikaseh arni] lamb cooked in lettuce with cream sauce

ΦΡΟΥΙ-ΓΚΛΑΣΕ φρουί-
γκλασέ [frooi-glaseh] dried
assorted fruits with sugar

ΦΡΟΥΤΑ φρούτα [froota]
fruit

ΦΡΟΥΤΟΣΑΛΑΤΑ
φρουτοσαλάτα [frootosalata]
fruit salad

ΦΡΥΓΑΝΙΑ φρυγανιά
[frigania] toast

ΦΡΥΓΑΝΙΕΣ φρυγανιές
[frigani-es] French toast

ΦΥΛΛΟ ΠΙΤΤΑΣ φύλλο
πίττας [filo pitas] filo pastry

ΦΥΣΤΙΚΙΑ φυστίκια [fistikia]
peanuts

ΦΥΣΤΙΚΙΑ ΑΙΓΙΝΗΣ
φυστίκια Αιγίνης [fistikia
Eyinis] pistachios

ΧΑΒΙΑΡΙ χαβιάρι [khaviari]
caviar

ΧΑΛΒΑΣ χαλβάς [khalvas]
halva, sweet made from
semolina, sesame seeds,
nuts and honey

ΧΑΜΠΟΥΡΓΚΕΡ
χάμπουργκερ [khamburger]
hamburger

ΧΗΝΑ χήνα [khina] goose

ΧΟΙΡΙΝΟ χοιρινό [khirino]
pork

ΧΟΙΡΙΝΟ ΜΕ ΣΕΛΙΝΟ
χοιρινό με σέλινο [khirino
meh selino] pork casserole
with celery

ΧΟΙΡΙΝΟ ΠΑΣΤΟ χοιρινό
παστό [khirino pasto] salted
pork

ΧΟΙΡΙΝΟ ΣΟΥΒΛΑΣ
χοιρινό σούβλας [khirino
soovlas] pork on the spit

ΧΟΙΡΙΝΟ ΣΤΗ ΣΧΑΡΑ
χοιρινό στη σχάρα [khirino
sti skhara] grilled pork

ΧΟΙΡΙΝΟ ΦΟΥΡΝΟΥ ΜΕ
ΠΑΤΑΤΕΣ χοιρινό
φούρνου με πατάτες [khirino
foornoo meh patates] roast
pork with potatoes

ΧΟΡΤΑ ΒΡΑΣΜΕΝΑ
ΣΑΛΑΤΑ χόρτα βρασμένα
σαλάτα [khorta vrasmena
salata] boiled chicory salad

ΧΟΡΤΑΡΙΚΑ χορταρικά
[khortarika] vegetables

ΧΟΡΤΟΣΟΥΠΑ
χορτόσουπα [khortosoopa]
vegetable soup

ΧΤΑΠΟΔΑΚΙ ΞΥΔΑΤΟ
χταποδάκι ξυδάτο
[khtapothaki xithato] pickled
octopus

ΧΤΑΠΟΔΙ χταπόδι
[khtapothi] octopus

ΧΤΑΠΟΔΙ ΒΡΑΣΤΟ
χταπόδι βραστό [khtapothi
vrasto] boiled octopus

ΧΤΑΠΟΔΙ ΚΡΑΣΑΤΟ
χταπόδι κρασάτο [khtapothi
krasato] octopus in wine

ΧΤΑΠΟΔΙ ΜΕ
ΜΑΚΑΡΟΝΑΚΙ χταπόδι
με μακαρονάκι [khtapothi
meh makaronaki] octopus
with macaroni

ΧΤΑΠΟΔΙ ΠΙΛΑΦΙ
χταπόδι πιλάφι [khtapothi

A
B
Γ
Δ
E
Z
H
Θ
I
K
Λ
M
N
Ξ
O
Π
P
Σ
T
Y
Φ
X
Ψ
Ω

pilafi] octopus pilaf
ΧΤΑΠΟΔΙ ΣΤΙΦΑΔΟ
χταπόδι στιφάδο [khtapothi
stifatho] octopus with small
onions
ΧΥΛΟΠΙΤΕΣ χυλοπίτες
[khilopites] tagliatelle
ΧΥΛΟΠΙΤΕΣ ΜΕ
ΒΟΥΤΥΡΟ ΚΑΙ ΤΥΡΙ
χυλοπίτες με βούτυρο και
τυρί [khilopites meh vootiro
keh tiri] tagliatelle with
butter and cheese
ΧΥΛΟΠΙΤΕΣ ΜΕ ΚΙΜΑ
χυλοπίτες με κιμά [khilopites
meh kima] tagliatelle with
minced meat sauce
ΧΥΛΟΠΙΤΕΣ ΜΕ
ΚΟΤΟΠΟΥΛΟ χυλοπίτες
με κοτόπουλο [khilopites meh
kotopoolo] tagliatelle with
chicken
ΧΩΡΙΑΤΙΚΗ ΣΑΛΑΤΑ
χωριάτικη σαλάτα [khoriatiki
salata] Greek salad –
tomatoes, cucumber,
peppers, feta, olives and
boiled eggs with olive oil
and vinegar dressing

ΨΑΡΙ ψάρι [psari] fish
ΨΑΡΙ ΒΡΑΣΤΟ
ΜΑΓΙΟΝΕΖΑ ψάρι
βραστό μαγιονέζα [psari
vrasto mayoneza] steamed
fish with mayonaise
ΨΑΡΙΑ ψάρια [psaria] fish
ΨΑΡΙΑ ΓΛΩΣΣΕΣ
ΒΡΑΣΤΕΣ ΜΕ

ΑΥΓΟΛΕΜΟΝΟ ψάρια
γλώσσες βραστές με
αυγολέμονο [psaria gloses
vrastes meh avgolemono]
steamed sole with oil and
lemon
ΨΑΡΙΑ ΜΑΡΙΝΑΤΑ
ψάρια μαρινάτα [psaria
marinata] marinated fish
ΨΑΡΙΑ ΤΗΓΑΝΗΤΑ
ψάρια τηγανητά [psaria
tiganita] fried fish
ΨΑΡΙΑ ΨΗΤΑ ΣΤΗ
ΣΧΑΡΑ ψάρια ψητά στη
σχάρα [psaria psita sti
skhara] charcoal-grilled
fish
ΨΑΡΟΣΟΥΠΑ ψαρόσουπα
[psarosoopa] fish soup
ΨΗΤΟ ψητό [psito] grilled
over charcoal; oven-roasted
ΨΗΤΟ ΣΤΗ ΣΧΑΡΑ ψητό
στη σχάρα [psito sti skhara]
grilled
ΨΩΜΑΚΙ ψωμάκι [psomaki]
roll
ΨΩΜΙ ψωμί [psomi] bread
ΨΩΜΙ ΑΣΠΡΟ ψωμί
άσπρο [psomi aspro] white
bread
ΨΩΜΙ ΓΙΑ ΤΟΣΤ ψωμί γιά
τοστ [psomi ya tost] sliced
bread
ΨΩΜΙ ΜΑΥΡΟ ψωμί
μαύρο [psomi mavro] brown
bread

ΩΜΟΣ ωμός [omos] raw

Menu Reader:

Drink

ΑΕΡΙΟΥΧΟ αεριούχο
[aeriookho] fizzy
ΑΛΚΟΟΛ αλκοόλ [alko-ol]
alcohol
ΑΝΑΝΑΣ ΧΥΜΟΣ ανανάς
χυμός [ananas khimos]
pineapple juice
ΑΝΑΨΥΚΤΙΚΟ
αναψυκτικό [anapsiktiko] soft
drink
ΑΠΕΡΙΤΙΦ απεριτίφ [aperitif]
aperitif
ΑΣΠΡΟ ΚΡΑΣΙ άσπρο
κρασί [aspro krasi] white
wine

ΒΟΤΚΑ βότκα [votka] vodka
ΒΥΣΣΙΝΑΔΑ βυσσινάδα
[visinatha] black cherry
juice

ΓΑΛΑ γάλα [gala] milk
ΓΑΛΑ ΚΑΚΑΟ γάλα
κακάο [gala kakao] chocolate
milk
ΓΑΛΛΙΚΟΣ ΚΑΦΕΣ
γαλλικός καφές [galikos
kafes] filter coffee; French
coffee
ΓΛΥΚΟ ΚΡΑΣΙ γλυκό
κρασί [gliko krasi] sweet
wine

ΕΛΛΗΝΙΚΟΣ ΚΑΦΕΣ
ελληνικός καφές [elinikos
kafes] Greek coffee

ΖΕΣΤΗ ΣΟΚΟΛΑΤΑ ζεστή
σοκολάτα [zesti sokolata] hot
chocolate

ΚΑΚΑΟ κακάο [kakao]
cocoa
ΚΑΤΑΛΟΓΟΣ ΚΡΑΣΙΩΝ
κατάλογος κρασιών
[katalogos krasion] wine list
ΚΑΦΕΣ καφές [kafes] coffee
ΚΑΦΕΣ ΜΕΤΡΙΟΣ καφές
μέτριος [kafes metrios]
medium-sweet Greek coffee
ΚΑΦΕΣ ΒΑΡΥΣ ΓΛΥΚΟΣ
καφές βαρύς γλυκός [kafes
varis glikos] sweet Greek
coffee
ΚΑΦΕΣ ΜΕ ΓΑΛΑ καφές
με γάλα [kafes meh gala]
coffee with milk
ΚΟΚΑ ΚΟΛΑ κόκα κόλα
[koka kola] Coca-Cola®
ΚΟΚΚΙΝΟ ΚΡΑΣΙ κόκκινο
κρασί [kokino krasi] red wine
ΚΟΚΤΕΗΛ κοκτέηλ [kokteil]
cocktail
ΚΟΝΙΑΚ κονιάκ [koniak]
brandy
ΚΡΑΣΙ κρασί [krasi] wine
ΚΡΑΣΙ ΑΣΠΡΟ κρασί
άσπρο [krasi aspro] white
wine
ΚΡΑΣΙ ΚΟΚΚΙΝΟ κρασί
κόκκινο [krasi kokino] red
wine
ΚΡΑΣΙ ΜΑΥΡΟΔΑΦΝΗ
κρασί μαυροδάφνη [krasi
mavrothafni] sweet red wine
ΚΡΑΣΙ ΡΕΤΣΙΝΑ κρασί
ρετσίνα [krasi retsina] retsina
ΚΡΑΣΙ ΡΟΖΕ κρασί ροζέ
[krasi rozeh] rosé wine
ΚΡΑΣΙ ΤΟΥ ΜΑΓΑΖΙΟΥ

κρασί του μαγαζιού [krasi tou
magazi-**oo**] house wine

ΛΕΜΟΝΑΔΑ λεμονάδα
[lemon**a**tha] lemonade
ΛΙΚΕΡ λικέρ [lik**er**] liqueur

ΜΕΤΑΛΛΙΚΟ ΝΕΡΟ
μεταλλικό νερό [metalik**o**
ner**o**] mineral water
ΜΗΛΟΧΥΜΟΣ μηλοχυμός
[milokhim**os**] apple juice
ΜΠΥΡΑ μπύρα [b**i**ra] beer,
lager

ΝΕΣΚΑΦΕ νέσκαφέ
[neskaf**eh**] Nescafé®, instant
coffee
ΝΕΣΚΑΦΕ ΦΡΑΠΕ
νέσκαφέ φραπέ [neskaf**eh**
frap**eh**] iced coffee
ΝΕΡΟ νερό [ner**o**] water
ΝΤΟΜΑΤΑ ΧΥΜΟΣ
ντομάτα χυμός [dom**a**ta
khim**os**] tomato juice

ΟΥΖΟ ούζο [**oo**zo] ouzo
ΟΥΙΣΚΥ ουίσκυ whisky,
scotch

παγάκι [pag**a**ki] ice cube
ΠΑΓΟΣ πάγος [p**a**gos] ice
ΠΟΡΤΟΚΑΛΑΔΑ
πορτοκαλάδα [portokal**a**tha]
orange juice
ΠΟΡΤΟΚΑΛΙ ΧΥΜΟΣ
πορτοκάλι χυμός [portok**a**li
khim**os**] orange juice
ΠΟΤΑ ποτά [pot**a**] drinks

ΡΑΚΗ ρακή [rak**i**] strong
spirit, eau-de-vie

ΡΕΤΣΙΝΑ ρετσίνα [rets**i**na]
retsina
ΡΟΖΕ ΚΡΑΣΙ ροζέ κρασί
[roz**eh** krasi] rosé wine
ΡΟΥΜΙ ρούμι [r**oo**mi] rum

ΣΤΑΦΥΛΙ ΧΥΜΟΣ σταφύλι
χυμός [staf**i**li khim**os**] grape
juice

ΤΖΙΝ τζιν [tzin] gin
ΤΖΙΝ ΜΕ ΤΟΝΙΚ τζιν με
τόνικ [tzin meh t**o**nik] gin and
tonic
ΤΣΑΙ τσάι [ts**a**-i] tea
ΤΣΑΙ ΜΕ ΛΕΜΟΝΙ τσάι
με λεμόνι [ts**a**-i meh lem**o**ni]
lemon tea
ΤΣΙΠΟΥΡΟ τσίπουρο
[tsi**p**ooro] type of ouzo

ΦΡΑΠΕ φραπέ [frap**eh**] iced
coffee

ΧΥΜΟΣ χυμός [khim**os**] juice
ΧΩΡΙΣ ΚΑΦΕΪΝΗ χωρίς
καφεΐνη [khoris kafe**i**ni]
decaffeinated